MARIE HELVIN

The Autobiography

MARIE
HELVIN

The Autobiography

WEIDENFELD & NICOLSON
LONDON

First published in Great Britain in 2007
by Weidenfeld & Nicolson

1 3 5 7 9 10 8 6 4 2

A CIP catalogue record for this book
is available from the British Library.

ISBN-13   978 0 297 85311 4

Typeset by Input Data Services Ltd,
Frome

Printed in Great Britain by Clays Ltd
St Ives plc

Weidenfeld & Nicolson

The Orion Publishing Group Ltd
Orion House
5 Upper Saint Martin's Lane
London, WC2H 9EA
An Hachette Livre UK Company

The Orion Publishing Group's policy is to use papers that
are natural, renewable and recyclable products and made
from wood grown in sustainable forests. The logging and
manufacturing processes are expected to conform to the
environmental regulations of the country of origin.

www.orionbooks.co.uk

This book is dedicated to my beautiful mom,
Linda Lee Helvin, with deepest love –

He manu ke aloha, a ʻohe lālā kau ʻole
Me ke aloha pumehana

CONTENTS

The Author and Publishers wish to thank the following photographers by whose kind permission the illustrations are reproduced:

1.2 (left) Kanebo Cosmetics, Tokyo; 1.4 (top) Clive Arrowsmith/Vogue@The Condé Nast Publications (bottom) Hiroshi, Harpers & Queen/National Magazine Co. Ltd; 1.5 (top) James Wedge/Selfridges, (bottom) Tony McGee; 1.6 David Bailey; 1.7 Barry Lategan/Vogue@The Condé Nast Publications; 1.8 (top) Honolulu Star-Bulletin; 2.1 (top) Company/National Magazine Co. Ltd, (bottom) John Swannell; 2.2 David Bailey; 2.3 David Bailey; 2.4 (top) David Bailey, (bottom) Alan Davidson; 2.5 Richard Young/Rex Features, (bottom) The Helmut Newton Estate/Maconochie Photography; 2.6 David Bailey; 2.7 Association des Amis de Jacques Henri Lartigue; 2.8 David Bailey; 3.1 David Bailey; 3.2 David Bailey; 3.3 David Bailey; 3.4 David Bailey; 3.5 David Bailey; 3.6 David Bailey; 3.7 David Bailey; 3.8 (bottom) Dave Bennett/Getty Images; 4.1 David Bailey; 4.2 (top) Tom Bret-Day/CelebrityPictures.co.uk, (bottom) Alan Davidson; 4.3 David Bailey; 4.5 (top) Richard Young/Rex Features, (bottom) John Davies/Telegraph Media Group Ltd; 4.6 (top) John Davies/Telegraph Media Group Ltd, (bottom) Photography Nick Knight, W Magazine, 2003; 4.7 Vicki Couchman; 4.8 David Bailey

PROLOGUE

*'What we think is less than what we know; what we know
is less than what we love; what we love so much less than
what there is. And to that precise extent we are so much less
than what we are.'*

R.D. LAING, *The Politics of Experience*

*M*y marriage to Bailey ended one morning late in 1983. I
woke up happy that I had the house to myself for once – he was
away on some shoot in Milan. I got out of our Jacobean oak four-
poster bed and went downstairs past the studio, revelling in the
silence. Our home was usually teeming with models and make-up
artists, hairdressers and assistants and assistants' assistants, rock 'n'
roll blaring and the doorbell constantly ringing. It was exactly how
a photographer's house is meant to be – after all, Antonioni had
come to visit Bailey for inspiration for *Blow-Up*. But today – ah! –
silence.

I wandered down to the floor where we kept the parrots: rosellas
and hyacinth macaws and African greys and many others. As I drew
the heavy velvet curtains they started clearing their throats and
fluffing their feathers. We had almost seventy parrots. They were
officially Bailey's, but when he went away and our housekeeper Cezar
was off, guess who looked after them? I couldn't bear all the birds,
and it creeped me out when Bailey let them lick his tongue.

As I left the room I caught a glimpse of myself in the mirror and I
thought I heard a voice cackling, 'You're getting mighty meaty, matey!'

Could it have been one of the birds? Had they picked it up from Bailey? He was always saying that, sometimes to himself, but also to me.

I was twenty-seven years old, five feet nine and a size eight, at the peak of my modelling career, but whenever I relaxed and ate even a little of what I fancied, Bailey would clamp down on me. I called him the 'food police'. 'Mom,' I'd say on the phone to my mother in Hawaii, 'please don't send me any more chocolate-covered macadamia nuts, the food police are on to me!' It upset me when Bailey made critical noises, prodding my hips, but I was also grateful to him. I needed to watch my weight because my face and body were my career.

When you live and work with a photographer, believe me, they will always tell you when you look like shit. But it hurt me when Bailey, my husband, cast that professional eye over me. That's not to say that I didn't say things that might have pricked his pride, as well. Once or twice I called my much older husband 'Pop' by mistake.

I cut up a grapefruit and started thinking about what my best friend Jerry Hall had been saying to me – how Bailey was seeing somebody else. Yesterday she had asked me round for lunch at the St James's Hotel, where she and Mick Jagger were staying. We had a feast of caviar and champagne but afterwards she sat me down and said, 'Marie darling, I've been racking my brains over how to tell you this, but Bailey's seeing someone else.'

'So what if he is!' I told her. I didn't believe men expressed their love through monogamy. Of course he slept around. He was David Bailey. He never flaunted it in front of me, so it didn't hurt me. A fuck wasn't the same as an affair, I told myself. But Jerry was insistent that this was different. 'This time it's serious,' she said, looking at me with great concern. I realised she was probably talking about her own situation with Mick. But back then I wasn't familiar with the concept of transference. What she said got to me.

'This time you've got to do something!' she goaded me. She said Mick was really worried about me and Bailey, Helmut Newton was really worried about me and Bailey – all our friends, according to her, were freaking out about Catherine, this girl they'd seen him with in Paris.

It was true that I'd seen her appearing regularly in Bailey's photos. My intuition had told me there was something going on, but my head refused to accept it.

I was retreating mentally from Bailey. I'd pass on his trips and go home to Hawaii for a few weeks to be with my family. We were all grieving after the recent death of Suzon, my younger sister, at the age of twenty-three, and we needed to be together as a family, even though we could barely bring ourselves to talk about her, because the pain was so great.

My trips home coupled with his foreign assignments meant Bailey and I were spending less and less time together: no more than half the year, in fact. People say that if your marriage is tight, it doesn't matter if you spend time apart, but that's not true. A physical divide soon becomes a mental one too.

Sitting there in the kitchen I brooded on all this, Jerry's words ringing in my head. 'This time, you've got to do something!' So I did. I'd never done it before, and I'm not proud of it today, and just maybe if I hadn't done it everything would have been different. He'd had many other flings; maybe this one would have fizzled out like all the rest. But I went into Bailey's private sanctum, his darkroom, and started leafing through his photographs. I didn't even know what I was looking for, but my hands were shaking as I went through the piles of modelling shots, the sheaves of portraits. Finally I opened a drawer, and there they were: photographs of Catherine that were so intimate they made me gasp.

When I found those pictures, it was the beginning of the end of our marriage. So many tears and recriminations followed. Mick was furious with Jerry for having told me about Catherine, and yelled at Jerry about it, or so he told me. The incident was certainly the catalyst for our break-up. Bailey and I had loved each other so deeply and had so much fun together, but things had gone irrevocably wrong between us. In a sense, I suppose, looking back, we had reached stalemate. Our relationship was at a stage of make-or-break. Perhaps my finding those pictures that morning was a liberation for both of us.

Larynx

I never confronted Bailey about those pictures. I didn't know how. At that time I didn't have a voice.

What does it mean, not to have a voice? Well, time after time when I should have spoken up, I simply walked away, left the room, left the party, left the country. Whenever I was about to open my mouth Bailey would say 'PLEASE don't be one of those awful American women who is constantly whining, "We need to talk about our *FEELINGS*!"' (He would adopt a particularly grating US accent for 'feelings'.) I didn't want to be one of those women either. It's different now: therapy speak is considered acceptable today. My mistake was wanting to please him and his mistake was not listening to me. At parties if he upset me I would just do a vanishing act. I'd go and sit in the car. I could never bring myself to have it out with him. Anything for an easy life, I told myself.

Once, in Milan, there was an incident which just about sums it up. At the end of a day's shoot, Bailey and I, his Italian assistant and the Italian assistant's girlfriend had drinks in the lobby. I got bored so I went up to our hotel room. The assistant's girlfriend came up with me and we chatted a bit and I showed her some dress or something. But I was tired so I said I was going to bed, and to make her go away I pretended to be fast asleep. She hung around looking at my clothes. I heard a knock at the door: it was Bailey coming up to bed.

I sneak a look up from the bed where I'm pretending to be asleep and I see him there in the doorway making out with this girl. All arms and tongues. I just kept on pretending to be asleep.

What could I do? I was paralysed. I couldn't call out. This is what I mean by not having a voice. I never ever confronted Bailey. I just didn't talk to him for about five days, and I was like ice. My answer to every question was a tight-lipped 'No', and I wouldn't even look him in the eye. No wonder, bit by bit, our marriage decayed: there was no communication.

Sometimes instead of speaking out I would be mischievous instead. When I was angry with Bailey I used to put one or two rabbit doo-doos in his bowl of peanuts. Bailey had bought me some rabbits from Palmer's pet store in Camden Town and he let me keep them indoors, hopping freely around the whole of what had formerly been Bailey and Penelope Tree's dining room.

'How were your peanuts, Bailey?' I'd say, clearing away the empty bowl.

'Delicious, thanks.'

It was the predicament of many women of my generation, this voicelessness. But it was also a personal problem for me. I even had it as a child. I was cast as Maria in my school production of *West Side Story*, but when the curtain went up nothing came out of my mouth, and an understudy had to stand in the wings singing while I mouthed my way through the show.

I got over it gradually, this choked-up silence, by standing up to Bailey, being hired to make speeches at award ceremonies, going on TV, even taking six months of singing lessons because some producers wanted me to have a go at being in *Nine*, a musical about the life of Fellini. The musical didn't get put on in the end, but I felt an extraordinary release from doing breathing exercises and learning to project vocally. It was amazing. I learned the thrill of beginning to use my larynx. When I found my voice it was really loud – in fact, deafening!

But first, how did I become this person who was so confident on the catwalk and in her head but so lacking in courage that she could barely shout at her own husband? It goes back to childhood, I guess. All things do.

ONE

MADE IN HAWAII

'Hawaii is a state of grace.'

PAUL THEROUX, *Hotel Honolulu*

Nineteen fifty-six was the year they dropped the first hydrogen bomb on Bikini Atoll; the year desegregation began in the States, Elvis Presley topped the charts, and the Soviet army stormed Hungary. It was also the year my family moved to Hawaii. Pop went on ahead, to find us a place to live and a job as an insurance broker (the dullest job in the world in the most exotic place in the world). The rest of us followed on the SS *President Wilson*.

'We're coming to your home!' The stewards were banging on our cabin door, shouting to wake us up. My little sisters Suzon and Naomi were too sleepy to move, and my mother, who had been seasick for weeks, just groaned. But I scrambled out of my berth, put on my Mickey Mouse ears (I was a devoted Mouseketeer) and ran on deck immediately.

It had been a three-week passage from Yokohama, and I'd had great fun running around the deck and making friends amongst the passengers. Mom even had pinned a sign to my shirt saying 'Please do not feed candy'. (My nickname at that time was 'Chibby', a cute approximation of 'Chubby'. According to my father I was an eating machine.) Scrambling up the companionway, I couldn't wait to see the island that was to be our home. I tumbled into the warm morning air and there across the shimmering turquoise sea I could see an enchanted coastline glittering with tiny lights.

'They've put the lights on to welcome you,' the steward told me. I was only four and I believed him. The idea that we were welcome in this new place entranced me. It was my first glimpse of the islands of Hawaii and one of the most magical sights of my life.

The Hawaiian archipelago is the only place I would ever truly call home. There are eight islands, and I am from Oahu, where Honolulu the capital is. I arrived there a '*malihini*' or 'newcomer'; later I earned the title of '*kama'aina*' ('long-term resident'). But I will always be, in Hawaiian terms, a '*Hapa-Haole*' – half-white. '*Haole*' means, literally 'white-skinned ghost' – it was the word the islanders used to describe Captain Cook and his crew when they landed on the archipelago, looking so pale it was assumed they must be long dead.

When we arrived in Hawaii its native royalty were long gone, and it was an American territory (though its flag, the Kae He Hawaii, has the Union flag incorporated into it, because, it is said, the British explorer George Vancouver presented a flag to King Kamehameha I on behalf of George III). In 1959, shortly after we settled there, Hawaii became formally designated the fiftieth state of the United States of America, and at school we swore allegiance to the American flag every morning. My identity is typically twentieth century: I was born in Tokyo in Japan, but I hold an American passport and I have lived in London for thirty years; I am a citizen of the world but a native of Hawaii.

This is normal at home, where everyone seems to be derived from many races, or 'chop suey', as we say. Hawaii is a truly multi-cultural society where various cultures flourish side-by-side. Almost all the kids I went to school with were a mix of French, Chinese, Hawaiian, Irish, Portuguese, Japanese – sometimes all in one person. I never had to define myself in Hawaii, so it was strange to me when people in London kept trying to pin down who I was and where I was from.

My parents' story was like Puccini's *Madama Butterfly* with a happy ending. My father was a young American GI from Norfolk, Virginia. He met my mother, a Japanese translator, when she was working at the American Officers' Club in Sapporo. Pop wasn't an officer but he wangled his way in there anyway. He has the good manners of a true southern gentleman, and the looks, my family often remarks, of Robert Duvall. It was a love match and, unusually for those times, Mom's parents gave permission for her to marry an American. Perhaps they felt it would help counterbalance the tragedy of one of their sons, who was killed in action shortly after they prevented him from marrying his American sweetheart. When General MacArthur pulled the GIs out of Japan after the occupation, Pop had to go, leaving my mom pregnant and alone. But, unlike so many, he returned.

Pop had always been keen to leave the South where he grew up. His father was a tough police detective; his mother Marie, however, was a gentle soul. I have no real memories of them but I do recall once seeing, when we visited my grandmother in Virginia, a local curiosity known as 'the snake pit', a hole dug at the bottom of the back yard. The snakes kept in this hole were used in dramatic local Southern Baptist ceremonies. They had their venom extracted, and were taken into church where they would be encouraged to bite the ministers; when the ministers survived it was taken as proof of a miracle. This was all too much for Pop, who became a lifelong atheist.

Like all his friends, he used to run errands for local gangsters (he swears one of them was connected to Al Capone), delivering brown paper packages containing liquor – or even morphine – around town. The restrictive local Baptist licensing laws meant there was a thriving black market. Hungry for adventure and keen to get away from home, he joined the army as soon as he could.

He was stationed all over Europe, including Chester, where in 1944 he was billeted on a farm near Tatton Hall and ended up 'sleeping in the chicken coops'. He was in the 744 Division of the Special Field Artillery Unit, and then assigned to the Third Army, led by General Patton in France, Germany and Austria. When the war ended he met the Russians in Linz. He was reassigned to the 11th Airborne and was sent to the Philippines, awaiting the invasion, but then Hiroshima happened.

My mom always talks about the shock that was felt on hearing Hirohito announce defeat over the radio; to many, he was a God in human form. No one had ever heard him speak before. After Hiroshima and Nagasaki Pop was sent to Hokkaido, the Japanese territory so northerly on a clear day you could see Russia. It was there that my parents met. In the post-war period when Japan was beginning to embrace the West, Mom was beginning to embrace Pop.

Mom's upbringing was also unconventional. She was born in Otaru in the Hokkaido region of Japan, the mountainous snow country and Japan's northernmost territory, where the Ainu people come from, as well as all the best Sumo wrestlers.

She was the last in a family of ten and born to a mother who was in her fifties. This was then considered a scandal in Japan, so she was given away to one of the older daughters; my mother grew up believing her sister was her mother and her mother was her grandmother. Later, this was one of the things that bound me and Jack Nicholson, and also Eric Clapton, who both had very similar family experiences. But more of them later.

Mom won a scholarship to study opera in Italy and learned enough English to equip herself for her international career as a diva. But because of the war she hadn't been able to take up the scholarship. She used to serenade us with 'the hills are alive with the sound of music' so loudly that you could hear her through the whole valley – to the intense irritation of our neighbours.

My maternal grandmother was, to me, terrifying: ancient-looking, severe and constantly murmuring imprecations in Japanese. When my sister and I giggled at her she used to chase us around with a broom. Little did I realise that she was a medium and a healer; a local wise woman. According to my mother she could go into a trance and levitate, bobbing gently up and down off the floor. They say these powers get handed down from mother to daughter, though I don't have that particular talent. I am sensitive, though, to places, spirits and energies. Staying at Sudeley Castle with my boyfriend Mark Shand I couldn't sleep all night because of the strange vibrations and the smell of something long dead. Perhaps it was to do with the ghost of Katherine Parr, who remained unburied for years after her death. In fact they later found a dead mouse under my bathtub, but I'll blame Katherine Parr for the fact that I couldn't sleep a wink and for all those raised eyebrows amongst our hosts when I came down for breakfast so late.

I have also always been nervous of electricity, though I only found out recently that my mother's father died in an accident at the Russian-staffed fisheries he owned – by electrocution. In the film *The Ice Storm* directed by Ang Lee there's a scene of death by electrocution which is very beautiful, sudden and dramatic. I suppose anyone would want their end to be so painless and poetic, but it resonated so deeply within me I felt almost as though I saw my death foretold.

When I was born in Tokyo, I was taken immediately to the US embassy to become a naturalised American. My pop christened me, in the southern tradition, with 'Lee' as my middle name, after the Confederate general. My siblings all have the same middle name, too; even Mom adopted it when she cast off her Japanese birth name, became an American citizen and chose the name Linda Helvin.

At first we made our home in Japan but soon, with the Korean war ongoing, Pop became uneasy and, thinking of what had happened to the Europeans in Shanghai, decided it would be safest to move his young family to the US, first to Washington DC. I remember the journey: we took the very smart Stratocruiser, the premier service run by Northwest Airlines. Mom and I slept in one of the special first-class bed compartments, situated where the overhead luggage lockers now are, and when we unzipped it in the morning everyone on the plane looked up at us, very impressed. It's one of my first memories. Despite what my father says about my chubbiness I must have been quite a cute child because the air hostess put a badge on me and let me help her hand out the drinks. (I loved it – the authority!)

Settling later in Virginia didn't work out, though. Mom felt a subtle hostility against her, as if she was perceived as having stolen one of 'our boys'. Pop went to college on the GI bill and worked selling insurance services to the US armed forces, but he wanted an out too, and craved somewhere isolated and free. And so we ended up in the middle of the Pacific Ocean.

Feet

It was an idyllic childhood. I walked to school barefoot, and I came home barefoot. Shoes were for rainy days, and then only slippers. Depending on what I wanted to eat, I would take a different route home, either walking past the lychee or guava trees, or where the mangoes grew, so I could devour them whole, skins and all (it's a Pacific island thing). I didn't bother with papaya. Too many seeds.

Sometimes I took a detour to see the sleeping grass, which grew in small patches along the Kalanianiole Highway. It lay in the sun with its leaves open, until I slid my bare feet over its ticklish top, when the leaves would curl up and shrink. Imagining the grass knew what I was doing, I would run away and hide, waiting for the leaves to open up before sneaking back and brushing my foot over its cool, delicate little leaves all over again.

By the time I was thirteen the soles of my feet were so tough I could stub out a cigarette without shoes. When my friends and I went looking for *opihi* (limpets) along the shoreline at low tide at Hanuama Bay, I would crack them with my bare feet and eat them. My feet have stayed strong ever since. When my friend the designer Bruce Oldfield came to stay with me he was squeamish about the island's 'wildlife' (for which read cockroaches), so if I saw one scuttling past me towards him I would step out and squish it under my heel. No problem.

I never liked people to see my feet when I was modelling; I had to do a close-up during a shoot once, and I asked Grace Coddington, the *Vogue* fashion editor, to step in for me. 'Why, what beautiful feet you have!' people said to me afterwards, but the credit should have been all hers.

All through my life I've been happiest barefoot, slapping my soles on the marble floor round at Jerry and Mick's or slopping around in sandals at home. In London it hasn't always worked; the paparazzi had a field day when I left Langan's Brasserie barefoot late at night once, carrying my Manolos in my hands. And once when I was dating the actor Neil Pearson I jumped barefoot into a taxi to go over to his home. The taxi driver almost refused to take me, uncivilised Hawaiian that I am. But I like my feet on the ground.

*

Do children ever appreciate their luck? We could pick fresh papaya from the back yard for breakfast, but I preferred to get a stack of pancakes dripping in butter and coconut syrup. Pop was a dedicated health nut, and would squeeze us fresh vegetable juices, which we'd swallow under duress. We preferred Tang, the orange powder drink marketed as 'the astronaut's choice'. We used to pray for a McDonald's until Pop, to put us off, told us the beefburgers were made of mongoose scraped off the highway. We believed him absolutely, and never asked for one again.

Hawaii is noted as a particularly healthy place to live. A Hawaiian born in 2000 can expect to live to an average age of seventy-nine years – a figure higher than any other US state. However, I'll be surprised if I don't pay the price for one unhealthy childhood habit: playing in the street following the DDT fumigation machine, which has long been banned in America. We used to chase behind it, dancing in the billowing clouds of smoke, pretending to be lost in an enchanted netherworld. I can still smell the toxic fumes and it makes me choke to remember.

Another more wholesome favourite game was to hike up to Jackass Ginger – a *mauka* (mountainside) gully covered in lush verdant jungle. We would weave, tie leaves into a mat and then during the rainy season we would slide all the way down the stony crags on our bony little butts. 'It rained last night!' we would shriek to each other. 'Let's go mudsliding!' I still have an odd discoloration on my bottom – like a permanent bruise – which shows up in certain photographs.

The atmosphere on Hawaii is balmy and tropical. The hot air hits you in the back of the throat as soon as you get off the plane, salty from the sea and fragranced with tuberose and *pikake* (jasmine). I never wore proper clothes; I would go to school wearing a huge baggy T-shirt with my bikini underneath so I could go to the beach straight after classes. I loved the sea but I was always aware of its power. Every child in Hawaii learns these golden rules: keep to beaches with lifeguards; never swim at sunrise or sunset when sharks feed; and never swim near bloody fish. Hawaii is at risk from tidal waves and I was taught to keep an eye out for the tide, and never, ever to turn my back on the ocean. Years later when I was staying with Mick and Jerry in Mustique I was horrified when she suggested going for a dip with the children at dusk. 'Don't you know this is feeding time?' I told her, but quietly, so as not to terrify the children. And why would she know? She's a gal from Mesquite, Texas.

Sheltered though the islands are, we witnessed all the defining moments of the sixties. President John F. Kennedy came to visit, with Jackie, and we went out to wave flags for them. I was too small to see what the fuss was all about, really, but I was hoisted on to my father's shoulders and waved at their motorcade. The day he was assassinated I was at school, and our principal announced his death over the tannoy with tears in her voice. The teacher started crying too, and we were all sent home. I have to confess I was happy just to have free time. I let myself in through the back door, which was always unlocked, and raided the fridge and watched TV most contentedly. Similarly, I was nonplussed when I saw pictures of women burning their bras in *Life* magazine. I really wanted a bra. What were they doing? I thought they were out of their minds.

Feminism wouldn't enter my life till much later. But there was no escaping the Cold War. Every other day at school we had a series of safety drills. We were taught to recognise the siren for tidal waves, when we had to head *mauka* – upland, because we were *makai*, by the ocean. We learned the signal for civil defence – and nuclear fallout. When that siren went we all had to hide under our desks – though I rather feel a wooden tabletop wouldn't have saved us from Armageddon. Every house was encouraged to build a fallout shelter, but my father refused. Figuring it wouldn't help much anyway, he built us a new *lanai* (patio) instead. Many of my friends had a fallout bunker at home, but we had a really nice *lanai*. My father planned, if things got really bad, that we would move to New Zealand and eat canned beans on the beach. 'Doesn't that sound great, girls?' he'd say. He's a free-thinker, my pop.

Every Christmas he would encourage us to support a different cause. One year, we sent literally hundreds of cards to Joan Baez who was in prison for evading the part of her tax bill that was earmarked for the Vietnam war. Each card was marked 'From the Helvin Family'.

I heard about the moon landing from the news when I was waiting for my favourite TV show to begin. Neil Armstrong took a ukulele to the moon with him, they said. That's neat, I thought, then – goody! 'It's time for "Captain Hono-lulu"!' came the theme tune, and I did my Captain Honolulu dance with my arms above my head. It was one giant step for mankind, but one small cartoon break for me. Later Apollo 11 crash landed in the ocean near Hawaii, which was a very big deal as it meant that, for once, Hawaii was in the news every day.

My twin passions, as a child, were nuns and horses. Pop had insisted we all learned to ride and I adored it. I kept locks of my favourite horses' manes in a little shrine in my bedroom. I even wrote to Walter Farley to ask if I could found a branch of the Walter Farley Black Stallion club. I told him I had hundreds of friends who wanted to join. When I received – my first letter ever! – a hundred badges in a manila envelope I didn't know what to do with them. I gave one to each of my sisters, Naomi and Suzon, and the rest ended up under my bed, where illicit candy was hidden too.

It was our family tradition to dedicate a special day, now and again, to a particular child. 'You've done well at school – let's have a Marie Day!' Pop might say, and I always chose to spend my day down at the stables with him (he had insisted all of us learn to ride), before having a sandwich together, filled with avocado, yoghurt and alfalfa sprouts, at his favourite health food restaurant. The tradition was inspired by the Japanese custom of a name-day, and it also gave me and my siblings the chance to have some one-to-one time with Mom or Pop. Mom would take me shopping, or she would give me a Toni perm, straight out of the box. I don't think my hair ever recovered. Neither of my sisters dared let Mom do it to them; it was one of the penalties of being the eldest.

The obsession with nuns was partly a reaction against my father's militant atheism, which was so strident he never let me go to church, even when my friend's elder siblings got married. It was also because of Bernadette Soubirous. I would skip school and sneak home to watch television during the day, when I figured the best television must be on. I was right: I watched *The Song of Bernadette* with absolute rapture (and it is still one of my favourite movies today). I thought Jennifer Jones was so pure and gentle; beauty for me became bound up with goodness and sacrifice. There was a Catholic school near my home called the Star of the Sea, and every day after school I used to run down to see the nuns and offer to carry their books from convent to class. I have no idea what they made of this scrawny little barefoot ten-year-old beaming up at them, proudly carrying their books. Suffice to say my parents never found out.

I idolised Jennifer Jones because she was dark, like me, but so beautiful. This was a time when the majority of female film stars were blonde and voluptuous, and little girls who didn't conform to that physical type had very few role models to follow. I loved Hayley Mills but she looked so different to me I couldn't imagine ever having all the adventures she had. So I used to fixate on alternative women who looked a bit like me: Debra Paget (in *Bird of Paradise* she jumps into the volcano to appease the gods and save the island. I could associate with that: again, beauty and sacrifice went together) and the dark-haired wench on the Sun-Maid packet of raisins. And when I was very little and watched the Mickey Mouse Club, Annette Funicello was always my favourite. I would sing along to the theme tune, as millions of other children did all across America 'M-I-C – See you real soon! K-E-Y – Be good now! M-O-U-S-E . . .' Annette was little and chubby and had frizzy Bozo-the-clown hair, just like mine after the Toni perm. It's important to children to see people on television and in the media who represent their ethnic and physical type. Bianca Jagger paved the way for me coming after her, I feel, as even though she was not a model, her iconic beauty meant that the dark exotic look began to be celebrated.

It makes me so happy to hear from younger models like Yasmin Mills, who is half-Indian, and Yasmin Le Bon, who is half-Persian, that seeing me in *Vogue* inspired them to have confidence in their own beauty. 'Marie Helvin broke a lot of barriers,' Yasmin Le Bon told Bailey on film in his Channel 4 documentary.

But back to my childhood cultural consumption. The big TV was the focal point in our living room. My father would be smoking a cigar in the Papa chair with his feet up; my mom would be on an elegant yellow silk sofa. The kids – we three girls and my new younger brother Steve – would be in lion-cub poses on the floor. I got first pick of where to lie on the floor because I was the eldest. Normally I would lie on my left side, and Suzon my sister would lie in my mirror image on her right. Pop sat between us on his throne, these little bodies splayed on the floor around him. My nickname when I was a teenager was KIA for Know-it-all, because I was always telling people what was what. My little brother Steve was Stevie Wonder, Suzon was Little Flower, the island goddess, and Naomi was Mighty Mouse. Pop still calls her 'Mighty' now, even though she's married to a French ambassador.

We were all watching the *Ed Sullivan Show* when the Beatles came on. I loved them, and the first record I ever bought was 'I Wanna Hold Your Hand'. I scorned Elvis, with his sideburns and greasy hair, and sided with the Beatles every time. I went to the cinema to see *A Hard Day's Night* and, because it seemed to be the thing to do, screamed all the way through; I was hoarse when I came home. Never in a million years did I think that I would meet any of them, much less become friends with any of them.

In many ways I was very Hawaiian. We moved many times, as Pop's new career in land investment took off. But in my early years we were just about the only *Hapa-Haole* household in the neighbourhood and at my first school there were no other children who were mixed like me: they were all Hawaiians and Samoans. After school I had extra classes in traditional Hawaiian dance and music – hula and ukulele. I was especially lucky because my teacher was a special ancient *halau* master. Every day after school we would have to eat *poi* (made from pounded taro root – like eating glue!) to get into the Hawaiian spirit, and then we'd practise our string-plucking, hip swaying and hand gestures. It's a uniquely Hawaiian tradition, a recounting of history and legend, and I used to practise for hours in my bedroom after dark, doing the hand movements in the shadows cast by the street lights.

It was such a magical, mythical place to grow up. I didn't have Mr Winnie the Pooh (is that the one that eats honey?), instead I had the Menehunes, tiny leprechaun-like creatures who were very industrious. I remember Pop once pointing out a bridge in Hanapepe on the island of Kauai and saying, 'The Menehunes built that.' I was also fascinated by *heiaus* sacred burial grounds hidden across the islands by ancient elders. Native Hawaiians treat these sites with respect and care and removing anything from them, a stone or even a plant, is punishable by state and federal law. They are sacred spots, rife with spirits. When I was a child there was a lot of controversy over the building of a huge hotel on a plot of ground that turned out to be a *heiau*. Several construction men were injured before work was suspended. The site was eventually shifted by a few metres, and blessed by a *kahuna* (keeper of ancient knowledge). Spirits are still alive in island life.

When the volcano erupts, we say its goddess Pele is angry, stamping and panting. According to mythology, just before the volcano is about to blow, she appears as either a very old lady or a young beautiful woman, hitch-hiking a lift at the roadside. You pick her up, turn round to look at the back seat of the car, and she's gone . . . I told you it's a magical place.

When Sonny and Cher came to visit I was chosen by a radio DJ to perform 'Aloha Oe' on the ukulele, written by Queen Liliuokalani.

I remember Sonny being rather taken with me, though I thought he was just a short old man – what was gorgeous Cher doing with him? I also won the state competition for the most original flower garland or 'lei' – I made mine from bits of lava, and made my hands bleed, in fact, by stitching it together. I was photographed in the paper with our first governor, Governor Quinn. It was a great day.

But there were distinctly American hobbies too. I was a dedicated Girl Scout, moving up the ranks from Brownie to Junior and Cadet, though I never became a Senior, because by that time I had become a hippie – of which more later. Winning badges was my *raison d'être* and my sash was covered in them: riding, marine biology, hiking, sailing. To get the flying badge, you had to go up in the cockpit of an aeroplane, and I made it happen by pestering the boy who sat next to me at school, whose father was a pilot.

Camping trips with the Scouts were the ultimate treat, and we went all over the island pitching our pup tents on mountains, jungle and beach. Every night, guaranteed, one of us would shriek, 'Crab attack! Crab attack!' I loved it when we sat round the campfire cooking American scout food, called 'Some Mores'. You made these by sticking a marshmallow on a twig and roasting it over the fire, then stuffing it between two Graham crackers and a square of Hershey's chocolate, so everything melted together. Candy was forbidden at home so I took it whenever I could get it. Once, we were meant to have a bring-and-buy sale but instead of selling my chocolate contribution I squirrelled it away and ate it all myself. Sweetness was something I craved. One All-Butter Dutch Cookie from Mom's cookie tin was, to me, heaven. After that she would hide it in the very top cabinet in the kitchen. I was famous for going on the Search when I got home, for food or loose change. Finding all the drawers open and cupboards ransacked, my parents would sigh to one another, 'Marie's been on the Search.'

My sisters and I were all skinny little rakes, and my mom was not a great cook. Those two facts were not unrelated. Mom claimed it was because she had grown up with servants and had been banned from the kitchen. She would leave us things on the stove to have for a snack when we got home from school, maybe sliced tomato with sugar sprinkled on it (which was a combination created during the deprived wartime era, and we certainly never ate it – our mother was from a different time and culture, you see), *onigiri* (a rice ball with tuna in the middle and covered with toasted seaweed), a pot of corn on the cob or sweet potatoes (which my mother lived on when she was hiding out in bunkers during the war), or tuna sashimi with soy sauce and hot rice from her pre-programmed rice cooker. Once it was a whole pot of fresh crab's legs, with lemon and butter on the side. It was always interesting to see what she'd left steaming on the hob for us but, really, she had no idea about cuisine. I soon took over supper after I had campfire cooking lessons with the Girl Scouts. 'Are you doing dinner tonight, Marie?' my pop would say hopefully. Nowadays my mom has renounced cooking entirely. She orders out all the time – and doesn't even own any pots and pans.

Mom totally embraced America: after her experience of the war she was happy to leave and start again in a shiny new fun culture. She never spoke any Japanese or tried to introduce us to that side of our history. Adjusting to American ways wasn't easy all the way, though: Pop insists that once, at a tea party in Washington DC, she became confused and tried to eat a teabag. Her English is perfect – she was a professional translator, after all – but sometimes, when she's angry, the words just become incomprehensible. My sisters and I used to laugh at her; sometimes this melted her, and she would start laughing too; other times it just angered her further.

Mom is a very gracious lady, but she's strong-willed also. When I swore at her once, she hit me on the head with the nearest thing to hand – a *Yellow Pages*. Another time, after I had been skipping school again, she confronted me in the kitchen, and this time when I answered back she grabbed an egg and broke it over my head – only this punishment backfired because I liked it so much I went straight to the shower and pretended to be Farrah Fawcett in her famous commercial. 'This shampoo is better than a raw egg . . .'

Hawaii was a sheltered, friendly island and they were innocent and trusting times. You could have broken open the lock on our front door with a hairgrip. We kids used to hitch-hike everywhere, and we would play all day on the beach unchaperoned. Mom would leave me in charge of my siblings with a dollar and we would share a giant bag of Fritos corn chips and three bottles of Diamond Head strawberry soda. The rest we would spend on candy. That combination of salty and sweet, with the seawater dripping down my face and hair into the chips and into my drink, is one of my most vivid taste-memories. Mom would then collect us happy tired kids before sundown.

There was only ever one unpleasant incident. One night as I was getting changed I saw that the teenage son of one of our neighbours was watching me. He was standing in the street literally peering in my window. When I told my pop he was so angry we couldn't restrain him from storming round to visit this no-good neighbour of ours with a baseball bat. Later, we discovered he had cause: my younger sister Suzon came to me and confided to me that he had asked her to touch his dick. I was so furious I broke her confidence and reported him to my parents. It emerged he was a pest to the whole neighbourhood and he was later arrested but judged mentally unfit for incarceration. Sometimes I catch sight of him in the street or at a gas station when I go home – that's how small the island is – and it makes my skin crawl. Hawaii may be one of the few tropical islands in the world where there are no snakes, but, metaphorically, the adage holds true: every paradise has its serpent.

*

'There is nothing in a caterpillar that tells you it's going to be a butterfly. Who knows what a man can become?'

R. BUCKMINSTER FULLER

When did you first 'do it'? It's a question there's no escaping. Once, at Sting and Trudie's house, we got high after dinner and started swapping confessional secrets about the first time.

'How did you lose yours, Marie?' they asked.

I told it like it was.

'I lost my virginity on the Slippy Slidey.' Trudie still teases me about it when I run into her. But what else could I say?

The Slippy Slidey was great fun, a long stretch of plastic sheeting on which kids would slide on water from the hosepipe. I loved it until I had a freaky accident one day when I was about seven. Somehow I got all tangled up on the way down and my knee hit my crotch. I landed in a heap at the bottom of the sheet. There was blood everywhere. I remember walking home crying, my legs bandy like John Wayne. Mom comforted me and explained as best she could but I didn't really understand what a broken hymen was.

No wonder it was so easy when I lost it for real, many years later. Though I was young, precocious even, when it came to the first stirrings of sexual attraction which I experienced while sitting on Marlon Brando's lap.

This happened at my Uncle Don's house. Uncle Don wasn't really my uncle, or even my official godfather. He was my 'Calabash' uncle though, which amounted to roughly the same thing, and I loved him. He was a great friend of my pop's, a real character and entertainer. He was an impresario by profession, and produced the most famous Polynesian dance revue, though he also did many other things. In fact, he was the first to employ my pop when he came to the island. Pop, Uncle Don and Batman worked together. (Yes, it really was Batman – the actor Adam West, then known as Bill Anderson, who later went on to star on TV. My parents used to point at Batman and say, 'Look, it's Uncle Bill!') Uncle Bill married one of the four famous Frisbie girls (the beautiful daughters of a Scots merchant seaman and a Tahitian beauty) and so did Uncle Don. His home was always full of interesting people. There I once met O.J. Simpson, young and at the height of his talent, but the man who really made an impression was Marlon Brando who had flown over to buy the island of Tetiaroa near Tahiti, one of many from the acting community that regularly made the five-and-a-half-hour hop over the ocean from LA to Hawaii.

There was a buzz around him at the party, as you might expect, and I found him fascinating. With childish chutzpah I pushed my way through the crowd that surrounded him. 'Who are you, cutie?' he growled and swept me on to his lap. I sat sideways, long little ten-year-old legs dangling. While people took snaps of us I felt obscurely happy perched there on this handsome actor's knee. I didn't know what this feeling was, only that I liked it.

I've often noticed that certain people who make a special impression return in my life later down the line. It feels to me like a magical thing, this process, though I don't know whether to call it chance, serendipity, or karmic coincidence. Bailey, for example, I sat next to in a restaurant two years before we 'met' for the first time. Marlon Brando was no exception. Fifteen years later I used to hang out on the estate on Mulholland Drive he shared with Jack Nicholson. People in my life recur and recur and recur – as you'll see through the course of this book. Is it accidental? More likely there's an invisible power at work under the surface of our seemingly random connections. I believe, ultimately, in fate.

Someone else of interest that I met at an early age was the Russian dissident poet Yevgeny Yevtushenko, then famous because of his poem 'Babi Yar'. He came to Hawaii on a worldwide lecture tour, miraculously managing to obtain permission to travel from the Soviet regime, and to me he seemed like a heroic escapee from Khrushchev's regime. He was blond and tall and wore a Beatles cap; he cut an impressive figure. I found it amazing that a real-life Russian was visiting our island: after all, these were our enemies in the Cold War, the whole reason we had built our nuclear shelter (or rather, our new patio). I attended his lecture at the University of Hawaii, which I hitch-hiked to get to – I was only a young teen, but I was desperate to be older. After his lecture, which was about his poetry and full of inspiring thoughts about peace in our time, I plucked up the courage to go and speak to him. 'Why do you want to bomb us?' was my childish question. I had been brought up to think all Russians wanted us dead as soon as possible. He was very gracious and friendly, and, wishing I could invite him home as I did all visiting people of interest, I innocently gave him our home phone number. I knew it was unlikely he would ever come back to Hawaii, but I hoped he could have a beer with Pop if he did.

I was a gawky, dreamy adolescent, and never thought of myself as beautiful. I was tall, with lots of frizzy matted hair (I swam in the sea so much I never bothered washing it), glasses and skinny beanpole limbs. 'Sticks', they used to call me at school.

I thought I was hideous, though I can't have been too bad. At school I was voted Queen of the May on Aloha Day, though when I look at the picture now I see that the standards were quite low. I don't look good, but my handmaidens sure don't either!

My one asset was that I always had good, clear skin. I was a slow developer – even Hayley Mills had more of a chest than me, I noticed to my chagrin. I owned a training bra with plenty of room for growth (the stitches could be unpicked to let it out – I was so desperate to let out a stitch!) but growth was not forthcoming. So I habitually stuffed it with loo paper. I became so practised, in fact, that once I carelessly grabbed green loo paper. How mortified I was when I realised I had shown a green front to the world all day ...

The first most important purchase I ever made was my blow-up bra. This I cherished. I wanted it so much I scrimped the money together by going round knocking at the door of every house in the neighbourhood, asking if I could wash their cars at fifty cents a time. Finally I had enough for my dream bra, which cost five dollars. This came equipped with a straw so that you could blow your tits up as big as you wanted. Some days I would be in a hurry and one side would be blown up more than the other. Sometimes I would huff and puff into the straw and go into school with enormous boobs; other days I didn't bother so much. It wasn't exactly a consistent system, but I loved that bra all the same.

My mom was relieved, I think, when school showed us a sex-education movie, sparing her from explaining it all herself. The boys were sent into one room – God knows what they saw – and we girls went into another room where they played us a Walt Disney-type film about the birds and the bees. I was not to know it but on the other side of the world, fifteen years earlier, a young David Bailey had become fascinated by Walt Disney animated movies, just as he was discovering sex too. On our first *Vogue* location shoot together, the famous pictures taken in Australia are a kind of Disney dreamscape, featuring me with a giant inflatable cartoon turtle nuzzling my shoulder.

Later he would make me scrape my hair back with Tenax hair gel or even KY Jelly into a very tight bun, which I disliked – it made me feel so exposed and as if I had nothing to play with round my shoulders. For him it was getting rid of superfluous elements, slimming things down to just my face for a high-impact shot. 'I look just like Jiminy Cricket,' I told Bailey laughingly at the time – and he gave me a look as if to say, 'That's it exactly.' Both of us shared a strange subliminal link between cartoons and the end of innocence.

I always had a lot of attention from boys and they used to like to walk me home, carrying my books and then hanging around the house till my father chased them off the front porch. They were all local tough boys (or *Mokes* in Hawaiian) with names like Baba Cruz or Keohokalole. I bet most of them are cops now. At school they were always punching me and poking me to get my attention. I used to come home black and blue. I guess it was their way of flirting, but I hated it.

I stuck with the boys for adventure, though. At low tide we used to sneak past the KAPU (Keep Out) signs across the rocky bay and into Doris Duke's estate, Shangri-La. There was a unique freshwater swimming pool there, which would fill up at high tide. We would go crazy, splashing about in the pool, but we knew we always had to keep an eye out for the turning of the tide because if we became trapped, we would drown. No other girls ever came on these daredevil expeditions.

There were lots of cute girls at my school, girls who, unlike me, wore shoes and had straight hair. To me they were like dolls, with pretty hair and pretty manners. I was fascinated by them, and I hoped that by hanging out with them some of their prettiness would rub off on me. I didn't have any elder sisters and I needed to find out how to be a girl.

I had a succession of fixations on girls. I'm not saying I was gay; I'd never heard of lesbianism. I just liked them, thought they were attractive and wanted to be their buddy. I would befriend them and they were flattered that I took an interest in them, and they would become, over time, my best mates – my slaves, even. They would hold a place for me in the cafeteria, make my favourite peanut butter, honey and banana sandwich, do my homework for me – all the little rituals of girls' friendship. One was so devoted she would iron my hair for me every morning before school.

I was considered an interesting person at school, because I always did my own thing – and I never played by the rules. At an early age, little gangster that I was, I became expert in forging my parents' signature, so I could skip classes. I would get dropped off at school by my mom, and hide in the bushes until her car had gone. When I got a bit older, I'd go off exploring with a friend, maybe to a bookstore to look at teenage romances, or hang out in a coffee shop making one cup of coffee (a treat – it was forbidden at home) last all day. All the while, we'd be keeping an eye out for the police – because truancy was illegal.

My parents never stayed cross with me for long; perhaps they were specially tolerant because they were young parents. In their spare time they were always doing the Hawaiian thing and playing sport: Mom bowling and playing golf and tennis, and Pop body surfing and weightlifting. He used to line us skinny girls up to do bust exercises, in fact.

Pop once broke his arm at Sandy Beach. When he came out of the water holding his arm we thought he was joking us, because he was a real tease. We only realised he was serious when he went to the lifeguard holding his arm screaming 'Eee-tai!' – the Japanese word for pain – and calling for an ambulance. It was so exciting to ride in the ambulance with the siren howling and the cars parting, and best of all the next day I was the centre of attention because everyone had heard about my pop and thought he was so cool because fathers didn't normally go body surfing down at Sandy Beach.

Once or twice they went off to Vegas together leaving me in charge of the family. I would cook 'Pot Luck', a dish I'd learned with the Scouts. It consisted of every can in the cupboard thrown into a great saucepan, mixed together with a pinch of every spice. At the time we all thought it was delicious.

As a pre-teen, I did what you could say was my first modelling work. My sister Suzon and I used to collect plumeria blossom from our garden to make leis (Hawaiian flower garlands) and we would hitch-hike up to Diamond Head, a panoramic lookout. There, we would pose for photographs for the tourists, charging them a quarter a time. It was a nice little earner and own business initiative. It was also a secret: my parents would have been horrified if they had found out.

In many ways I felt like an adult trapped in that little thirteen-year-old body. I always wanted to be older than I was. I was good at school (when I turned up) but I wanted to be in the older kids' classes, not my own. I befriended the psychology teacher and she let me sit at the back of her classes while she taught Jung. 'Who looks outside, dreams; who looks inside, awakes' was the phrase that first bit me, making me want to pursue this dreamy interior world that no one had spoken to me about before. My family was very loving, but very conventional – this was the first thing I encountered that hinted of a world outside and beyond.

I have a passion for Jung's work to this day. I also learned from this teacher about speed reading and memory enhancement. People say I have a great memory – Bailey always used to fire random questions at me: ('Who was that guy we met in Chichén Itzá?'). The reason I can remember ('You mean the Jesus freak with the big beard named Hank?') is all thanks to this teacher, who trained us, via visualisation techniques, how to develop photographic recall. Iron-ically, I can't remember her name, but she was important to me.

She also taught me how to get rid of non-essential data before it clogs up the mind. I take an instant gut decision: do I keep this memory? If not, I deliberately drop it from my mind. It goes out of my brain, along with all the old phone numbers, the trivia, the rubbish. A side-effect of this system is that numbers become impossible – they're like hieroglyphs to me. I can't add four with four.

One day Mom shouted to me excitedly, 'Phone call! Phone call!' It was – could you have guessed it? – Yevgeny Yevtushenko. He had returned to Hawaii and was coming round to pick me up and take me, and a friend of my choice, with him to a Monkees concert. It was like a dream come true.

As I remember it I got very dressed up for Mr Yevtushenko's visit. My mother helped me and together we put together an outfit made up of a white tank top with lots of silver thread in it – lurex, I think – and a silver tulip skirt, silver stockings and silver shoes. (Tights did not exist in those days.) I felt very grown up. Yevtushenko was with the Monkees' producers, Bob Rafelson and Bert Schneider. Bob went on to direct *The Postman Always Rings Twice* and *Five Easy Pieces*; Bert was also a film producer (he made *Easy Rider*) and a huge supporter of the Black Panthers. Years later I would meet Huey Newton at Bert's house; I was so intimidated by his powerful charisma and his intensity. Unfortunately I couldn't participate in his political conversation and he seemed to think I shouldn't bother living if I wasn't going to be an activist.

But there at the concert I was in my element – not because of the company but because we were watching the Monkees. I was in heaven! They were the first manufactured boy band, very much part of the Zeitgeist, and they were all really cute and I loved them.

After the concert Yevtushenko took me home and I vividly recall Pop sitting there in his easy chair while he and Yevtushenko talked. In my memory, Pop is wearing his boxer shorts, which makes me a little anxious – but he offered the Russian visitor not the everyday, cheap local Primo beers, but one of the larger, more expensive Michelob bottles. Was it all just a dream? Although it seems so clear to me I sometimes wonder if my imagination hasn't embellished this incident. It is something I have returned to mentally so many times – I spent a long time trying to write a play about it, in fact – that I can't be absolutely sure what actually happened after the concert. But this book consists of my memories, and they are true to me.

My first kiss happened when I was twelve or thirteen at a local playground hangout called Skateland, with a kid called Billy Tuando. He was from the Salvation Army Boys' Home, a rough little orphan, *Hapa*-Samoan, and Mom was not best pleased. I thought it was bliss, though, and remember the kiss fondly whenever I pass the spot in Hawaii – or I would do, if Skateland hadn't been replaced by the morgue and pathological institute. With that kiss, though, everything changed. Crushes on girls went out of the window and I started dating Hawaiian surfer dudes.

One of my early romantic encounters was nearly fatal. There is a famous saltwater natatorium in Waikiki (now on the National Register of Historic Places) and it had a small underground water hatch which was a well-known spot for brave kids to make out in. You had to hold your breath and swim through a short tunnel to get there, which I and my beau did, no problem, but once we swam through we found the tide was too high and there was no air to breathe. There was only a sliver of breathing space between water and rock, which we fought to get to. All romance vanished as we struggled – he kicked my neck in his rush to get out. We were lucky we didn't drown.

At around the same kind of time, I stole one of my parents' ultra-light True cigarettes and smuggled it into my bedroom. I lit up and posed with it in front of the mirror. I thought, I like the way I look smoking, and then passed out on the floor. Whatever makes you continue with a drug that does that to you? Sad to say, it was the first of a habit that continued until I was forty. Soon, I would be going to the drive-in with a boyfriend and chain smoking all the way through the movie with my baby brother Steve curled up in the back. My favourites were the Hammer films; I loved Vincent Price and particularly *The Masque of the Red Death*. Who knew I would later become acquainted with his co-star Jane Asher and her husband Gerald Scarfe. I also watched *Blow-Up*, which made no sense to me.

My party years had begun: drinking beer, getting high, making out. This last was quite fraught, though. I was so flat-chested all there was for the boys to get hold of was toilet paper. Once a guy told me, 'You have a body made for loving.' He sure didn't realise I was packing a bra stuffed full of Andrex, one side blue, the other side pink. Boys were certainly never allowed below the belt: I even put a safety pin on the zip of my jeans. When my parents went away I would host all-night parties, concocting an enormous pot of brew made from every can of beer I could find and a dollar's worth of ice from the gas station.

My baby siblings and I had had a habit of cycling out with our breakfast, a grapefruit maybe, or some toast, to eat in the sunny branches of a gigantic hau, an ancient tree with a vast trunk and branches that we had worked out how to climb. Now I started staying at home, saying I couldn't be bothered to join them. I'd rather be putting on make-up and going down to meet boys at the beach. 'You've begun to be very boring,' my little sister Suzon told me. In fact I had simply begun to be grown up.

*

'One pill makes you larger
And one pill makes you small . . .
Remember what the dormouse said:
Feed your head . . .'

JEFFERSON AIRPLANE, 'WHITE RABBIT'

'By means of microscopic observation and astronomical projection the lotus flower can become the foundation for an entire theory of the universe and an agent whereby we may perceive Truth.'

YUKIO MISHIMA

Have you ever stared at a flower so long it came to resemble an entire universe? Each petal a kingdom, each stamen a world in itself? Forgive me if I sound like an acid casualty. That's exactly what I was.

I stared at a daisy once for a whole afternoon, at a love-in in Tantalus in the high hills of Oahu, where we sat around in home-made tie-dye clothes endlessly debating the human condition and talking about Carlos Castaneda, or rather the teachings of Don Juan, the Yacqui shaman who inspired him. LSD was still legal in Hawaii when I was growing up. Lauren Hutton has written about how she was ordering it direct from Swiss laboratories until, as she puts it, 'That fuckin' Timothy Leary messed things up for us . . .'

We used to drop acid all the time, 1,000 mg, 1,500 mg and more, chewing wood rose and morning glory seeds (which have hallucinogenic properties very similar to peyote), smoking anything to get high and expand our consciousness. It wasn't about having a mindless hedonistic rush, like you get from cocaine; instead we wanted to become free mentally. I could have stayed looking into that flower for ever, but I snapped out of it when I realised it was nightfall and my friends were calling to me. I made it home on rather unsteady legs.

In those days you were either with them or with us; you were square or hip; you did drugs and went to love-ins, or you wore glasses and trained to be a doctor or a teacher. It was a call you had to make. Deeply caught up in the whole hippie rigmarole, I was hopelessly altruistic. I didn't want to study hard and become a politician. Instead I fancied I might become a conservationist and save the world through peace, love and protest songs.

I smoked dope from my early teens on – not the knockout skunk available nowadays that's hydroponically grown, vastly more potent and messes with your mind, but the milder weed of the sixties and seventies, called *pakalolo* in Hawaii and naturally occurring on the island. It was so commonplace I can't remember my first joint; my mother was even prescribed it by her doctor to help her break her caffeine addiction. It felt as if everyone was doing it.

Mysticism, yoga, Ravi Shankar, Indian food, Indian gods, bell-bottoms, body painting, long hair for men and women – all these were our fads at the time. Everyone was fascinated by India, but no one really wanted to go. We wanted the full Indian experience on home shores. We were all young and pretty unenlightened. I hitch-hiked to the Waikiki Shell, the outdoor amphitheatre, to hear the Maharishi Mahesh Yogi speak because he was the guru to the Beatles, but personally I was a little sceptical of all his talk about the electricity of human thought. I just didn't get it.

I did get Led Zeppelin though, and how. To experience the music fully I would drag my record player into my closet and shut myself in there with it playing full blast. It was my way of engineering a stereo effect, and getting kinda high on the music too.

'Mellow Yellow', Donovan's song, made it sound as if you could get high from banana skins and my friends and I spent a whole summer trying out different ways of baking and drying them, smoking them ... None of it worked. Finally we hit on hanging the skins on the laundry line for days till they were black and toasty and flyblown. 'What are they?' said Mom. We told her they were for a science experiment. Smoking them had only one effect, though: it made us sick.

Then one day the exotic 'windowpane' variety of acid – a teeny tiny bit of gelatine impregnated with acid – arrived in Hawaii from England. I remember going to take one with a friend. We had decided to split it between us but we couldn't work out how to divide it – like a fool I tried to tear it with my teeth and spent the rest of the day growing and shrinking like Alice in Wonderland.

My participation in counter-culture drug use meant I was exposed to things a fifteen-year-old shouldn't have to see. I held the tourniquet while my friend's older boyfriend injected heroin. He had invited me into the loos to smoke a joint and I followed him casually. Then he asked me to tighten a belt round his arm while he held one end of it in his mouth and started shooting up. It was awful to watch him – to see the needle pierce the skin and the blood rush into the syringe ... I have a lifelong phobia of needles, and I thought I was going to faint. I saw his pupils contract into pinpoints, in a way I have only ever seen once since, when one of my pet rabbits mounted the other rabbit and its eyes literally rolled in its skull. The man then slumped over the sink while I watched with horror and fascination. I got out of there fast. It was an experience that left me with a lifelong wariness of addiction. He had always seemed friendly and lucid but I soon discovered that not everything is as it appears to be. The devil is in the detail.

Once, when I was on a teenage date, I was astounded when the boy brought out a can of whipped cream, emptied it all out and then used the nozzle so we could get off on the aerosol. It was an unpleasant, numb high, and didn't last long, so the two of us packed up and went to the cinema to see *To Sir with Love*.

The place to hang out was the Jungle, three streets in Waikiki full of dealers and pot-heads. It seemed to me like the epitome of cool. Now those streets are gone, replaced by skyscraper hotels. My main passion was for live music, and I saw the Doors, the Yardbirds, the Kinks, Led Zeppelin, Cream, the Stones – all of them stopped over to play Hawaii on their way to Australia or Japan. David Carradine and Barbara Hershey had a jug band, and I went to see them at the Crater Festival. I thought they were just the coolest thing. Her look was beach girl on acid, with great flowing long hair: Wow. But my favourite American band was called Blue Cheer, after the acid pill. Their claim was that they were the loudest band in the world and when they set their gigantic speakers up, we shook around on our metal chairs as if we were being electrocuted. I am nearly deaf in one ear: maybe it's from spending all that time getting as close as possible to the speakers.

Years later, when Jerry was visiting me in Hawaii, we went together to see the band Journey. I had to force her to come, and it was deafening rock and roll – but she had a neat solution. She tore the filters off her cigarettes and put them in her ears! I thought it was the cleverest thing.

The great venue was the Waikiki Shell where I'd heard the Maharishi, and it was there I saw Jimi Hendrix. (Later, when I graduated from high school from the same stage, all I could think of when I walked across the red carpet holding my diploma was: 'This is where Jimi stood!') At the University of Hawaii I saw Frank Zappa playing with his band the Mothers of Invention. I even got an invitation from the band, who were really ugly but also kinda cool, to come and visit them the next day, so I grabbed a friend, skipped school and went straight round to their rented house in the Jungle. But of course the Mothers were all dead to the world. It was only nine in the morning. Bitterly disappointed, my friend and I loitered around in one of the coffee shops, prohibited though they were, trying to avoid the police.

One night I went along to a friend's apartment in the Jungle and saw that a cinefilm was playing, projected on to an improvised screen made from a white sheet. I had ditched my glasses by this time and I couldn't see what was happening in the film, but I could hear an unusual thudding noise, like the sound of a wet fish being slapped. I went closer and peered at the screen, really peered at it, and the people in the room – there were about twenty-five of them – started laughing at me. Because what they were watching was a porn film, and the noise was the noise of people's bodies slapping against each other. They were doing it doggy-style! It was a real shock to me. (We only had cats at home, after all.) I was pretty horrified but I played it cool. I wanted to look older than I was, right?

Though I didn't know it then, this porn experience was probably the catalyst for what happened shortly afterwards. I went home with a couple I met at the Jungle, so we could all get stoned. But after a joint or two the man and his girlfriend jumped on me. Perhaps they didn't know I was only fifteen, or perhaps the porn film had seemed to them like a sort of initiation – but either way, I didn't like it. I ran out of there pretty fast.

I took drugs because they made me feel adult and connected to the wider world. They influenced music, literature, movies – drug culture defined the sixties. It was as simple as that. You could not avoid it. If you weren't involved in drugs it felt like you weren't living life to the full. Drugs were my way of coming of age and escaping the confines of the islands. For Hawaii had begun to seem like a very small place.

'When are we going to get off the Rock?' my friends and I would say to one another. We had what we called 'Polynesian paralysis'. When the Stones came to Hawaii we heard them being interviewed on the radio, and when the DJ said, 'How does it feel to be here?' one of them replied, 'Where are we again?' It was only a joke but my friends and I were so hurt. Was Hawaii really such an insignificant place?

I started to obsess over foreign culture. I had read the complete works of Dickens by the time I was sixteen, and it was the food he wrote about that really fascinated me, and gave me a tantalising insight into the alien culture. What were 'crumpets' and 'scones'? What was 'pease pudding' and 'ginger beer'? They sounded so exotic to me; I longed to try them. (I did know what kippers were because my father had them every Saturday for breakfast and the entire neighbourhood evacuated.) What was fog? Vog, volcanic fog, was what we had, which came rolling over the sea from the volcano Kilauea, over on the big island. Perhaps London was still choked by 'pea soupers'. What about 'cobbled stone streets'? What the hell was a cobble? My curiosity about London was also piqued by the Yardley cosmetics adverts, which showed tall leggy girls on roller skates with Twiggy-style fake eyelashes. A beautiful blonde girl with pigtails would be standing making a call from a beautiful big red phone box and then: 'Hey hey, we're the Monkees . . .' They would all appear and start singing. It was all so exciting. I yearned to travel.

Whenever someone foreign visited the island I was desperate to meet them. Once it was the celebrity hairdresser Vidal Sassoon. He was then at the height of his fame because he had created the famous haircut on Mia Farrow for *Rosemary's Baby*. *Life* magazine said it was the most expensive haircut in the world because he had been flown over from Europe specially; before that he was already famous in London for creating the Mary Quant style. One night he appeared on the Hawaii TV news and explained he was doing a US tour and was looking for models for his demonstrations. He meant business: he had booked an auditorium that accommodated thousands. And he was going to pay his models. I was in!

Mom helped me get dressed up for the audition. We washed my hair, which was halfway down my back by this time, and very thick. There were hundreds of girls at the audition but he took one look at me and he said, 'HER! I want her.' I was over the moon.

A few days later, I was on the stage. Blinded by the lights I couldn't see the thousands in the audience, only my mom in the front row. The great Vidal covered me up with a towel and started hacking away. Call me stupid, but I had been caught up in the whirl of the experience and this was the first moment I realised, Oh, he's going to cut my hair. After a few minutes of vigorous chopping sounds I felt a wetness on the back of my neck and touched it – it was blood. He was using a new razor technique and had nipped my skin; it didn't hurt, but it shocked me. I looked at my mom and her face was horrified. A big tear fell off my chin. I realised he was giving me a really drastic crop, and I burst out sobbing. I was embarrassed to be crying like this but the more embarrassed I was the more I cried. I practically howled as I received the applause from the audience. I ran backstage and looked in the mirror and there was a shorn page-boy standing in front of me, with the harsh geometric short back and sides. I was devastated.

I received my earnings – a hundred dollars – in one bill, which I'd never seen before. I was really tempted to put it in a frame, but instead I bought a beautiful English Raleigh bike, which was to me like a Concorde. It was stolen within two days. I was so mortified by my haircut I didn't want to leave the house for weeks.

Years later, I met Vidal in Japan when I was a model. I mentioned the incident to him and he said, 'Oh my God! You're the girl who wouldn't stop crying.' He soon booked me to model for him and, perhaps as some kind of recompense, he made sure to give me exactly the haircut I wanted, which was, I remember, the Mushroom.

The Vidal fiasco didn't inspire me to become a model, and I had no idea it would become my career and my way of finding the adventure I craved. I was just a schoolgirl hippie who painted herself silver on the weekends. No joke: I had a gay Hawaiian friend called Ray, and he and I bought silver oil from a theatrical shop which we painted all over each other's bodies. God knows what was in the paint – it was probably pure poison, mercury oil – but it looked fantastic. I wore a silver bikini too. Our entire skin would glow, and did so for years afterwards, no matter how hard I scrubbed.

Ray and I were hired, sometimes, to dance at music festivals and parties, our silhouettes projected on to a great white cloth. We called it 'interpretive' dance; by that we meant basic gyration and lots of

Kali-like Indian-style posing. I decided modern dance might be my calling and wrote to Merce Cunningham and Martha Graham in New York – but with no success. I carried on dancing, though, stoned out of my head and painted silver, my bikini bra stuffed with loo paper. A photo of me in this state was printed on the back page of the main Hawaii newspaper – but my name wasn't on it and my parents didn't see it, thank God. They had no idea; I was living a double life.

*

'And it's one, two, three,
What are we fighting for?
Don't ask me, I don't give a damn,
Next stop is Viet Nam;
And it's five, six, seven,
Open up the pearly gates,
Well there ain't no time to wonder why,
Whoopee! we're all gonna die.'
COUNTRY JOE AND THE FISH,
'I-Feel-Like-I'm-Fixin'-To-Die Rag'

It was around this time that I became politicised. Paris was in flames with the student riots, and the Beatles were in Rishikesh hanging out with the Maharishi writing *Abbey Road*. But what had most impact on me was the devastating Vietnam war. If I can pass anything on to another generation it would be the horror of being just on the periphery of these events.

Honolulu, the stopover between the States and the East, was at that time the major command HQ, second in importance only to the Pentagon. It was also the official R & R (rest and recreation) centre for the military. Everywhere you went there were soldiers or swabbies, as we called the sailors, and sometimes their wives and babies too. You could spot them because they always looked more conventional than anyone else, the men with buzz cuts, the women in neat dresses. They were the antithesis of me and my straggle-haired hippie friends. At Fort DeRussey, right in the middle of Waikiki, you would often see soldiers reuniting with their loved ones after their tour of duty, their arms outspread, all so happy to see one another – and yet I hated them. They were the enemy within that was fighting this awful, needless war.

Sometimes in the Jungle I would share a joint with soldiers straight out of Hanoi, or Phnom Penh. All they wanted to do was get high and forget, to be a nineteen-year-old again, while I wanted to cross-question them, put them on the stand. I was angry with them for fighting but I felt sorry for them too. I thought it was unfair that they were outcasts from the whole of the rest of the culture.

My friends' older brothers were conscripted, going off in their droves to be brutalised, wounded and sometimes killed. It was a terrible time to be an American. Every night on TV there was a graph that listed scores of names under the headings 'Dead', 'Presumed Dead', and 'Missing'. It also said what state each of the fallen came from; we could see what was happening to the boys from Ohio and they could see what was happening with us very much like the US coverage of the Iraq war today. I was inspired to join peace protest marches – and besides, it was a great way of getting out of school. My father actually urged me to cut class to go on the marches.

If we were driving along the highway and there were any pro-war demonstrators on the side of the road, Pop would give them the *maka-ele-ele* look – that is to say, his Hawaiian patois word for the stink-eye – and encourage all of us kids to shout obscenities at them, much to my mother's horror. When senator Hubert Humphrey stood against Nixon he would shout 'Dump the Hump!' at any homes we passed with a window sticker for him.

Pop was vehemently anti-war – in my home Jane Fonda was considered a heroine – just as he is adamant today about the illegality of the Iraq war. Pop was so anti-Vietnam, he encouraged me to do anything to protest against it. If I had wanted to do anything extreme he would have backed me one hundred per cent. He would have been thrilled. Instead, however, I planned to join the Peace Corps, which he was not so thrilled about, since he thought it was too closely connected with the Kennedy administration. But many a time I wandered over to their recruitment office on the campus of the University of Hawaii, hoping to join when I was old enough.

I must have turned up on twenty or twenty-five anti-Vietnam rallies, and became known as a peace protestor. So it wasn't, perhaps, surprising that when I tried to get a US passport later that summer it was very difficult. The CIA were taking their monitoring duties very seriously at this time, after all.

When I wasn't at rallies, I was down at the beach waxing surf boards or making out at the drive-in. I had lots of flirtations but one serious boyfriend: Russell, an American beefcake a few years older than me with long brown hair and a very cool pair of cowboy boots. Skipping class one afternoon, I went over to his place and let him take me into the bedroom for the first time. I was ready to lose my virginity.

As we made love on his bed he put on some classical music, which was so alien and beautiful to me it made me cry. I grew up in an American home in the sixties where all we heard was Frank Sinatra or Ella Fitzgerald, and I had no idea about Tchaikovsky. We sang *Oklahoma!* in my music class at school. Now I've grown to love classical music and always cry at concerts – the music touches me so deeply. Lying there with Russell when it was all over I still had tears streaming down my face. I thought it was what real women did after sex – that was what they always seemed to do in black and white movies. As Simone de Beauvoir said, 'One is not born a woman, but becomes one.'

I graduated easily, passing all my classes and even skipping a grade. The only class I ever failed was PE – the ever so slightly butch PE teacher probably wanted to make me come back all through the summer just so she could ogle me in the shower, I tell you. After the ceremony, Pop took me and Michie my best friend out for a really smart dinner. He tried to order champagne but the restaurant said we were under-age – Pop gave them hell but we never got to try any. But it didn't matter because the real treat was still to come: my mom and I had tickets for a ten-day trip to Japan. The American tradition at that time was to give your kids a gold watch when they graduated, but I passed on that. Who wanted a gold watch? I knew there was a bigger world out there, and I was desperate to see it.

Finally I was achieving my dream of travelling. I always felt different to the other kids, and strange though it may sound I always felt I would become known in some way. It was as if it was my destiny. When I was doing detention in the library I had chanced upon a book entitled *How to Be a Success*. I liked it so much I stole it and learned it by heart. It was an early type of self-help book, full of advice such as 'Always feel confident in yourself' and 'If you can dream it, you can do it'. It was cheesy, I knew even then, but in its way it was real inspiration too. It encouraged me to think wider than Polynesia in a way that nothing and no one else around me did.

Mom and I got dressed in our finest for the plane trip, which was a big deal in those days. We even wore dresses and shoes! I said goodbye to my boyfriend Russell, and told Michie to take care of him while I was away. I had no idea, when I looked down from the aeroplane on to the glittering archipelago below, that I was leaving my childhood behind for ever.

TWO

JAPANORAMA!

'Ziggy really sang, screwed-up eyes and screwed-down hairdo
Like some cat from Japan . . .'

DAVID BOWIE, 'Ziggy Stardust'

———

'**W**ow! This place is cool. There must be lots of hippies here.'
That was my first childish thought as we drove past the bright,
colourful cars in the streets of Tokyo. How wrong I was. They were
not psychedelic hippie cars, but Tokyo's famous taxis. I was about to
enter cultural meltdown, only I didn't know it yet.

First we made it to our hotel overlooking the Imperial Palace
where my mother and I got changed and ready to go off to the
kabuki theatre. We only had ten days in Japan, and we wanted to
make the most of it. We dressed smartly and were on our way towards
the door when one of us said: 'Shall we have a quick nap? Just for
fifteen minutes?' We woke up the next day, lying side by side in our
twin beds, still in our smart clothes. Thus I discovered jet lag.

We rushed everywhere after that, around Tokyo and off on the
Shinkansen to Nara to feed the tame deer in the famous deer park,
and to the golden pavilion in Kyoto. My mom wanted me to try the
food, visit the holy temples and do as much sightseeing as possible.
But for the general populace it seemed we ourselves were a sight to
be seen. Heads turned to gape at us wherever we went, my tall
Japanese mother and her gawky half-American *halfu* daughter wan-
dering behind her wearing her hair untamed down her back and the
briefest of mini-skirts. To the neat, conservatively dressed men and

women of Tokyo I must have looked like a crazed, suntanned giant. The sight of my toes peeping out of my open sandals provoked shock and horror. People pointed at them and jabbered away in a language I didn't understand. It never crossed my mind they might think my look appealing; I simply felt self-conscious – and very alien.

The city overwhelmed me with its dirty, smelly air and preoccupied people. The buildings were so tall – we didn't have skyscrapers in Hawaii then. This was the first time I had been to a city since I was about four years old, and I felt lost and suffocated amongst the crowds of women, many of whom were wearing traditional kimonos. Once I even passed out in a department store. I became claustrophobic, crushed in the throng of people. I really struggled to breathe; nowadays it would be called a panic attack. I yearned for home.

But I also enjoyed a few cosmopolitan treats. My mother had given me a hundred dollars to buy anything I wanted, and from Mitsukoshi department store in the Ginza I selected for myself two items I thought very sophisticated: a fake leather mini-skirt and a matching vest with poppers.

Towards the end of our trip, while we were in the hotel coffee shop, a lady we didn't know accosted my mother. Very elegant and poised, she was talking to my mom in Japanese – I couldn't imagine what about. Finally Mom turned to me, 'She's a model scout, honey. And she wants to know if you're a model, or if you'd like to become one.'

I was incredibly flattered and surprised but the answer, of course, was no. I was hoping to go to the University of Hawaii in the fall, to take a liberal arts degree, and I was eventually hoping to take courses in marine studies or oceanography, if my credits were good enough. I couldn't be a model; I liked being in the water, under the sun, in the open air, with my friends. I loved waxing my guy's surfboard and getting high – I was a beach chick. I was going home to my gorgeous boyfriend Russell and all my friends; my life was quite full, in fact, so no, Thank you, but no.

The gracious lady, who had been a model herself, bowed and

smiled. Again, she conversed with my mom in Japanese. Mom seemed animated. It appeared this woman knew one of my mom's cousins, and more than that she was going to meet me and Mom the next day so she could take us to a special Japanese tearoom for an unusual kind of cake that Mom loved. En route we were going to call in at Kanebo Cosmetics' head office, just put our heads around the door . . .

The next day she was as good as her word. We were swept into the Kanebo Corporation building, thirty-odd storeys high. I found it tiresome, frankly, standing around in a boardroom with lots of men in suits, and I was very irritated when they pronounced my name 'Malie' and kept on saying it: 'Malie, Malie, Malie!' But when we left the gracious lady – Mrs Imai was her name – insisted I took with me her *meishi*, her business card. 'Call me to arrange your three-year modelling contract,' she said cheerfully. The answer was still 'no', but a seed had been planted in my mind.

*

I returned to Hawaii ten days later and found everything had changed. My friends and family were waiting on the runway and they garlanded my mom and me with welcome home leis as we stepped off the plane. There was my beautiful Russell with his long brown hair, his blue eyes . . . but why did he look so sheepish? My best friend Michie was standing very close to him and wouldn't quite look me in the eyes. I knew something was up. Within a few days I found out they had started an affair. She had looked after him, all right. I lost my first boyfriend and my best friend in one coup.

In retrospect it is easy to write off teenage heartache as trivial, but at the time I was devastated. My heart was broken. The first time it happens to you is the time you remember and you re-experience it whenever you break up with someone. My upset was compounded by the fact that all my friends tried to cover for Michie and Russell – everyone seemed complicit in the deception. I lay on my bed with Walter Farley's Black Stallion badges underneath it and sobbed. I never wanted to see or speak to any of them ever again. Suddenly leaving home and going to work as a model in Japan was a tempting option.

Would my life have been very different if I hadn't gone to work for Kanebo then? Perhaps. Tourism is Hawaii's main industry and at home I would probably have paid my way through university by working at the Sea Life Park, being the girl in the bikini who swims with the dolphins while holidaymakers clap and take pictures. But the die was cast and this life slipped away from me; I entered an alternative universe where I made different decisions. It just happened that way. This was my path.

I begged my father to call Kanebo, and he and my mom negotiated my contract over the phone. It took about a month to finalise – my parents insisted on lots of clauses to protect me from being overworked and so forth – and during that time I moped at home, playing with my younger siblings and dreaming about the future. I sent Kanebo the modelling shots I had done for Uncle Don's magazine *Young Hawaii*, and eventually they signed me up with an exclusive modelling contract for three years. No sooner was that done than I was off in a plane again, and wondering what I had let myself in for.

Perhaps, when Kanebo saw me again, they would discover my bad points, such as my wonky smile (those teeth were not these teeth I have now, reader, I assure you!) and frizzy hair. Perhaps they would send me back as faulty goods. I arrived, sixteen and totally green, in Tokyo with one Samsonite suitcase containing *How to Be a Success*, three bikinis and tons of unsuitable clothes: tie-dye, beachwear, sandals. I took no make-up with me apart from one black eyeliner pencil. I didn't even bring any shampoo – I just thought I'd wash my hair with bath bubbles or whatever came to hand. I had heard of conditioner but I thought it wasn't for me, only Farrah Fawcett. The one thing that equipped me for city life was my prized pair of proper shoes, which Mom had bought me on our first trip to Tokyo. They were low court shoes with a buckle on the toe: my Benjamin Franklin shoes. I wore them everywhere until they fell apart.

My first job was for Kanebo's Christmas poster campaign. They put a long dark wig on me, and gigantic spidery false eyelashes, and gave me an electric candle to hold. I tried to look soulful, with my eyes stretched wide open and my back as straight as a poker. The poster went up all over Japan. The photographer was Kishin Shinoyama, who was a superstar in Japan at the time and went on to be a great friend and mentor to me. But that day, my first day's modelling, I thought he was very weird, with his loud expostulations in Japanese and his strange hair, which he wore in a wild Afro. The studio was also disconcertingly full of crowds of people from the hairdresser's assistant to the advertising CEO.

But after that nervous start, my early modelling days were a breeze. I was never expected to do anything for myself; Mrs Imai, the elegant lady from the coffee shop, had become my manager-chaperone, and I lived in her apartment and she took care of every detail of my life. I was driven to the studio, dressed up like an acquiescent doll, positioned to look cute, and photographed. Still a minor, I even had regulation 'milk-and-cookie' breaks during the day. Modelling is so easy, I thought – which goes to show how much I had to learn. I saw it all as fun. I wasn't an ambitious model yet; I was just a young girl having a good time, being photographed.

Culturally I was completely at sea, however. Several times, I met women in traditional kimonos with female names and befriended them, only to find out months later they were men. It didn't bother me, but I must have been really innocent not to realise earlier. (Years later I became friends with Amanda Lear whose gender everyone discussed endlessly. Bailey was constantly trying to take nudes of her and encouraging her to part her legs just a few inches, though she was always too clever to give in. I couldn't understand what the fuss was about – as far as I was concerned she was a she and she could have had a hedgehog between her legs for all I cared. I adored her and we had lots of fun. She used to say to me, if I wanted to remember something, 'Tie a knot in your eyelashes, darling!')

I marvelled at Japan. I'd never seen a vending machine where you could put money in and get a hot sake back. Or a hamburger, or hot spaghetti – wow! But I didn't speak the language, and Japanese society at that time was very conservative. There was no youth culture, no counter-culture: it was very ordered. There was no hippie fraternity, no love-ins, no be-ins – drugs were taboo and illegal, punished by severe penalties. I didn't dare talk about grass, let alone acid. And I couldn't seem to find anyone who wanted to listen to my Led Zeppelin albums.

I acquired a nickname but I hated it: Pineapples. Boys used it mainly, calling flirtatiously: 'Here comes Pineapples from Hawaii . . . How're you doing, Pineapples?' Maybe the girls called me that as well, behind my back.

Despite my adult pose I was still a child and needed help and guidance, but I found none. Some of the women who surrounded me were, in fact, very cold. They should have been simpatico with a kid like me, but they regarded me mainly as a threat – or a money machine. It never occurred to me that other women might be jealous of me. Instead I misguidedly attempted to befriend them, and showered my earnings on these so-called girlfriends, buying everyone treats. I didn't know what to do with all the money I was earning and, as the eldest in my family, I had been taught always to share. I was wrong to try and buy their friendship, of course, but they were wrong to accept my gifts. The more they took from me the less they liked me – despised me, in fact. Many a time I was ripped off by these hangers-on keen to help me spend my pay packet.

Much later I happened, quite by accident, to get my own back when travelling in Japan with Bailey, Serge Gainsbourg and Jane Birkin. One of the women who had exploited me appeared out of the blue, chaperoning us in a nightclub and introducing Jane and Serge before they performed. I really gave her the cold shoulder. She was in Antarctica. 'Marie, why are you being so mean?' breathed Jane. 'That's not like you!' But what goes around comes around . . . Turn, turn, turn.

Yet I also met women I respected and who were kind to me, such as Kuroda-san, the most beautiful of all the show models, who taught me how to move on the catwalk. I didn't know how: the only prior experience I'd had was at a Hawaiian beauty school camp, where they had a fashion show at the end of the weekend and I proved a total dunce on the improvised catwalk. 'Go, go, go, Marie!' shouted the compère, so, misunderstanding the expression, I raced as fast as I possibly could, practically running to the end and back again. So I had a lot to learn. Kuroda-san explained to me how to undo a jacket with one hand and fling it off the shoulders with one controlled motion, and, generally, how walking on the catwalk was completely different from walking down the street.

In some ways Japan was magical. For a few weeks in the spring, I walked through the boulevards mesmerised by the trees heavy with cherry blossoms and of course it was an exciting period for me: I was independent for the very first time. I could go out when I wanted and stay out as late as I liked. I had my own money and my own life. It was like being a college freshman, except the whole town was mine to explore and I quickly got over my loneliness.

I found even a little glamour intoxicating, and loved being flown to Guam or Saipan to model bikinis, and then to the mountains of Hokkaido to model ski-wear, where I saw snow for the first time. It was fun to see the place of my mom's birth and I loved the stodgy dumplings and the delicious Sapporo beer – and the restaurant where each table had its own 'Genghis Khan' grill, which reminded me of my beloved Scouts campfire cooking.

I also took part in Kanebo's extraordinary shoot in Death Valley. As a child I had been addicted to Ronald Reagan's *Death Valley Days* on the television and was thrilled to visit that godforsaken place. We three models – myself, an African-American-Japanese girl (like myself, a daughter of the US occupation) and a Dutch girl – together with Shino, as I now called Shinoyama-san, as well as make-up, hair and crew, flew to Los Angeles and hired Winnebagos in which we drove down to Death Valley, where we stayed in hotels for two months. They had great difficulty getting a permit to shoot, because not only had it been designated a conservation area, but Antonioni had recently filmed *Zabriskie Point* there and the damage he had done to the environment was well known. In fact, we could see his handiwork glinting on the mountain ranges, jagged shocks of fuchsia and gold where his helicopters had disgorged paint for the film's special effects.

I marvelled at the painted peaks, at the vast salt lakes and deserts. Nature here was inhospitable; my sneakers fell apart after I walked on the cracked salt terrain. It was an unearthly place, and perfect for our shoot, which afterwards became iconic in Japan – Death Valley was even nicknamed 'Shino-Tani' – Shino's place.

Taking a break from shooting we trundled off in the Winnebagos back to Las Vegas to see *Hair* ('The American Tribal Love Rock Musical') which had come there on tour. I was desperate to see it and lied about my age so I could get into the theatre. But what a shock it was to me when I saw full-frontal nudity on stage. I thought of myself as a hippie, but the truth was I was rather amateur at being one.

Back in Tokyo things got a lot better when I finally found a kindred spirit in Tina Chow (then Tina Lutz). I saw her on the catwalk when Imai-san took me to a show. She was breathtaking – and I recognised we were of the same mould. She like me was a *halfu*: half-American, half-Japanese; her first language, too, was English. Mrs Imai thoughtfully introduced us to one another after the show, and a friendship was born.

Imagine my delight when I discovered that not only did she speak perfect English but also that she lived just around the corner from Mrs Imai's apartment, which I now occupied alone. Tina and Bonnie, her elder sister, still lived with their parents, and the whole family were so kind and welcoming. They were a lifesaver, because they understood how Japan must appear to a young American like me and were able to help make sense of it for me. Tina's mother was Japanese aristocracy, and her father was an American who dealt in Japanese antiques. (There's a paparazzi photo of Bailey and me leaving Heathrow in which I'm carrying an incredibly ornate antique ivory walking stick that makes the whole picture look very glamorous, but in fact I was just transporting it for Tina's father.) Bonnie became a friend too, and the girls really took me under their wing. I used to wander round to their home when I was lonely.

'Let's go for tea!' Tina would announce, and we'd go to a hotel for long elaborate Western teas of smoked salmon and cucumber sandwiches and cakes, tea with lemon on the side and – my favourite! – huge cream puffs. Here she advised me on where to go and what to do and, most importantly, whom to trust. 'You're hanging out with a very fast crowd,' she told me once, early on. 'I think you'd better drop them.' She was right: if I had been busted doing drugs in Japan I would have been deported or locked up immediately. Tina and Bonnie kept me on the rails. I played along with it gratefully and never told them about my druggie past.

Tina looked, to me, how I thought a model should look: big eyes, full lips and huge cheekbones in a tiny little face. She wore her hair scraped back and her eyes heavily made up – a gorgeous look very much based on Marisa Berenson's. Marisa was all over American *Vogue,* and we knew that not only was she a beauty but also from an incredible lineage, including Bernard Berenson the art critic. Her grandmother, to cap it all, was the couturier Elsa Schiaparelli. We idolised Marisa.

Tina was really into make-up and beauty and through her I learned that I had to understand what I was selling and the job I was doing. She was always showing me with feminine delight the new Estée Lauder compacts that she had bought. Bonnie and I were not quite as girly and we would giggle at her as she showed us how to apply blush and 'contour'. Tina was a pro. All three of us had great fun when we went up to Expo '70 in Osaka where we modelled for Pierre Cardin and met him and his girlfriend, Jeanne Moreau, who was lovely, and fell on us with delight as fellow English-speakers in a place where everyone else was incomprehensible.

There was only one problem: Tina was the face of Kanebo's rival company, Shiseido. I know it drove our respective companies nuts that we were such good friends. But it never occurred to us to be competitive. If anything we thought it was funny that there was such antipathy between these two old Japanese cosmetics giants.

It was through Tina that I met Issey Miyake, the renowned fashion designer. We became close friends – years later I would do a show for him during the Paris Collections, and my sisters and brother modelled for him too in Hawaii once; my whole family adored him. In Japan we went out together many times, once to a Fugu restaurant, where they served that lethal delicacy. The Fugu fish, potentially 1,200 times deadlier than cyanide, can only be dissected by a licensed chef, and requires a 30-step prep. I ate it before anyone told me what it was – and to be honest, it tasted pretty much like any other fish to me. Another time we went to a Chinese restaurant, a special sashimi place. When Issey's sake arrived it was ruby red. 'What's in that?' I asked. He told me he very occasionally drank sake mixed with turtle's blood because it made his dreams vividly creative.

Interesting people were starting to come my way. I used to bump into Hoki Miller, Henry Miller's wife, who was always witty and vivacious, at one of my hangouts, the Baby Doll, the smart restaurant and clothes shop on three floors. I became so comfortable there I could just turn up on my own and be sure I'd find someone engaging to eat with. People were always willing to speak to me because I was an oddity: very young, from another place and on my own in the country. Generally they were kind and protective towards me. I found companionship in all sorts of odd places, and I jumped at friendship with anyone who could speak English. I went swimming with Satchi Parker, Shirley MacLaine and Steve Parker's daughter. We barely said more than 'Hi' to one another but I felt a bond with her because she was American. I also met the conductor Seiji Ozawa, who would go on to lead the Boston Symphony Orchestra – and I remember having a conversation with him about the film *Midnight Cowboy*. 'You're an American,' he said. 'Does this underclass really exist in New York?' I bluffed my way out of that one.

One week I turned up at the studio and saw that Shino had a very handsome Frenchman assisting him. It was Pablo Picasso's son Claude (whose sister Paloma would later become a great friend of mine). He was interested in photography and had come to Japan and sought out Shinoyama. He was long-haired, sophisticated and in his mid-thirties, and I delightedly said yes when he asked me out to dinner.

He took me to a smart supper club, where I was enthralled by the entertainment: a singer, a magician and a tame kind of striptease where no one took their clothes off. We got on well and went out for dinner a few times. At the end of one supper I noticed Claude was sketching something on his napkin.

'What's that?'

'It's you,' he replied, 'sitting in bed eating a croissant. It's how I see you,' he added softly. I realise now that this was a gentle kind of seduction, but at the time I was too young. I was more interested in rock boys. Bad rock boys.

In fact it was about this time I fell in love with a charismatic Japanese rock star called Shoken. He was a very pretty man, really tall, almost six feet, quite dark skinned, with skinny jeans and long dark hair. He was in a band called the Tempters, and his rivals were a band called the Tigers. (Wouldn't it have been great if Tina had been going out with a Tiger?)

We had a two-year relationship, a serious one even though it was conducted in his broken English and my pitiful Japanese. (This did improve, though, as I learned the language at one-to-one evening classes with students from Keio University, with an idea that it might count towards a credit if I ever took that liberal arts degree.) With Shoken, sex wasn't particularly satisfying; as far as I was concerned coitus didn't ought to be interruptus. I used to go along to his daytime gigs in clubs, but, since there was no youth culture, there were never any parties to go to afterwards. Instead we went sedately out for a sushi dinner, or maybe to an *onsen*, a hot spring. I think he liked to show me off, and I was pleased to be seen with him. He was a superstar, a boyband hero.

This, however, meant that his fans, screaming little girls, followed me everywhere, hating me. His management made sure I wasn't too obvious and didn't sit in the front row at his gigs so the fans weren't disillusioned. Finally this came between us: when he dumped me he said his management was saying he shouldn't be seen with just one person. I was heartbroken for a few weeks, but we drifted back together in one of those uncomfortable on/off relationships. Later he went on to become a very successful actor, most notably in Akira Kurosawa's *Kagemusha* in 1980.

Meanwhile I was starting to take modelling more seriously. It was Shino who jolted me out of my childish amateurism. I was always chattering during shoots, and he would put his fingers on his lips and say warningly, 'Malie! Silence is golden.' I would quieten down a bit then because I loved and respected him and I didn't want to make him angry. By this time we had become good friends and I knew his beautiful half-American half-Japanese wife June Adams. But I still didn't think of modelling as work. It was more like play.

One day, though, Shino took me to one side. What was I doing, he asked? Why wasn't I taking any interest in the process of modelling? 'Contribute to this image!' he said severely. 'Don't leave it all up to me! It takes two – the model has to serve the artist.' His outburst really upset me, as I hated to see him disappointed in me. I started to learn how to do my own make-up, how to do my own hair and how to work with a photographer. By the time I met Bailey I understood how symbiotic a model and a photographer's relationship could be.

Shino and I worked well together after that, and consistently: both of us were contracted to Kanebo. He became a close friend and mentor: he even photographed my naked family album.

The average Western reader will do a double-take at that last phrase, so perhaps I'd better explain. The Japanese have a very particular concept of nudity that sees it not as salacious, but innocent and artistic. National figures such as writers, artists, singers and actors are often depicted naked in posters – all the private parts airbrushed out, or crossed through with magic markers, of course. The nudity must not be too real. All the most famous and respected actors do it. You could be the Nigel Havers of Japan and you'd have had a nude portrait taken. It's not only the famous, but ordinary families, too, have nude pictures taken by professionals, in a style that's sexy but wholesome also.

My family album came about when I went home with Shinoyama and my three siblings and I flew to Molokai, a sequestered Hawaiian island. Public nudity is illegal in America but here we found a beach so deserted no one would report us. There, on an inaccessible shore that could be reached only by mule, an elderly priest called Father Damien had once run a colony for sufferers of Hansen's disease (formerly known as leprosy, but we knew not to call it that). It was called Kalaupapa, and it was the only centre for Hansen's in the whole South Pacific; Father Damien has since been beatified. The atmosphere there was very eerie. One of the photos from our shoot was of me extending my hand in a gesture of friendship to the youngest resident of the refuge, a man who had lost his nose, lips and fingers.

We saw another of the residents pushing about a wicker baby stroller with, tucked up inside, a little dog wearing a bonnet – a poignant sight, since the inhabitants there, I deduced, were not allowed to have children. In fact we saw many strollers with little piglets or puppies snuggled in them. The people there were, by the time we visited, free to go but they had been there so long that they didn't want to leave, or didn't know how.

There on a deserted beach we frolicked about for the camera without our bathing suits; the result was a beautiful and distinctly Japanese collection of family photos. It was a great success, published under the title *Marie's Seven Days in Molokai* – though we never saw any of the profits, as was so common in those days.

Pop never saw our album, though – but neither has he seen *Trouble and Strife* either, of which more later.

By the time Shino took those pictures I was already beginning to be famous as a model in Japan. It always used to be Tina who was mobbed by autograph-hunters when we went out for tea, but now people were beginning to know my name also. They would come rushing out of shops as I walked by, calling out not just 'Tina Ratz' but also 'Malie Helbeen! Malie Helbeeeeen!' I thought it was funny; I enjoyed it. Perhaps they also knew me as *The 11 p.m. Show* cover girl. It was a racy kind of after-hours chat show; I doubt Tina's parents were impressed I was on it. It was a strange kind of job too: I just stood there on camera smiling at the beginning and end of each commercial break – live! – every night for six months. I was as mute as a doll onscreen. When Pop came to visit me in Japan he told me that when he watched it he shouted at the TV: 'Say something, goddammit! Say something!'

I was increasingly well known, but I was still surprised when Kanebo organised a 'Sign Kai' – a signing session for me in a department store – and about a thousand people turned up. I don't know why so many people wanted to go see a gauche child. I think there had been a great PR campaign behind me, though I couldn't quite tell because I didn't speak the language. I suspect they were promoting me as an exotic 'Princess of the Islands' or something – after all, Hawaii was a fantasy paradise for Japan, and much was made of my background. I was always pictured with a plumeria (frangipani) blossom in my hair. This was well before Jalpak (Japan airlines) made the island accessible with countless flights. It was then still romantic and inaccessible, a place of dreams.

So at the Sign Kais I scrawled on fans' posters and their magazine spreads for a whole day with a magic marker. Then Kanebo came to me with a serious message: I had to make my signature smaller. This I duly did. I signed miniaturised pictures, and a portrait on a card that I gave away to thousands of people. I did this all over Japan, from Hokkaido to Kyushu in the south.

I felt comfortable with fame; it came naturally to me – and perhaps that comfort, that ease, made it happen. Besides, I was too young to expect anything else, too unknowing to do anything but take it in my stride. When you're young you get used to things very quickly.

Also, I liked doing signings in department stores because I knew there would be – yummy! – a giant cream puff waiting for me at the end in the food department. I was just a kid, remember.

Tina and I had fan clubs, we got mobbed in the streets – and we were always being chased by men. Tina, though only a year older than me, was courted by established men of the world, conductors, photographers, film directors: traditionalists. I attracted aspirant druggies, dudes who were into the music scene.

Perhaps we were both so sought after because being a *halfu* was considered desirable. Japan was fascinated by the West, and we were fantasy figures, at once alien and familiar. The upshot was magazines wanted our pictures, and men wanted to get into our pants – even much older men. We got used to fighting them off.

I realised I was famous when my pop came to stay with me once, after I had been in Japan for almost two years. He booked us adjoining suites at the Imperial Hotel, but when he turned up, the staff at the front desk were outraged. They wouldn't stand for me, their perfect little princess, sharing a room with someone who they assumed was a dirty old man. I was very cross and embarrassed and made it quite clear he was my pop. It was my first taste of how the public imagination gets carried away with what it perceives you to be.

Legs

In Japan I felt like a giant, since I was often several feet taller than Japanese men and women. This was the reason I was treated like a freak when I first visited. It was also the reason why, over time, I became a star there.

It can take a while before you realise what your advantages are. Having long legs was tricky when I was younger. My pop used to tease me with the song: 'Here comes Marie/She's so tall/She sleeps in the kitchen with her feet in the hall.'

Then my legs got me into trouble at school where I made myself conspicuous by rolling up my skirt into a tiny mini. The school even called my parents to complain about it. My parents totally supported me, saying it wasn't that my skirt was short, it was just that my legs were long. They didn't know I was secretly rolling the waist over on my way to school.

Later in life my legs would do a lot of work for me. I had my knees painted blue by Kansai Yamamoto, I modelled countless pairs of tights, and posed for Bailey in nothing but a lime green swimsuit and cobalt-blue stockings.

I started wearing stockings and suspenders habitually because of Bailey. I hated the fuss of all those fastenings and hardly ever got them right; they would often fall down most unexpectedly. I grew up without stockings or even underwear, which I often don't bother wearing even now. But Bailey, like many men of his age, found suspenders a real turn-on – and that was good enough for me. Sometimes he would ask me not to wear a suspender belt but to use a ten-pence piece to hold them up – like a wartime belle. Needless to say, by the time we got wherever we were going the stockings were always sagging round my ankles.

And perhaps my legs achieved, in the end, a kind of high-kicking immortality. I was told that Allen Jones the great British pop artist used them as the model for his erotic sculptures, in which women's bodies form the support for a piece of furniture. (These, in turn, inspired the women-shaped white tables in the Korova Milk Bar in *A Clockwork Orange*.)

Anyway, by now in Tokyo I had discovered the asset I was standing on. I was going places on those legs.

*

As I walked around Tokyo I got used to seeing myself on billboards. I didn't think anything of it, really – the girl up there with all the make-up and big hair seemed barely recognisable as me. Instead I preferred looking at the fabulous posters of one of Japan's 'living treasures' – the great novelist Yukio Mishima. Shino had taken these pictures, in which Mishima was shown naked to the waist with a stunningly well-defined body (it was unusual in Japan to see a body so toned). He was holding a sword and wearing a headband with a medieval Samurai inscription on it, his face radiating nobility and determination.

I was always desperate to find books to read because all the hotels seemed to stock was Harold Robbins – not my thing at all. My lifesaver was a publisher called Charles E. Tuttle, who produced English editions of the Nobel Prize-winner Yasunari Kawabata's *Snow Country*, which I loved, and Kobo Abe's *Woman in the Dunes*, which I also pounced on. And then there were my favourites, Yukio

Mishima's *The Sailor Who Fell from Grace with the Sea* and *The Temple of the Golden Pavilion*, both in editions by Tuttle. (Who was that dear Mr Tuttle? He did me so many favours by publishing those books in English.) So I knew Mishima's work as well as his face. Everyone did: he was a superstar, a knockout.

I had the habit, on my days off, of dropping in to Shino's office in Roppongi, the trendy part of Tokyo, where all the places I wanted to hang out were the boutiques and patisseries were. I had become really friendly with Shino's PA and I would pop in to see her for tea. One afternoon I breezed into the room and did a double-take. There was that noble, determined face, familiar from the billboards ... it was Mishima-san himself, sitting there with her.

'Oh I'm sorry,' I gasped, 'I'll leave ...' But they both asked me to come in, so I raced over and sat next to him. It was likely he would have seen my TV commercials, or the famous Death Valley shoot, and I got the impression he possibly recognised me. He was very well dressed in a suit, extremely elegant and controlled. He was courteous above all. He spoke perfect English and seemed interested in my impressions of Japan. I told him I loved Samurai movies but I thought the air was really stinky, which made him laugh.

I sat with him for about forty-five minutes, loving every second. He and Shino's PA were drinking Scotch and I asked if I could have a little in my Coke. He looked at the PA, she nodded in acquiescence, and he poured me a drop or two, very delicately with his baby finger outstretched, which I thought was very chic. I remember really hoping he wasn't about to leave. I think I had a little crush on him. (Later I went on to have a real thing about Ken Takakura, who starred in *Black Rain* alongside Michael Douglas, and *The Yakuza* with Robert Mitchum, becoming one of the first Japanese actors to cross over into Hollywood. He and Ken Watanabe, the actor who followed after him (and was Academy Award nominated for *The Last Samurai* with Tom Cruise) both looked a little like Mishima, and all of them share a look of manly power that I love.)

When I got home I was so excited to have met him I couldn't think whom to tell first: I met Mishima-san! Afterwards, for a

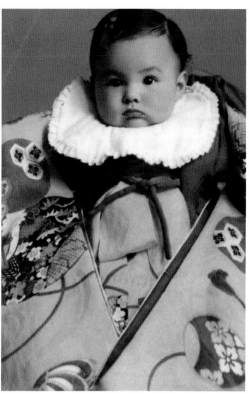

This was taken in Tokyo for my US passport. According to Mom, I was terribly fat and looked just like a boy sumo wrestler, which is why they put the bow in my hair. This Japanese kimono get-up was backless and is traditional for baby pictures.

I was the eldest of four children growing up in Hawaii with two sisters (Suzon and Naomi) and brother Steve. Mom is holding Steve; Suzon and I are modelling stockings of sand; Naomi was too young to be fashion-conscious then.

かぎりなく ひろがる愛の祈り…メリー クリスマス

MERRY CHRISTMAS

カネボウ化粧品

The start of my professional modelling career! The first ever shoot for Kanebo Cosmetics. I was about 16 and had no idea what I was doing – hence the caught-in-the-lights rabbit expression. It was taken by Shinoyama, the first of many he was to take of me.

With Mom and Pop, all of us looking glamorous and happy.

With my darling sister Suzon

This was the first shoot I did for *Vogue*. Unfortunately, none of the photographs from this session including the cover was ever published as *Harpers & Queen* came out first. The series was shot by the mad but lovable Clive Arrowsmith.

This was my first cover shot in London, taken by Hiroshi in 1971 during my trip here with Kansai Yamamoto. David Bowie saw the cover and pages inside and was so inspired by the look and design that he went on to hire both Kansai as designer and Shibayama as his make-up artist to devise the look for Aladdin Sane.

I did a swimsuit campaign in the Seventies with James Wedge for Miss Selfridge. Imagine my surprise when this one came out!

pin-up

Sunshine at Miss Selfridge

£2.95

Marie Helvin

Taken by Tony McGee, this was the packaging for my clothing line. We sold all over the world for three years and only stopped when the fashion for stretch bodywear ended.

This was a portrait shot by Bailey on a large-format plate camera. The shutter speed is very slow, so you need to hold your position and expression for longer than a normal camera. You also have to get used to the photographer standing aside the camera rather than behind it. Not to have that barrier can be very disconcerting for a non-model.

opposite page I am wearing Kansai Yamamoto whilst sitting on this incredibly uncomfortable log, trying to keep my balance to avoid falling into a disgusting green pond full of God knows what. The only reasons I look so serene is down to the Zen-like atmosphere the photographer Barry Lategan is famous for creating.

This photograph of me was taken at the Diamond Crater Festival in Hawaii in the late 60s. My dance partner was a Hawaiian-Filipino man called Ray, and we both painted ourselves silver with paint that we bought from a theatrical shop. No matter how hard I scrubbed, I glowed for many, many years.

With my one-time boyfriend Mark Shand, brother of the Duchess of Cornwall, at Queen's Tennis Club. I was with him for four years and I had a wonderful time with him and his family.

while, I kept dreaming that I was going to meet him again. It was a moment of my awakening to the possibility of the older man.

Years later, I accompanied Bailey to an Olympus Cameras weekend at the Hôtel du Cap in Antibes. All the greats were there: Annie Liebowitz, Lartigue, Don McCullin, Ralph Gibson, Sarah Moon – but most exciting to me one of the guests was Eikoh Hosoe, the photographer who had taken the series of iconic images of Mishima called 'Barakei' ('Torture by Roses'). Bailey and Helmut were rather taken aback – and, I like to think, possibly a little jealous – when Eikoh and I became immersed in conversation about our memories of the great, doomed author.

*

Meanwhile the earth was moving for me. Quite literally, in fact. I experienced my first Japanese earthquake on the third floor of a department store on the Jinza. There was a rumbling noise and minor panic amongst the shoppers and – a horrid sensation – my eyesight went a little hazy. I looked out of the window and I saw a building across the street tilting from side to side, in a special way designed to counteract the tremors, and I knew the block I was in was moving too. It was just another one of those things about Japan.

I was beginning to find Japanese men very attractive, and acquired a new boyfriend called Mori. He was a traditional singer, a little older than me, and he performed wearing a sober suit. He had a very beautiful voice and I adored him, but although the relationship was strong it wasn't strong enough for what happened next.

I discovered I was pregnant by Mori. I totally panicked. I didn't want a child and neither did he. I went to him, distraught, and he found somebody who would perform an illegal abortion. Even birth control was outlawed in Japan at that time, though of course in practice it was widely used. Mori and I used condoms, though they had proved themselves all too fallible.

On his instructions I went alone to Shibuya station and took a train out of Tokyo to a hospital in the suburbs. A doctor met me there and put me in a special room away from all the other patients. I remember putting my legs in the stirrups, which itself was a shock because I had never had any kind of examination like it before. I got a shot in the arm so I couldn't remember anything; when I woke up, the job was done.

That didn't mean it was easy. I didn't speak the language and I had no control of the situation; I have no idea what they did to me. Often I have wondered if that operation contributed to the numerous gynaecological problems I suffered from in later life. I asked my gynaecologist once if the connection was likely and she said, 'Well, let's just say, nuns don't get these problems.' The abortion was over very quickly, but its legacy stayed with me a long time, though not for reasons of guilt. It was absolutely the right thing for me at the time, and I am horrified whenever I read that a country or a state is rewriting its abortion laws to make them more difficult for women to obtain. As far as I am concerned, women should not have control over their bodies taken away by legislation. I am definitely pro-choice.

I rested that day, and I cried, not so much from pain but because I was so alone, by myself in this big private room. The doctor came in to see how I was doing and when I said I was OK he invited me to join him for dinner. For some company, I said yes, and found myself having dinner with a Japanese abortionist and his friend a French priest, who arrived dressed in a black soutane and a crucifix. It was one of the weirdest days of my life.

A great regret to me is that, like so many lost young girls, I didn't tell Mom about my abortion. I didn't even tell my chaperone Mrs Imai, just in case she told my mother. I automatically assumed Mom would be furious; it never occurred to me that she would show sympathy. Almost twenty years later, when I was at home in Hawaii one lunchtime drinking champagne with her and my sister, I told them, quite lightly, about my secret abortion. To my horror Mom burst into tears straight away. She was devastated, and said she felt unworthy, as if she had failed me because she had been unable to help me. It must have been horrible for her finding out that I hadn't trusted her when I was in trouble, and I regret not doing so. I always tell my young goddaughters, and any teenage girls that ask 'Don't be afraid to tell your mom anything. She'll always love you.'

Instead I suffered in silence: I didn't even tell Tina, or Bonnie. Mori and I never talked about it after it happened. At that time to call Honolulu was a big deal, in the sense that everyone would be waiting by the phone to talk to me and it would take forty-five minutes to an hour. We pre-arranged all our phone calls, tending to speak on Sunday nights, which was Monday morning at home. Pop would wait by the phone for me before he went to work. I always spoke to everyone in the family in turn: Mom, Su and Naomi and little Steve. I knew they missed me and I missed them. I also knew my parents worried whether they'd done the right thing in letting me go.

Homesick, I started to blow my pay packet on going home to Hawaii for the weekend. Once I discovered first class there was no going back. The flight attendants even got to know me by name. Sometimes I'd be the only person in the whole first-class section, I'd also spend my money on presents: fashionable things for Naomi and Suzon and Japanese food for my mom (I couldn't buy clothes or shoes because all the sizes were too small for me). I also started to get into comfort food, partly because the abortion had left me feeling sorry for myself.

I gorged on all the rich dishes I had never tried before: coherent foreign cuisines just weren't available in Hawaii. Italian to me was pizza and nothing else, and there wasn't an Indian restaurant on the whole island. In Japan I discovered soufflé and crème caramel, smoked salmon and wine, cream puffs, profiteroles, pastries. I went wild over patisserie. My mom had never allowed these things into the house (unless it was a birthday cake) because she was always on a diet. But I was living alone and I had to learn to feed myself, and I sure did.

The first time I returned home for a holiday I got off the plane to see my family standing at the gate gawping at me. I thought they must be dumbstruck by my new-found sophistication. I peered at them over my sunglasses and waved gaily. But they were quick to disabuse me: it was because I was so plump. 'You look as if you've been squeezed out of a sausage machine!' exclaimed my father. The Japanese fashion industry hadn't commented on my weight gain – they liked their models a little podgy and doll-like – but my mom put me on a strict diet of grilled fish and mineral water.

Back in Japan I collected my seventeenth birthday present – a tiny car, a Toyota Corolla that Pop had chosen for me after I convinced him I needed one desperately. In fact it was an insane idea. I couldn't read any of the signs and my licence was the Hawaiian one I'd got aged fourteen. The only routes I ever took were ones I'd driven in taxis. Once, driving my Toyota home from a fashion show, I found myself sitting in a traffic jam that lasted so long I began to wonder what was going on. I turned on the radio and tuned to the English-speaking US armed forces station. It was a terrible announcement. Along with four of his faithful Tatenokai members, Yukio Mishima had barricaded himself into the Eastern Command military head-quarters, and addressed the troops below with a passionate speech in support of the Emperor. Then his loyal Tatenokai supporters had watched while he killed himself according to the ancient and hon-ourable ritual of *seppuku* (disembowelment). Morita, his closest friend, stepped in as the *kaishakunin* to perform the beheading. Morita then killed himself also. It later emerged that Mishima had been planning this suicide for about a year.

It shocked me so much, I felt physically ill. I realised with a jolt that I was driving really near the Japanese Eastern Command military headquarters, where it had all happened. This was why there was such a traffic jam. I sat there, stunned and saddened that the gentle man I had met had come to such an end. You can never really know someone else's inner life, or the quiet torture that lingers in some souls.

I came to acknowledge I would always be a stranger in Japan. I tried to find my familial roots, spending the odd weekend with my aunt, who had raised my mom, and her husband, who owned a *ryokan* in Hamamatsu. Uncle Chu, an ex-army officer, raised *kingyo*, the prized goldfish crossbred to have huge bubble heads. I used to watch as they swam towards him for their daily individual massage.

(He even named one in my honour because it had lovely big red lips!) I enjoyed absorbing this Japanese culture, but the etiquette and rituals remained fundamentally baffling to me. Doubtless living in Tokyo for two years polished my relaxed island ways, and gave me better manners and a scrupulous sense of cleanliness, politeness and hospitality, but I never connected with the place spiritually – in fact I felt increasingly frustrated there. Mori and I split up – boyfriend troubles, again, making me keen to move on – and to cap it all another driver crashed into my little Toyota. It was a write-off. When I heard that the gifted designer Kansai Yamamoto was taking a show to London, I implored him to take me with him. I was desperate to see the city of Dickens and all my rock gods: Led Zeppelin, the Kinks, Cream.

'Sorry,' he said, but he was doing an authentic kabuki show with only one or two Japanese models. 'You're lovely, Marie, but no.' I was not about to give up, however. I went to see him again the next week and begged him. Again he said no. Looking back, my behaviour seems strange. If I wanted to go to London so much, why didn't I just buy a ticket? But young people didn't travel as freely then as they do now; gap years and round-the-world tickets were then unheard of.

Finally, Yamamoto relented. He called to say he wanted me to come with him to London after all. But he had fierce stipulations. I was to be paid expenses only. I had to study the rudiments of kabuki movement: how to simper like a male actor impersonating a female, and how to strut like a proud kabuki warrior. And in London, I wasn't allowed to speak to anyone, as it was imperative that the whole tone of the show was pure Japanese, and no one must know that one of the models was actually American. I also had to shave my eyebrows off. It was all fine by me. I was going to London.

THREE

WHAT PART OF NOH DON'T YOU UNDERSTAND?

Nineteen seventy-one was the year my mother was throwing her knickers at Tom Jones (or wishing she had the courage to do so). It was when Jim Morrison was found dead and Idi Amin came to power. In Britain, Ted Heath was in and so was decimalised currency. And it was also the year Kansai Yamamoto launched his fashion show on London. Allow me to set the scene.

The lights were dim. The crowd was hushed, expectant. Row upon row of London's fashion crowd – editors, agents, pop stars and a photographer or two – were sitting in the Chelsea boutique waiting for Kansai Yamamoto's show to begin. Come on then, they silently demanded. Impress us. And a loud noise rang out:

'Click!'

It was that hollow sound familiar from Noh theatre, a percussive noise like a tap from the beak of an enormous woodpecker.

'Clop!'

Again it came, this sound.

'Click! Clop!' Faster now, the sound echoed in time with the music, which was staccato, abrasive. Finally it became clear where the racket was coming from: a woman entered, centre stage, bringing the click-clop (*karan-koron* in Japanese) with her: it's Marie, wearing the noisiest Japanese clogs in the world.

Well, I had to do it. Kansai Yamamoto had stuck to his stipulation that I needed to learn the basics of Noh and kabuki theatre. I learned how to walk in exaggeratedly high *geta*, Japanese wooden clogs, in time to the music, as if they were some kind of percussive instrument.

So there I was on the catwalk, my face contorted into a Noh mask, my body stooped over with a bundle on my back that was meant to represent a baby. It was avant-garde, this show; more like acting than modelling. Gradually the other girls joined me on the floor: Beatrice Welles (Orson's daughter), Carina Fitzalan-Howard (who would become Lady Frost), Caroline Coon (who founded Release, the drugs charity). Cathee Dahmen and Anjelica Huston were also up there, beside me – fellow Americans. Not that I could openly embrace her as such – I was keeping very quiet and publicly pretending to be Japanese, as Kansai had instructed. I tried not to speak and if I did, I used a wobbly pretend Japanese accent.

We are all wearing high rubber Japanese collars, very traditional, sculptural pieces. (Their influence can be seen in the costumes for Francis Ford Coppola's *Dracula*; Eiko Ishioka was said to have been inspired by this collection of Yamamoto's and she won an Academy Award for her costume design on the film.) The effect was really dramatic – but what did the discerning London crowd make of it? Impossible to say. They were immobile, silent. Perhaps they were bored. Perhaps they were wishing they were at Mick Jagger's wedding to Bianca in the south of France, which was also happening that day.

The photographer Patrick Lichfield was acting as Mick's best man, otherwise he would have been at the show. It was a sell-out; Kansai had cannily publicised the performance by making all of us girls parade up and down the King's Road in costume. I had to go stomping along in PVC boots with a fat blue wedge, shorts, and a T-shirt with a Noh face on it: if you pressed the nose it made a loud 'Waaaaa!' noise. My eyebrows were gone, my face was whitened, my hair slicked down, and all available body parts were covered with *irezumi* (temporary tattoos). Oh, and my bare knees were painted blue. It was all the work of Shibayama-san, the respected Japanese make-up artist, whom I knew well by that time. But never had she made me look like this before. I felt totally embarrassed under this outlandish get-up. Never would I have believed that, in due course, I would make my home off the King's Road, in one of the houses we paraded past.

But back to the show. As the grand finale we all entered wearing cloaks made of rainbow-coloured silken string. We were somewhere between noble Japanese warriors and alien sprogs. I took centre stage and began to rotate my neck, flinging the heavy, colourful headpiece round and round. Despite all the rehearsals it still made me feel faint as I swung my head, faster and faster, shaking the headpiece like a lion's mane. What in the world was London going to make of this spectacle?

This mane-flinging ritual always elicits appreciative whoops and shouts in Japan. Would the Brits receive it more coolly? Would they even clap? I gave it everything I had; I gave my neck hell. As my vertebrae-crunching performance slowed to an end the audience leaped to its feet. The lights came up and they cheered and roared with approval. It was official. We were a hit.

Being a London sensation was fun. We, the Japanese team, were fêted for the whole three weeks we were there: lunches, dinners, parties. The futuristic look of the show was such a hit that the whole collection sold out at Boston 151 on the Fulham Road, and agents clamoured to sign me ('Do you have representation, Miss, er, Helvin?'). It was like something out of *A Star Is Born*. Both *Vogue* and *Harpers & Queen* wanted me on the cover.

Grace Coddington, fashion editor of *Vogue*, had been in the audience, as had Barry Lategan, the photographer who discovered Twiggy. He said he wanted to photograph me and asked me to come along the next day to a shoot they were doing with Maudie James, Cathee Dahmen and Moira Swan. Maudie was always on the cover of *Vogue*; even an outsider like me knew these were the top London models of their day.

At the shoot Barry asked Barbara Daly the make-up artist to make us look 'like flowers'. She painted our faces with pastel colours: round, intensely pink blobs on our cheeks, peachy orange lips, green eyeliner and yellow eyeshadow. She was an extremely talented make-up artist, who went on to do the make-up for Kubrick's *A Clockwork*

Orange and *Barry Lyndon*, but her tools were like nothing I'd ever seen before: a box of Caran d'Ache pastels. She used them because at that time it was the only way to get these vivid colours. Shibayama was fascinated when I told her what tools Barbara used and together we went to an art shop in Covent Garden where she bought a jumbo tin of Caran d'Ache in all colours of the rainbow. She probably used them up painting the face of David Bowie.

Why him? Well, when *Harpers & Queen* came out featuring me on the cover in Yamamoto, David Bowie saw the magazine and the pictures of me in rock 'n' roll kabuki designs, and loved what Yamamoto was doing. It was an inspiration, he says, for Ziggy Stardust. I think he really meant it because he then hired Yamamoto and Shibayama to design his Ziggy look and they went on a world tour together. So the Caran d'Ache were put to good use.

I later got to know David a little, but I've never discussed the *Harpers* cover and pictures with him. I don't think he would have recognised the white-faced character with the shaved-off eyebrows as me, even. I was playing a role, after all; the looks I later became known for – the sexy woman on the satin sheets, the fresh Hawaiian girl with the leis round her neck – were totally different. I think he would be surprised to know I was the kabuki alien in the rainbow robes.

To returning to the shoot with Barry Lategan: it was a baptism of fire. Barry worked slowly to attain perfection, taking about twenty Polaroids of every pose before photographing it. Polaroid cameras have a really slow shutter speed – it's about as demanding as working with an old plate camera – and I had to stay stock still; adapting my breathing so it was imperceptible. I needed not to be still so much as to evoke stillness, and this was something that had to be learned. It was all new to me, and on top of it the Polaroids were also taking a while to develop and Barry would tuck them under his armpit to hasten them along. Holding a pose while waiting for what seemed like the hundredth Polaroid to develop, worn out by the previous night's show and probably low on blood sugar (London food was revolting!) I fainted clean away. But Barry was kind about it and showed me how I could hold a pose for longer if I swayed gently on the spot, to keep the blood moving – a trick soldiers use on parade.

Back in the dressing room the other girls were icy towards me, this American upstart drafted in at the last moment. Sitting in the dressing room there was a tense atmosphere. To break the silence I asked, 'So what do you guys do, er, in the eve-nings?' (I only remembered to put on a Japanese accent halfway through the sentence, so perhaps it sounded a little strange.) 'Oh, we all sit at home watching *Coronation Street*, love,' replied one sarcastically, not even lifting her eyes as she buffed her nails.

I realised that knowledge about modelling was passed down in a guarded and almost secret way (I'm making it sound like *The Da Vinci Code*) and I was determined from that time on to share any tips I had, about make-up or agents or anything else, freely, with any girl who needed it. In future, if luck came to me, I would make sure to spread it round. I would be generous with my good fortune. I was a hippie: I was all for karma.

Only Cathee Dahmen – who was also an American (part-Native American, in fact) and a model for Antonio the renowned fashion illustrator – was warm to me. I let her into my secret. 'I'm not Japanese,' I whispered to her. 'I just have to pretend I am. I'm an American like you!' She helped me with the etiquette of my first *Vogue* shoot and after the shoot she invited me back to her home for supper. I walked in and there at her kitchen table was Romeo. I nearly fainted for the second time that day. It turned out her husband was the actor Leonard Whiting, who was Romeo in Franco Zeffirelli's *Romeo and Juliet*. I had been on a school trip to see the film, and my classmates and I had spent the whole time whispering about how cute Romeo was. Now here he was offering me pasta. I was beginning to like London a lot.

Cathee and Leonard went on to become really close friends of mine, and so did Barry Lategan. A calm, gentle man, he was fascinated by the East and worked in a Zen-like style. When I went back to Tokyo we corresponded a bit – a working bond had been forged. I can't have behaved too badly that day I fainted because he always says nice things about my style: 'Marie's got a sense of grace in her – graceful and responsive, she always behaves in the most decorous way.'

Later he took the famous photograph of me sitting on a log wearing a silk Yamamoto tunic and holding one of his hand-made Japanese umbrellas – a picture of pensive Eastern delicacy. Soon after, Paul and Linda McCartney would recreate that photo for a Wings album cover.

The *Vogue* photographer Clive Arrowsmith was totally different to Barry. In fact he was different to everyone – a real eccentric. A few days later I was on my way to a session with him at Vogue House, and I was standing in the lift on the ground floor, when a cowboy in a Zapata sombrero came through the front door and raced towards me through the lobby, two pistols tucked into his low-slung belt. Keen to avoid this demented intruder I pressed the button to shut the lift doors. Too late. He stuck a bronco boot in through the door and squeezed in next to me. As the lift soared upwards he twirled his guns like a rodeo star, grinning at me.

As I fled out of the lift towards Grace Coddington, she stopped me in my tracks as she smilingly gestured to the cowboy. 'Have you met our star photographer Clive?'

He captured in his shoot that day the dynamism of my kabuki moves – a direct contrast to Barry Lategan's fragile flower look. But the photographs were pulled off the front of *Vogue* when the *Harpers & Queen* issue came out first, with me in Yamamoto on the front cover. Naïvely, neither Shibayama nor Kansai had realised that these magazines, keen competitors, weren't both going to feature the same model with exactly the same look on their covers.

It was a period of many fashion discoveries. I noticed the thing to wear was hot pants – all the other girls in the show were wearing them, tiny Daisy Duke-style shorts that barely covered their butts, just like the girls on roller skates I had so admired in the Yardley commercials. When I asked where I could buy my own hot pants, they all chorused, 'Biba.'

I found the boutique on Kensington High Street and was mesmerised by the massive posters of a breathtaking Ingrid Boulting, photographed by Sarah Moon, with elegantly dark kohl-ringed eyes. I wanted to look soulful and romantic like her – didn't everybody? I'd never seen such photos before. It seems strange to think I was to become friends with both Sarah and Ingrid. (Years later I was sitting in Rome by the hotel pool with Ingrid when the producer Sam Spiegel introduced himself and asked her to audition for a role in *The Last Tycoon*: she got it and starred opposite Robert De Niro.) In the store I found my pink suede hot pants and some matching suede boots with a high, chunky heel and a zipper on the side, which I bought in every colour – pink, red, yellow . . . I had found something worth spending my money on. When I flew home my entire Samsonite suitcase was stuffed with Biba boots.

I had a chance to get out of my pop-kabuki robes and wear my new hot pants when Michael Chow, who produced the show – and was two years away from marrying my best friend Tina – took us all out one day.

Our first stop was the Grenadier, a very old-fashioned pub in Kensington, where they offered us something to eat that came on a stick. I took a bite – and suddenly realised the thing on the stick was a sausage. Waves of nausea came over me, instantly. I am my father's daughter: I have never eaten proper red meat, only fish and chicken. I wanted to bolt to the toilet to throw up but it was a crowded, narrow, olde-worlde pub and I was trapped. I spat the sausage discreetly into my handbag. I wonder what Barry Lategan would say about that graceful response.

Later Michael Chow took us on to Tramp nightclub on Jermyn Street. There I noticed a gorgeous girl on the dance floor, blonde and alluring, wearing hot pants even smaller than mine, and dancing by herself, transported by the music, whirling about in a smoky haze. I'd never seen anybody do that. I'd missed out on the whole dance scene – because in Tokyo I was too young to go to clubs – and I was entranced. I said to Michael, 'Who's she?' and he explained it was Patti D'Arbanville, who was Cat Stevens's girlfriend. I suddenly clicked. It was she whom the song was about: 'My Lady D'Arbanville . . .' It was the number one song in London at that time, and everywhere I went it was playing. It's a song that always takes me back to that period of discovering London.

We had a great time and Michael dropped me off outside the hotel in Cadogan Square. But I couldn't get in, because it was one of those little old-fashioned hotels that locks up at night. I stayed there ringing the doorbell until a very grumpy old porter eventually came down and yelled at me, 'Do you know what bloody time it is?' I was so shocked I burst into tears. I wasn't used to being told off like that. Then I made my way slowly up to bed in one of those rickety old London elevators.

I was getting ready to go to sleep when I heard a tapping at my door. 'Malie . . .' It was Kansai Yamamoto's voice – what could he possibly want at this time of night? Maybe he wanted to discuss my kabuki moves. I opened up and welcomed him in. He perched on my bed, and began to try and seduce me in a typically Japanese way, indirectly, through insinuating terms of speech, going round the block three times before coming out with it. 'You know, Malie, I would like to become close to you,' I think he said. It took a while for the penny to drop. It never occurred to me that this person who employed me would make a move. 'Close to you, skin to skin . . .' he continued.

I pushed him off immediately, laughing politely. 'Don't be silly, Kansai!'

He laughed, too, as he made his way out of the room. It wasn't a big deal, and there was no awkwardness afterwards. I think he was just trying his luck.

At breakfast the diminutive pots of jam were a source of fascination for me. I collected four every morning; by the time I left I had about sixty mini jam pots to take back to Hawaii.

Cathee and Leonard began to invite me to dinners and parties every night and I was very happy to be out with them. I started coming back to the hotel later and later. After the first time I just gave the grumpy old night porter the finger.

In that short first trip to London I absorbed so much and met so many people: Peter Blake, Michael Chow, Barry Lategan, Twiggy and Justin de Villeneuve. I even had dinner in San Lorenzo's, where, years later, Bailey would propose to me.

But I hadn't quite got my bearings yet. On the way out of London to the airport I gazed at the ordinary little houses on the side of the highway and wondered if any of my British idols lived in them. Perhaps Robert Plant lived in that little semi-detached bungalow? Or Jimmy Page in that one? Maybe that was where Ray and Dave Davies lived? What I had learned, though, to my great disappointment, was that no one in England said 'Tally-ho!' or even 'Pip pip'.

It was a magical trip, and made a big impression. As I boarded the grim Aeroflot plane for the long-haul flight to Tokyo, I felt sure I would return. We stopped over in Moscow, where I went crazy and bought lots of matryoshka dolls. All the way home I ate real English cherries that I'd bought in a brown paper bag from a street stall. I had never seen cherries like that before, fresh with the stalk still attached, and I spent the whole journey spitting out cherry stones and pooting, probably. Charming. I also made sure I had a window seat. On the flight out I had sat in the aisle and been squished by the hugely overweight Russian air stewardess whenever she moved past. Not this time. I was wising up to some things.

A Pale Skin

You could call my complexion *café au lait,* and I tan really easily. So much so in fact that I was known as 'the tan queen' for I could go brown over the course of just one day in the sun, if a tanned look was required for a shoot. Whatever deep dark colour I am in pictures, it's all my own. There was no fake tan or body make-up available in those days. So I fried myself instead, using my own sun lotion concocted from baby oil mixed with a few drops of Mercurochrome. I never used any sun protection and I have terrible sun damage, now visible in freckles and discoloration across my décolletage.

And when I had to do a job that required paler skin, I found a way of sloughing off my tan quickly, by avoiding baths and moisturiser for a couple of days and then taking long hot baths. The colour simply flaked off me, like the skin from a snake.

I looked different to all the other models at castings in London. Sometimes too different. Barbara Daly recalls how the limited outlook in early seventies England made life difficult for me: 'Photographers would say, "She's amazing, but I don't think we can really work with her, because she's not what we're used to."'

Occasionally at castings when I showed up at the desk they would look at me in shock and I'd realise that by my name they expected a French- or Germanic-looking woman. They'd say, basically, thank you and goodbye, and I'd leave, embarrassed.

Even ten years later when Iman started out in the business she said she was made to feel 'like a piece of polished mahogany'. I saw pictures of her before she was launched in New York, in fact, when Bailey got a letter from his old friend the diarist, photographer, and socialite Peter Beard. 'Look at these,' said Bailey, and chucked over a packet of photos of a gorgeous African woman with endless elongated limbs. She was holding a staff and wearing a *kikoi* and Peter claimed this beauty he had discovered was the daughter of a goatherd. Later we discovered of course that this was a charade he had cooked up: she was actually highly educated and had been a student at Nairobi university and was the daughter of a diplomat.

The story was a brilliant PR ruse and made her famous overnight. But in New York there was still discrimination on the streets. I was over there in the early eighties and we left a party together one night. When we tried to hail a cab, she said, 'You do it. I stand no chance of getting one.'

Regarding my ethnicity, well, what do you want me to be? People projected so many things on to me. The press called me all sorts of things, from the irritatingly inaccurate 'Asian supermodel', to the imaginative 'part-Japanese, part-Danish-American tiger lily'.

By the end of the seventies my look wasn't so puzzling to people any more. 'An American-Japanese exotic, striking beauty. It was the look for the times, don't you think?' says Manolo Blahnik. 'She was the seventies.'

FOUR

MODEL BEHAVIOUR

'People come into your life for a reason,
a season, or a lifetime.'

I knew I was a really successful international model when I started living in airports. Working in Paris, Milan, New York and London, sometimes all in the same week, I was either cruising on a ticket pre-paid for by the client, or, occasionally, queuing for standbys and ending up stranded in departure lounges. I was in and out of Düsseldorf, Tokyo, Honolulu. Flying to Japan by the cheapest airline, Sabena, I discovered that Brussels airport was the best to sleep in – it was really cosy – and found that a good place to pass the night wasn't on a bench in a draughty concourse, where you always felt someone could creep up on you at any moment, but in the warmth and relative safety of the ladies' toilet. Oh, the glamour of modelling.

Arriving at UK passport control, I would don a pair of dowdy spectacles and put my hair in pigtails. I would claim to be a student who needed another stamp to get into the country (I would always have my library card ready with my picture on it – hoping they wouldn't read the small print and see that it was from Kalani High School of Hawaii) just to finish my thesis. It always worked.

Finally I would arrive home at my flat tired out. Days later I would be off again, perhaps to Rome for the couture collections, or back to New York ... Each time I dreaded the constant lying at passport control.

My life was lonely and transient, even though my career was blossoming. The London agent Eileen Green had written to me in Tokyo saying it was unheard of for a model to be asked to be on the cover of both *Harpers & Queen* and *Vogue* in the same month, and that I would be in demand if I came back to London. Also – and this was her stroke of genius – she enclosed the maximum length work permit (three months), stamped and ready to begin from my date of arrival. That, and the fact that Shoken, my on-off rock star boyfriend had dumped me again, this time for a club singer, made me think realistically about returning to London.

I broke my contract with Kanebo easily. Mrs Imai, who could see how much I wanted out, even conspired with me and helped me find another one-off job with a rival clothing company. As soon as the pictures were published, Kanebo dropped me. I was free to go. I think most people, my parents especially, were a little surprised that I was moving still further across the world. I turned up in London with nothing except my contacts from my previous trip, and my confidence.

I had also learned by now that Europeans loved the theatre of the Orient, as they called it (I've never been keen on being called 'oriental' myself; it makes me sound like a carpet) so I also brought a kimono with me. It was a gift from both my aunts and Uncle Chu in Hamamatsu. I picked it out for its beautiful black, gold and white design (it was in fact a widow's kimono, but I liked it so I let that go) and came with all the traditional undergarments: five underslips, an obi (belt), three smaller ties, white socks and slippers.

It took me about an hour to put it on, and I only wore it once in London, and once when Eileen Green took me to Paris. It caused a sensation both times but then I decided to quit doing the theatrics for the Europeans' benefit and to be more true to myself. The kimono languished at the bottom of my suitcase until I gave it to a Red Cross shop. They didn't know what it was, but they took it anyway.

Four months after my first visit, I came back with a different accent: an American twang. Imagine everyone's surprise when the silence-is-golden 'eastern beauty' whose catchphrase had been 'me no speak' started shouting 'How's it, man?' My true voice was now coming through, whether people liked it or not. London was different, too: no one was wearing hot pants any more, for a start. So I copied Cathee Dahmen and bought some fashionable clogs – proper wooden Dutch ones – and wore them with my jeans. I was always a sexy dresser; even in Japan I wore clingy lace and velvet dresses in the evenings. But I wanted to be like the other girls so I got clogs.

Cathee and Leonard had kindly had me to stay with them in their flat in Albert Mansions in Battersea, and so had Barry Lategan, who was a great friend and mentor to me. I stayed in his flat in Rosetti Studios in Chelsea while he was away, during my very first days in London.

From his flat I took a taxi to my new agent's office. 'Bruton Place please, sir! Do you know where that is, sir?' The taxi driver started laughing at me. I couldn't work out why, until he told me no one ever called him 'sir'. I had been brought up by my father to call everyone female 'ma'am' and everyone male 'sir' – *everyone*, from the President to a street cleaner. It was just good Virginian manners. But here it evidently wasn't the custom. It seemed to have tickled the cab driver, though, because he wouldn't accept any money and drove off still laughing to himself. Once, later, I had a cabbie who was really moved when I called him 'sir' – the English evidently took the whole honorific system very seriously.

Eileen Green's agency was based in her mews house on Bruton Place – the same house, in fact, that Brian Epstein once lived in, which impressed my inner Beatles fan enormously. As I walked down the street, trying to work out whether I should call Eileen Green 'Ma'am' or not, I saw a tall dark gawky girl coming in the other direction. She looks like a model, I thought – and sure enough, it was Anjelica Huston. We embraced each other, thrilled to see each other again after Kansai's show. We spent the day together with Eileen and a sweet young model who could only have just turned sixteen called Bambi (there was a vogue, around that time, for models to give themselves one extraordinary name, like Firefly, Vanilla, Pamplemousse – or Twiggy).

Bambi patiently explained the currency to me and Anjelica, talking us through all the different-sized coins. I have always been haunted by the thought that she was the 'Bambi' who was murdered along with her whole family in 1985. It is highly likely that it was her – the ages correlate – yet I find it hard to accept that a lovely young beauty like her should have come to such a tragic fate. She was kind to us that day, and so was Eileen Green.

Soon Eileen had work pouring in for me. She was a softly spoken Irish mother hen – not for her the glamour of the other agents, who were always throwing models' parties (in New York in the eighties one agency was such a social hub it was nicknamed the Pussy Farm). Instead Eileen was a fantastic agent and highly protective of her girls, and I stayed loyal for many years. Being my main 'base' agent she managed all the jobs that came in internationally, although I also had representation in every single fashion capital then, as models do today.

Besides Cathee Dahmen and Anjelica, I got to know a few of the other models that Eileen represented, my 'stable mates' as they were called. Years later, when Tessa Dahl (mother of Sophie) was briefly on her books, I was in the office when I overheard Eileen having a terrible row on the phone. Frustrated, she passed the phone over to me. It was Roald Dahl on the other line, ranting on with some story or other about how his daughter was being treated. I knew his name but it was his wife Patricia Neal who was the star to me – no one in Hawaii had ever heard of this Willy Wonka person. 'Oh hello, sir, it's actually Marie Helvin on the line.'

'Oh yes,' he said, sounding mollified. 'You seem like a very nice young lady, judging by your pictures.'

I made a nest in London, renting a furnished one-bedroom flat on Cathcart Road in West London – a modest space but huge by comparison with most models' accommodation. My landlords were an elderly couple called Hardting, a Polish man and wife who were sweet to me, bringing me heavy Polish pastries because they thought I needed fattening up (I think they had no idea what job I was doing) and taking me out, once, to Daquise, the Polish restaurant in South

Kensington. There was only one moment of discord, an incident I cringe to remember.

Being a young single girl I had no pictures with which to decorate my walls, and if I saw an arresting image in a magazine I would tear it out and stick it up on the kitchen pinboard. They were provocative pictures, not pretty ones. There was Andy Warhol's 'Electric Chair' print, Nick Ut's photograph of the Vietnamese girl running naked suffering napalm burn, and there was one of Hitler. It wasn't a photograph per se, but a likeness, an impression. I found it vaguely mesmerising, a challenging image, and I pinned it up next to the others. They were images I used to look at and think about as I ate my breakfast. But the next time Mrs Hardting came to check on the flat and saw it in the kitchen, she went crazy.

She started shouting in Polish, and then told me, very seriously, that I must take the picture down at once. She rolled her sleeve up past her elbow. There on her arm was a concentration camp number. I was absolutely horrified at what I had done. How could I have been so crass, so insensitive? But somehow, though I intellectually understood the horrors of Hitler's regime, I had grown up too far away to appreciate them in human terms. Hawaii is one of the most geographically isolated places in the world, remember – and this was the first time I had met someone who had actually survived the Holocaust. (Incidentally, however, if I had waited around on Hawaii I would have done so: Vladimir Ashkenazy came as a visiting professor to the University of Hawaii soon after I left.) And though we studied these subjects at school, it was only in a cursory way – the curriculum was catching up with history, as it still is today, even in the UK. I didn't see visual images of the atrocities until a year or two later when I watched *The World at War* series, narrated by Sir Laurence Olivier.

I was mortified, and took the picture down at once. Mrs Hardting knew I hadn't been deliberately callous, and forgave me.

She was tolerant, too, of my many house guests. Models were constantly staying with me, arriving with a suitcase, crashing on my spare bed in the living room, and jetting off the next day, or dropping in for a few weeks and leaving me some pocket money in rent.

One of my favourite visitors was Anjelica, who was a kindred spirit. We were both Americans, we had grown up in the same era, and we shared the same pop-culture background – that is to say, we both smoked weed. After a drug-free Tokyo it was a great thrill for me to have friends like her and Bob Richardson, her boyfriend. One of my first shoots in London was with Bob (father of Terry Richardson). We shot six pages of *Honey* magazine. I remember Anjelica's black eyes peering round the door as I did the shoot.

When she came to stay with me it was the era of the Three-Day Week, so our power came and went. When it came, we would watch T-Rex on *Top of the Pops* on television, and when it went, we would sit there together in the candlelight, studding our jeans and smoking joints. The studs came from Kensington Market in all different shapes and sizes – stars, diamonds, rubies – and all the studding was done by hand, on my denim shorts and her jeans. We laughed about our modelling work. Anjelica was so dark and mysterious that she was often typecast in gothic roles.

'Why do I always have to play the vampire?' she wailed.

'Why must I always be the token exotic?' I would reply.

We spoke about our futures. She always wanted to act. 'I want to be . . .' she once said, exhaling a pungent cloud of smoke, 'immortal.' Then we dissolved into hysterics.

For dinner we would go to the Indian restaurant around the corner and share a bottle of Mateus Rosé, a drink I wouldn't now give to my cat. At the time, though, we thought it delicious. Then I would take the bedroom and she would crash on the bed covered with the Indian throw in the living room.

Soon after we were both booked to do a fashion show in Paris, and I flew over and we checked into the rooms the fashion team had booked us at L'Hôtel, the grand old place on the Left Bank where Sarah Bernhardt stayed, Oscar Wilde lived and died and where the show itself was taking place. I went up to her room to share a joint – I normally didn't while I was working, but this time I thought, Why not?

Big mistake. I went twirling down the catwalk, a beatific smile on my face. That particular catwalk show demanded a loose flowing walk from its models, almost a dance, but I took it too far. Faster and faster I went, waving my arms giddily until suddenly I twirled right off the stage and fell into the lap of a very grande dame in the front row. It was the editor of *Harpers & Queen*, the Alex Shulman of her day, and she was not amused. I slid off her lap and on to the floor, grinning, and somehow managed to pull myself up and waltz off the stage. The show's producers were waiting in the wings for me, furious.

'We will NEVER work with you again!' they roared. 'You stupid girl!'

Here, Anjelica stepped in to defend me. 'Don't speak to her like that,' she said. 'How dare you? You'll make her cry . . .'

This incensed the producers even further, and they chased both of us out of the hotel – we were practically thrown out with our bags. Bob and Anjelica stayed on in Paris, and did lots of beautiful pictures for French *Vogue* (none, incidentally, making her look like a vampire). I headed off to London, still high, and I remember trying very hard not to giggle or dance as I went through immigration. As anyone who's ever smoked grass will know, the harder you try to be serious, the more you want to laugh. I learned my lesson, though. Cannabis and the catwalk just don't go together.

At this time in the early seventies cocaine wasn't much in evidence in the modelling world. It was only in the eighties that it exploded, completing the triumvirate of coke, money and greed. My early days of modelling were much more innocent. No one had ever heard of anorexia or bulimia – it was as if they didn't exist, though the symptoms must have pre-dated the diagnosis. But contrary to what people assume, I don't think it's possible for a successful model to have either illness because their schedules are always too tough. How could you get on a plane and fly to four different countries in a week if you were starving yourself? I've never knowingly met a successful model who was anorexic or bulimic.

I wasn't concerned about my weight, which was naturally skinny.

I was about 115 pounds, and five feet nine inches tall – you could see my hip bones clearly. In fact I was so used to being thin I felt I could eat almost anything I wanted, and when I got to London and discovered the wonders of Mars Bars I was soon eating one every day. (I thought I was doing well to restrict myself to just one!) But soon enough, Eileen Green sent me to a diet doctor on Harley Street. I was an editorial model and I couldn't afford to gain any weight. Also she wanted me to get down to 105-110 pounds; I think it was pretty standard practice for all models on her books to be sent to Harley Street. The diet doctor (who, incidentally, was as wide as her frickin' office) prescribed me some pills – the regular amphetamine kind. I took them for about a month but I stopped when Barry Lategan and Beatrix Miller, the editor-in-chief of *Vogue*, both said I was getting too thin.

Through Leonard Whiting I met John Walker, part of the American singing duo the Walker Brothers. We went out for dinner a few times and once dropped into Scott's flat off the Fulham Road, which was puzzling to me because it was almost entirely empty of possessions, with only a guitar propped up against the wall. John was sweet but we never had a relationship.

I had a great friend in Michael Chow, who was establishing himself as a restaurateur as well as an important patron of contemporary art. He was always introducing me to interesting people. Once, we went to a Chelsea restaurant called the Casserole, where tables were arranged around booths. I shuffled into our booth, sat down and suddenly realised that opposite me on the other side of the table was Peter McEnery – the man who had given Hayley Mills her first kiss! I suddenly felt like a child again, flooded with memories of watching my favourite Hayley Mills films at home in Hawaii, and I could barely speak to him.

Sometimes Michael would pick me up on Sundays, and we would do two galleries in the morning, before going out to lunch with his friends: Peter Blake, perhaps, or Richard Hamilton or Tanya and Michael Sarne (he directed *Myra Breckenridge* and she went on to found Ghost). After lunch we would do two more galleries – Michael always wanted something new, something more. With him I also started the habit of going to see three movies, back to back. I can't do this any more: two is my limit.

Once Michael invited me to a dinner at a Japanese restaurant in St Christopher's Place. The other guests were Tsai Chin, Michael's older sister the actress (most recently seen in *Memoirs of a Geisha*), Calvin Lockhart, the most handsome black actor in the world at that time and none other than Muhammad Ali. He was in his prime and so beautiful I was, again, totally tongue-tied. I wish I could say he twinkled at me, but no.

Ali was my father's ultimate hero. Nothing I ever did impressed Pop much – he's not wowed by my fame or fortune – but he was seriously proud of me when I rang and told him I had had dinner with Muhammad Ali.

I got proof of it, as well. I asked Ali for his signature for my dad on a piece of paper. Then halfway through the dinner I thought, Anyone could have done that squiggle. So I got him to write: 'To Marie's Pop. She has asked me to write this for you. I am looking forward to seeing you in Mozambique.' (Pop was hoping to see him in the Rumble in the Jungle there the following month.) Before dessert, I asked Ali to write 'Hello, Linda' for my mom, too, just to make sure. He dealt with all my childish requests with remarkable patience.

Another time I went to dinner at one of Michael's restaurants in Queensway, where he was entertaining a great group of people at a round table. The conversation was busy and I barely noticed, on my left, a dark, gruff photographer. It was Bailey. 'Pass the rice, me old China,' he said to me. What did that mean? I thought it sounded vaguely offensive. I wasn't Chinese. I didn't recognise it as Cockney slang. Although he was vaguely flirtatious with me, in the way that he was with everyone, I didn't take any notice of it because I knew he was going out with Penelope Tree. 'Penelope would adore you,' he told me. For his part, he thought I was flirting with him: I had bought a sexy dress from Bus Stop on Kensington Church Street and the strap kept falling down. He can barely remember anything more than this of our first meeting: neither of us were particularly taken by each other. And they say romance is dead.

*

'So Man, who here seems principal alone,
Perhaps acts second to some sphere unknown,
Touches some wheel, or verges to some goal;
Tis but a part we see, and not a whole.'
ALEXANDER POPE, *An Essay on Man*

How people enter and leave each other's lives is so mysterious, all you can do is be relaxed about the process. To quote Deepak Chopra: 'Whatever relationships you have attracted into your life at this moment are precisely the ones you need in your life at this moment. When you are ready to do a new thing, in a new way, you will do it with new people. There are people waiting for who you are becoming.'

This was a period of so many discoveries and initiations, such a tumult of new experiences that I was always thrilled when I got a sweet slice of home. Sometimes it might be a parcel of dried mango or Famous Amos cookies in a 'care package' from my mom. Best of all, members of my family would come to stay with me. First to visit was Mom, who had never come to Europe before. She arrived in a flurry of excitement, declared there was no such thing as jet lag, and insisted that we go to Harrods that very day. So we dropped her bags and went straight there. When we got home again she fell into a very deep sleep. The next day I tried to wake her, shaking her gently, calling, 'Mom? Mom!' but it was no use: she was out for the count.

When she was still asleep the day after I ran in and out of her bedroom hollering, 'MOM!' Eventually I panicked and called my father. 'Do you think she's OK?'

'Well, honey, I don't know. Have you checked she's breathing?'

When she finally came round she didn't know what all the fuss was about. We had a great time sightseeing and she became addicted to Indian food which did not exist in Hawaii at that time apart from at the Hare Krishna centre. She wanted it morning, noon and night. She was also delighted to meet my new friends. Patrick Lichfield made a particularly good impression – of course he did. For all his pedigree (he was second cousin to the queen) Patrick was a supremely easy-going man. I had been shooting a fashion spread with him and he invited me and the stylist out to lunch afterwards. 'I can't,' I said, 'My mom's been staying with me and I have to take her to the airport.'

'Don't be silly,' he said with his habitual magnanimity. 'I'll send my driver to collect her and she can come for lunch too.'

So the three of us had an early brunch together at Burke's, the club he part-owned off Bond Street (later Bailey took me there to see Dudley Moore perform – he was tiny, but so, so handsome). We had smoked salmon and scrambled eggs, which my mother had never tried before, and Bloody Marys. (The next year I took her to Paris where she had her first proper croissant, a million miles away from the 'crescent rolls' you got in Hawaii.) She went off to the airport very happily.

My next visitor was my younger sister Suzon, who came with a schoolfriend to stay after they graduated. They meant to go back-packing round Europe but in the end only got as far as Paris. Suzon then extended her stay with me, and Michael Chow gave her a job as the cloakroom attendant at his restaurant Montpelier Place, across from Harrods. She loved it – 'Rod Stewart gave me a huge tip last night!' – and at the same time, during the day, she took a part-time course at the Sir John Cass school of art. I was so happy to have her with me, and enjoyed playing the role of big sister once again. It was my turn to introduce her to all the new things she wouldn't be aware of, like Greek food and French cinema. Michael took us both to the Tower of London, to the maze at Hampton Court and the Houses of Parliament.

Suzon always had strong mothering instincts, and later in life she made it her goal to adopt a huge brood. Even here in London she found an orphan to look after – a stray marmalade cat. We christened it Mr Willard after the boy in the cult film who has no friends but rats, and Mr Willard remained in my home, even after Suzon went back to Hawaii.

When I went to Paris to model Yves's ready-to-wear collection, I took Su with me too. The designers at that time allowed you to choose whether you wanted to be paid in money or clothes, and normally I always took the money (agents preferred it that way, otherwise how would they get their commission?) but this time I wanted Su to have some pretty clothes. She came with me to the Rive Gauche boutique in Saint-Germain and chose, right from the rack, a turquoise velvet pleated skirt, which billowed out when she spun round in it. She was the real beauty of the family, with her delicate features, green eyes and naturally golden hair. She looked amazing in this velvet skirt, and wore it with gold sandals which I bought her from Manolo Blahnik's tiny one-room shop Zapata on Old Church Street.

People often ask me if I knew, at that time, that he was going to be mega-famous, the shoe designer of his generation. But I can't answer the question, really. I never thought in terms of the future, or who would make their name and who would fade away. I was proud of my friends being creative and talented and I knew we were all important in our way, especially the artists amongst us. But I never thought about my own immortality – I only kept my own cuttings because, like all working models, I had to. I never stopped to think if I had just met my future husband, and I certainly never thought that this was one of the few precious times I would have with Suzon before her life was cut short. I just lived moment by glorious moment, never looking forwards, or behind.

*

'You always have champagne at the shows. Always. Even at ten in the morning.'

KATE MOSS

My most favourite indulgence in the world is to have a glass of champagne as early as possible in the morning. I don't do it often, of course, but I love the giddy way the champagne hits you right in the head. It makes me feel Bang! It's showtime! It takes me straight back to being on the catwalk in Paris aged nineteen.

There was always champagne for the models backstage – glass upon glass of it, at any time of day or night. There were magnums at Thierry Mugler, jeraboams at Chanel, nebuchadnezzars at Kenzo. It never stopped flowing. If you were called at six a.m. for an eight a.m. show you would still get a glass put in your hand as soon as you walked through the door. It was as if they wanted the models to be permanently on a champagne high, to make us feel like we were on top of the world, the most exquisite beauties ... and it worked. Three glasses in, it is a lot easier to strut down a catwalk like a jaguar in a jungle, to feel your body was created to be admired – for an hour or two at least, until the champagne wears off.

But the fittings were a different affair, and much more sober. At Yves Saint Laurent's first atelier in the rue Spontini, the models would be hushed, whispering amongst themselves as they waited in a dressing room before taking turns to come through for a fitting. Yves and Pierre Bergé might indulge in a whisky and soda after sundown, but models were never offered a drink. Yves, a fragile, quiet man prone to giggling, was always charming and sweet. His black-and-white French bulldog Moujick would either be tucked under his arm or charging into our dressing room, snapping at our ankles. It was tempting to send him flying with a kick, but Yves loved him so much that was more than our jobs were worth.

It was at the rue Spontini that I first saw Loulou de la Falaise, Yves's friend and muse. What an entrance she made, walking down that wide curving staircase, whippet-thin and boyish in Yves's Le Smoking, a man's suit with a white shirt. Her hair, too, was cut into a gamine crop, yet she had a beautifully feminine face. I was entranced by her. I think all of us models were slightly in love with Loulou. She had such style, *joie de vivre* and charisma and was so cultured, switching from French to Italian to English in one husky sentence. She was quite unlike any of the harpies who normally surrounded the gay male designers. I would never dream that, years later, I would find myself desperately trying to extricate myself from a compromising position with her in a nightclub in Rome.

Yves's couture shows were small-scale in those days, and held several times a day at his atelier for a select group of invitees: film stars and very wealthy couture-buying women; there would never be more than two rows of little gilt chairs. In the shows he made a witty nod to the past by having us go on to the floor carrying cards with numbers on them, like the models from the fifties. I'd done this before, in Japan, so it was easy for me. But interruptions from the audience were harder to deal with.

'You! Number Twenty-two, come here!' I heard a low, sexy voice say as I strutted into the lights. It was Lauren Bacall, in the front row, reaching out to touch the jacket I was wearing. What could I do but pause to let her inspect me? She broke the seriousness of the show with great panache.

In later years when I met Bacall she was always charming. Once Jerry Hall and I were invited to a stiff society party thrown by Ahmet Ertegun, the head of Atlantic records. We didn't know many people amongst the haughty, older crowd and we went to sit on a banquette down at one end of the long long New York townhouse rooms, feeling rather out of it. Suddenly Bacall spotted us through the crowd of New York socialites and said in a huge voice, 'Let me see the girls!' The crowds parted and people looked at us in a new light. Remember, she had been a model herself before she started acting, and she was always interested in fashion. She came over and sat down with us. 'So, let's have a drink, girls.' It was lovely of her to make us feel included.

Yves had caused shockwaves by posing naked for the advert for his perfume 'Y'. The photograph by Jeanloup Sieff went on to become one of the defining gay images of the seventies but when it was released it was practically banned. I posed, alongside a beautiful black male model called Marion, for his next perfume campaign, a unisex scent – the first on the market – called Eau Libre. It failed to catch on – as so often happens with things that are ahead of their time.

In the early seventies I also did a lot of ready-to-wear collections and editorial work in Milan. Italian fashion editors really appreciated black models and so-called exotics – they had a much wider definition of beauty. I did well there and worked a great deal with Gian Paolo Barbieri – so much that I became known as one of 'Barbieri's girls'. I enjoyed his high-glam studio work, and would pose for him for hours in attitudes reminiscent of the work of the great directors of the thirties and forties. I might be lit from above like von Sternberg's *Blue Angel* or swathed in shadows, like the films of von Stroheim – it was very stylised glamour. And as with Bailey, there would often be a story behind his photographs, a rationale: they were never just empty poses. Once I did a shoot with him for the Italian fashion magazine *Linea Italiana*, which feature me and the seventies icon, the part-African-American, part-Swedish model Pat Cleveland, in a giant bathtub especially built for the purpose; he stood above us on a ladder instructing us to intertwine our bodies while keeping our heads above the water. 'Smile!' he shouted. 'Imagine you're Esther Williams! Both of you!'

Milan was also where I met Gianni Versace, then a young but clearly very talented designer working his way up, little by little, at fashion houses such as Cadet. Back in those days it was unthinkable for young designers fresh out of college to set up their own fashion house before paying their dues and serving an apprenticeship. I modelled Versace's clothes many times before the Versace brand existed; there are pictures of me wearing them in Italian *Vogue* but his name, of course, is not credited. Already, however, Gianni was supported by his family: his brother Santo was always around, in charge of the business side, and so was young Donatella, also being trained to go into the family empire.

If it wasn't Milan, it was New York. I had been invited to join an agency called Wilhelmina's, which was one of the top two in the city representing the extremely glamorous half-Puerto-Rican Bond-girl-to-be Barbara Carerra and, later, others including Patti Hansen, Pam Dawber (Mindy in *Mork and Mindy*), and Gia Carangi. The other top agent was Eileen Ford, who was more known for WASPy, all-

American beauties, like Cheryl Tiegs and later represented Jerry and Christie Brinkley.

On my first go-sees in New York I realised how European my portfolio was. The styled, glamorous work I had done with Barbieri looked very foreign to the American eye. Instead they wanted a young, fresh-faced, athletic look. I was booked to do beauty work with Borghese, the beauty company owned by the Revlon group, and when I got to the job they wiped all my make-up off. Hair had to be clean and shiny, not styled and set. The look they wanted was utterly natural; in all the poses I struck I seemed to be running or jumping or eating ice-cream.

I was often paired with another young, dark-haired model called Barbara Minty, who went on to marry Steve McQueen. We got used to turning up on a job and seeing one another and became friends. We laughed about the fact that simply being brunette was enough to classify you as a model who was 'exotic': these were days when the conventional ideal of beauty in America was Karen Graham, the Estée Lauder model. *Vogue* wasn't to have its first black cover girl till Beverly Johnson (also one of Wilhelmina's clients) in 1974.

I was also booked to do fashion shows for designers like Bill Blass and Oscar de la Renta, usually at the Pierre Hotel. I'd turn up in my sneakers and jeans and get changed into over-the-top ballgowns and flowing dresses. There was always a very marked dichotomy between the clothes I wore and the grand, grown-up clothes I modelled. This was before youth culture took off and young women like me were assumed to have no taste and no spending power – so no one designed for them. I sent any clothes that came my way back to my mom. Dolled up in Oscar de la Renta she certainly turned heads in Hawaii. She started winning best-dressed prizes at ladies' lunches.

It was in New York that I met Valentino, who was really warm and enthusiastic about me when I met him at a go-see for his fashion show. By contrast with the other designers he seemed so European and sophisticated. Bill Blass, whom I adored, would shout, 'Come on, kids! It's showtime!' to the models; Valentino would never be so down-home.

He was deferred to as *il dottore* or *maestro*, *Women's Wear Daily* had just dubbed him 'the Sheik of Chic'. He was kind to me and told me to call him when I was in Italy; years later I did, and I worked with him all over Europe. He has always been one of my favourite designers to work with. Much as I adored him, however, I was always amused that he claimed he 'discovered' me. I hadn't the heart to tell him I had worked with Yves Saint Laurent before him.

I found the urban life in New York slightly overwhelming and was in need of a friend. In those days before the age of cheap travel, there was more of a bond between two compatriots in a strange country, so it was quite natural for me to call a friend of a friend of a friend simply because he was Japanese and we were both living in New York. (It happened the other way round, too – I looked after lots of random friends of friends of friends from Hawaii who came to London. I even once helped a virtual stranger, a Hawaiian who was a fashion designer, to sell a small range at Browns! It was a reciprocal process, this looking after and being looked after.) That was how I came to befriend Hiroshi, who was then working as the artist Jasper Johns's first assistant.

Hiroshi was an amazing-looking man, with long, straight black hair down to his waist like a Cherokee chief. I used to visit him at Jasper Johns's studio, which was in a vast and gutted 1920s former bank on First and East Houston. Johns himself was usually away at his home and studio in St Maarten in the Caribbean, and I became friendly with his sister who was from South Carolina, near where Pop came from, so we had a similar background in common. Hiroshi would invite me into the studio, and show me the canvases in the cavernous, empty space, all light and height. I remember seeing one of his famous American flag paintings sitting on an enormous easel. Once I happened to walk through his bedroom and wondered why such a famous artist had so few belongings – I realise now he was going for the minimalist look.

Hiroshi became one of my best friends. He showed me New York and took me out to restaurants I wouldn't have dared to go to alone. If I was solo I would just have the cheapest, healthiest, most fat-free meal I could find, but hanging out with Hiroshi and the other Japanese assistants at Jasper Johns's was more fun.

Meanwhile I had reconnected with the celebrated American photographer Arthur Elgort, whom I had already worked with in London on British *Vogue*. He was a really kind man, and popular with all the models. In London he had taken me for tea at Fortnum & Mason; afterwards I had suggested we take a bus ride, and, hoping to impress him, led us confidently on to a bus. When we ended up at the Victoria bus depot I had to admit I had no real idea where any of the buses went. That foolishness was all forgotten when I caught up with him here in New York and Arthur welcomed me into his home, which was always full of visiting European models. He was good fun; he was non-threatening, too. He was married to a ballet dancer and soon after I arrived in New York he took me to the Met, where my naïve comment was: 'Aren't the dancer's feet noisy?' He was kind to me and all the models and so was his sister, who taught yoga in a big room in his studio – a great way to wind down after go-sees.

Working with Elgort brought a special thrill for me because I had developed a crush on one of his assistants. The man in question seemed to reciprocate and even invited me out on a date at a fish restaurant. I dressed up in my best clothes, which were all vintage (I liked the look but, more importantly, vintage was cheap then) from my red patent forties shoes to my little red beret. Unfortunately, he ordered me quenelles of pike, a dish that was so rich I spent the whole evening throwing up in the toilet. I was brought up in Hawaii on a very basic, simple diet and to suddenly discover the wider world of food was a shock to my system. I had never even seen fresh asparagus or broccoli before; they simply did not exist in Hawaii then.

The date ended in disappointment – running to the loos vomiting isn't really a turn-on – and I went home alone to the apartment in the residential hotel on Central Park West that I shared with a fellow model called Connie. 'I thought you told me to be ready to clear out because you were going to bring a guy home!' she said. 'What happened?' I just passed out on my bed.

But I did find romance in New York, with a blond, blue-eyed American model I knew already, called Jeff. This affair is a real source of regret for me: it was the first and the last time I ever went near a friend's boyfriend. I met Jeff and his girlfriend Ritva in Milan, and I used to stay with her in Paris sometimes and she would stay with me in London. No matter that she had moved on and got a new boyfriend now; being with her ex, Jeff, still felt like a betrayal of friendship.

Jeff and I had a brief and passionate affair (when Connie could be persuaded to leave our hotel room). And just as I was coming of age, sexually, so, it seemed, was the rest of America.

*

'The seventies was the beginning of the sexualisation of everything.'

POLLY TOYNBEE

Jeff and I went to see *Deep Throat* together – at his request, needless to say. I was happy to go along because it was a sensation at the time, showing at the local art-house cinema. Everyone was going to see it: from the average Joe to intellectuals. I thought it was a nasty little film – everyone in it was so unattractive and hard-looking. It didn't turn me on in any way; my aesthetic was more refined than that.

Nevertheless it was an important turning point. It was the symbol of the new, liberated approach to sexuality that would lead, eventually, to the erotic work I did with Bailey. Of course I didn't know, that night, that I was going to end up in a book myself years later that would cause a furore: *Trouble and Strife*.

Deep Throat was a tacky film – like so many others of those movies that are a *succès de scandale*. When Bailey and I went to see *Emmanuelle* we thought it was just silly; at *Realm of the Senses* (*Ai No Corrida*, directed by Nagisa Oshima and banned in the UK so we saw it in Paris) together we were both snoring in the aisles. The only time we woke up was the moment she cut his dick off – at which Bailey sat bolt upright, as any man would. *Deep Throat* wasn't much in itself, but it did symbolise the social change that was then happening. It contributed to an atmosphere of sexual freedom that I embraced, and so did Bailey. We all did.

I believed then – and still do – that sex is another way of being free, perhaps the ultimate way of being free. If you are liberated in your sex life then you are liberated in life generally. I don't think of sex as just a physical act, but as the definition of who you are. By that I mean that it can't be shut in a box and locked away: your sexuality is part of your life force and to deny it is to deny who you are.

This is not to say that I am promiscuous. Some of the best relationships I have ever had are platonic, with just as much intensity as a sexual partnership. These can be sexualised too, albeit in a different way; contact becomes superfluous when there is a mental closeness that goes beyond friendship.

These are my values, and they were created by the age in which I lived. I grew up during a time when sex had become a legitimate discourse, after the Kinsey report and the gestalt teaching of the Esalen Institute had started to filter into public consciousness. I had grown up going to see hippie gurus who preached love and sex, like Rajneesh, author of *My Way: The Way of the White Clouds*, whose followers wore orange robes, and Maharishi Mahesh Yogi, the Beatles' famous guru. I also read the work of Krishnamurti, a mystic who stressed the power of the individual to change society. All these influences were fermenting within me, and would, in due course, give me the confidence to break boundaries myself.

As it happened, a few years later I had an encounter with Linda Lovelace. She came for a session at Bailey's studio in Primrose Hill, along with her boyfriend and promoter Chuck Traynor (whom she would later vilify in her autobiography *Ordeal*). Bailey barely had any idea who she was – he's an artist, he doesn't think in terms of people's public status – but I was fascinated to see her in person. She was ordinary-looking, but dressed the part in teeny-weeny hot pants and thigh-high boots. I remember sneaking a peek through the door to his studio and seeing her sitting for him, straddling the same stool

Yoko Ono had posed on a few years before. Those pictures are probably now buried deep somewhere in Bailey's archive.

Back to New York in 1972. After a happy few weeks with Jeff I headed home to Hawaii for Christmas. Jeff really wanted to be with me and we had a great idea: he should come and stay. He was so charming, I was sure my family would love him, and encouraged him to get a flight over. My head must have been turned by the freedom I had in New York, because it never occurred to me to think it might be a bad idea to bring my lover into my family home.

But when he arrived Pop was appalled – quite rightly, I realise now, looking back. This was the first boyfriend I'd ever brought home and I expected him to stay in my bedroom with me? No way. He refused to let Jeff stay in the house. I was the first-born, and in a sense I still was Pop's little girl, and he didn't like the idea of a man staying with me in my childhood bedroom, with Naomi, Su and Steve in next-door rooms. It caused a massive row. 'She lives abroad! She's a grown woman! What do you expect?' shouted my mother, sticking up for me, as she always did for all us girls. They had started to row a lot, my parents – I think being outnumbered by Mom and we three daughters was too much for Pop to cope with. He didn't stay in the household for much longer, as it turned out. But that Christmas, Pop won out, and Jeff and I had to check into a hotel, the Illikai in Waikiki.

It was fun being in our own hotel room, but then Jeff and I had to consider how we were going to pay for it. I had invited him as a guest so I felt I should cover it; in the end my mother made a contribution too (my mother adored him, and he flirted outrageously with her). The financial mess was all rather embarrassing. Jeff flew off to Italy, and we planned to meet in Milan or wherever we could – but life intervened. 'Doesn't anybody stay in one place any more?' Jeff wrote to me from Milan. 'I wanted to come back to spend some time with you, but I've been offered a role in a film ...' And for me things changed when I heard the bad news from New York.

I rang Hiroshi to say Happy New Year, and to tell him when I was flying in to New York – but he sounded distraught. It transpired that his assistant, a young Japanese man I had got to know well, had been murdered in the street outside Jasper Johns's studio on New Year's Eve. It was a horrifying attack. He had been stabbed with pens and pencils – one had pierced his heart and he had died instantly. He hadn't even been carrying any money with him – it seemed to be a motiveless murder. It summed up all that was terrifying about New York street crime at that time. I was so upset I cancelled my ticket and didn't return to New York for about a year.

Twenty odd years later I had a call from Brian Clarke, the artist who is a close friend of mine. 'Do you remember Hiroshi?' he asked. Hiroshi was, no surprise, now head of one of the most prestigious galleries in New York. 'Well, he wants to know if you want your trunk back.'

Memories came flooding through me: that Christmas, leaving New York, I had dropped off my big shipping trunk containing all my New York belongings at Jasper Johns's studio. Hiroshi had evidently kept it safe for me all that time. I was really moved and grateful to him, but I was also hesitant. What would be in this Pandora's Box from my past? A portable record player, I knew that; albums; books; lots of Yves Saint Laurent (I had practically the entire 'Safari' collection). I took a snap decision and told him to chuck away the trunk or do whatever he wanted with it. I thought the poor man had probably held on to it for long enough, and besides, I don't believe in getting too attached to material belongings. And that period in my life was now closed. It was best to leave that box unopened.

'Marie? You've got a job in Paris, love. Get yourself on a flight – the ticket's pre-paid and waiting at the terminal – and ring your agents there now, won't you?' I did what Eileen Green told me. I always did. When I spoke to my French agency, Paris Planning, they told me that the job was for French *Vogue* and the photographer was Guy Bourdin, a man who was, in my opinion, an artist first and a fashion photographer second. His reputation for being difficult preceded him. It was whispered that one of his wives had hanged herself (his second wife would go on to do the same, in fact) and that he had no feeling for the models he worked with. But then again, perhaps the man just had limited English and so appeared very abrupt. Most people wanted to work with him but few got the chance, and the rumours about him might have been merely resentful, yet I was still nervous before our session.

At that time there were frequent tales of models being damaged: getting electrocuted, being poisoned by body paint, going on shoots in the desert and never returning. One of Helmut Newton's favourite models was murdered and mutilated. These stories haunted the profession.

Some of them were basically urban myths, though others were true. The industry was regulated as far as there is an association for agents, though there is no union for models (we're not a political breed) and we're always self-employed and reliant on our agents' protection. In Italy the system was most archaic: models were classed legally in almost the same professional category as prostitutes. There's not more than a syllable's difference between 'clothes horse' and 'clothes whore', after all.

And in our line of work, casual abuse happened all the time. Sometimes it was just careless accidents inflicted by hairdressers or stylists, like burns from heated tongs or allergic reactions to one of the many brands of make-up used. At a friend's house I saw models voluntarily having their ankles injected with something to slim them down – or rather I didn't see, since I left the room in horror. At a Claude Montana show all the girls' heads were covered with black masking tape, but when it came to removing it – ouch! – we were all screaming; after that I decided never to do another Montana show again.

Other practices were just demeaning. It was routine for make-up artists to spit on their brushes before applying them direct to our faces. Some of the more macho make-up artists would first expectorate with a big phlegmy noise. Most of us never uttered a word of protest, although I do remember doing a job with Jerry when she very politely and reasonably said to the make-up artist, 'Please, I would prefer you to use the water from the sink.' I was so impressed and proud of her.

Way Bandy, the American make-up artist extraordinaire (who worked with stars from Elizabeth Taylor to Raquel Welch and did all the *Cosmopolitan* covers with photographer Francesco Scavullo), was famous for giving his models beautiful skin. What was in the special elixir he mixed up and painted on their faces? I never worked with him but I knew the rumour: his spunk was the secret ingredient.

With Guy Bourdin I was particularly apprehensive because I knew a girl who'd had a session with him and paid the price. She couldn't work for months afterwards. The photograph was a fantastic image, a sideways view of her with her eyes wide open and bright pink powder being blown (by an assistant, off camera) straight into her eyes. Can you imagine what it did to her eyes? She washed them out so many times on the set that by the end they were totally dry. It took her a long time to get over it. It's an iconic photo, but does anybody know her name? Was it worth almost losing her sight over?

I can empathise with her, though. I know what it is like to be so involved in the shoot that you let anything happen. I think I might have even done it myself. Guy Bourdin was so respected I would have hung upside down and practically guillotined myself to work with him.

I've done things I shouldn't have done. Once, the editor of French *Vogue* Francine Crescent (through whom I later met Fellini) took the unusual step of asking me personally to take part in a shoot, before going to my agent. The photographer was going to be none other than Gina Lollobrigida. I said yes on the spot, of course.

But Francine Crescent was very angry when she saw the photos from the shoot. Gina had taken me to the rooftop of one of the highest buildings in Paris, where she had asked me to lean over the parapet and stretch out my arms as if I was flying. I had unhesitatingly gone along with it: I was carried away by the moment and by the excitement of being photographed by Gina Lollobrigida, who had starred in films with Sinatra and Bogart and whom all men of a certain age fancied, especially my father. But the photos showed what risks I'd taken. Francine Crescent took me to lunch in the canteen at French *Vogue* and lectured me sternly. 'You took a chance with your life,' she said. 'And by extension, you took a chance with my reputation and the reputation of my publication. Sometimes, a photographer will ask you to do insane things, and you must always use your better judgement. Don't hesitate to say no.'

On top of all this, the Lollobrigida pictures weren't that great. Her assistants had done most of the work, really – as is sometimes the way with celebrities turned photographers. It's certainly not worth taking risks, even when you're working with a star photographer. I also learned to trust the old adage: never work with animals. With Albert Watson in New York I had to hold the hand of a chimp, which was sweaty and grasped me with unexpected power. The photograph was grotesque. And in Germany I was asked to pose with a baby leopard. The handler was off-putting enough, his arms ripped from elbow to wrist with scar tissue, but the animal itself was a distressing sight, huge and heavily sedated. I was instructed by the art director to lie down and support its head in my hands. I tried to but when my arms slackened, the poor creature's head slumped sickeningly, like a dead animal's. I walked out.

The phone rang again. 'Marie?' came the deep rasping voice. It was the head of Paris Planning, Gérard Marie, who later went on to marry Linda Evangelista. 'Get yourself down to the Champs-Elysées. Guy Bourdin has requested you have a manicure at Guerlain.'

It was the first time I'd ever had a manicure, and I found the whole thing thrilling. I was staying at the cheapest hotel and making my *café complet* breakfast see me through the day, so I luxuriated in having a manicure at a top salon that lasted an hour and a half. Guy Bourdin had apparently stressed that my nails should be cut unfashionably short and square. Curiouser and curiouser.

When I got to the shoot I realised why: it was a beauty shot, a close up. All they wanted in the picture were my fingertips, lips, a portion of my nose, perhaps. Guy was pleasant, hard to converse with because of the language barrier, offhand and very Gallic – but why shouldn't he be? He just liked my hands. Talk about an anticlimax.

There were some famously naughty men working in Paris at that time, Eileen Green warned me. 'The French mob' were a pack of photographers including Patrick Demarchelier, Jean-Jacques Bugat or Alex Chatelin. They were said to seduce all their models; supposedly there was a couch in their studios for the purpose. 'Go home straight after the job, now, love,' Eileen would say in her lovely Irish lilt. Already I wasn't listening to her, because by that time I was going out in the evenings having a wild time at dinners with other models and photographers. Her mumsy protectiveness was now beginning to grate a little; and besides, was unnecessary advice, for my heart, by that time, was taken.

Through Leonard Whiting I had met a gorgeous young actor: Bruce Robinson. He had played Benvolio in *Romeo and Juliet* with Leonard Whiting and they used to regale us with tales of how they were both chased around the set by a randy Franco Zeffirelli. When we were first introduced Bruce was very much in love with Lesley-Anne Down, a gorgeous, wild child actress, the 'It' girl of her time, who went on to become famous for her role in *Upstairs Downstairs* but had at that time just been voted 'The Most Beautiful Teenager in Britain'. Whenever her name was mentioned, it was prefaced by this tag. What chance did I have if he was going out with such a girl?

But when their relationship foundered, Bruce and I shared a stolen kiss in the back of a taxi. It was, to purloin Wilde's phrase, the perfect pleasure because it left us both unsatisfied. Soon after we began an affair, snatching time with each other whenever we could. I adored him and his dark, moody romantic looks remain for me a benchmark of male beauty. I always go for the brooding, Heathcliff type. I was wild about Bruce, and we spent most of our time together in bed.

When I watched Princess Anne's wedding to Mark Phillips on the television, it was with only half an eye. Although it was the afternoon, Bruce and I were in bed together at the time, at my little flat in Draycott Place, passionately embracing while the stuffy ceremony took place in the background.

Hungry, we went round the corner to a wine bar we liked and gorged on a ploughman's: cheese, a hunk of bread and grapes (this was way before tapas arrived in London). When we got back to the flat, the wedding was still going on. I think we decided to go back to bed again in honour of Princess Anne.

Bruce and I never settled down – in fact, I didn't even visit the house he shared in Camden, though after seeing his living conditions as represented in his autobiographical film *Withnail and I*, I now have an inkling of why he didn't invite me round. And just when we were becoming close, it would be time for the Milan collections, or the Paris ready-to-wear shows, or it would be time for me to go home again.

When I set off for Hawaii, Bruce ran after me in the rainy street and presented me with his goodbye token: an old-fashioned hardback book, *Once Upon a Time – The Fairy Tale World of Arthur Rackham*, which I still have. Inscribed inside, he had written, 'Dearest Marie, Thinking of you. All love, Bruce. London, November 1973. Raining (lots) and a tear (one).'

I would hop back to Hawaii from Tokyo twice in that year, 1973. The first time was to see Elvis's now-legendary concert, Aloha From Hawaii – the first time a live international satellite link-up had been used. I'd never been a fan, but when I saw him perform live, responding to the adoring crowds, I was blown away. His charisma even made you forget that silly white jumpsuit.

Sitting next to me at the concert was none other than *Hawaii 5-o*'s own 'Zulu'. Yes, the actor Gilbert Kauhi, who played Jack Lord's sidekick. Between him and Elvis, it was quite a night.

Two months later I came back for another gig: The Stones. I was a real fan and adored every minute. Seeing pictures of Bianca in the paper. I thought she looked fabulous.

FIVE

IN LONDON, IN LOVE

*'Women were brought up to believe that men were the
answer. They weren't even one of the questions.'*

JULIAN BARNES

⌐

$\mathcal{T}$hey were fatally beautiful shoes. A pair of black-and-white co-
respondent dance shoes with a pattern tooled in leather; a dandy's
shoes; the type of shoes Fred Astaire would have worn to dance with
Cyd Charisse. I couldn't stop staring at them, across the aisle on the
aeroplane.

Bailey (for it was he who was wearing these shoes) caught me
looking. He shifted around a little in his seat, looking tired and
scruffy in a leather jacket and jeans. He was on the final leg of his
journey back from some socialite party in Acapulco; hence the shoes.

'Didn't bother changing 'em,' he said.

'I really like them,' I replied shyly. 'They make you look like Fred
Astaire.'

Bailey gave me a look; an appraising sideways glance that said,
'Are you daft in the head, then?' A look my father would describe in
Hawaiian patois as a *maka-ele-ele* look. Damn, I thought to myself
and resolved to keep my big mouth shut. So we fell into an awkward
silence, and the jet engines rumbled on. For conversation I turned
to Patrick Lichfield instead, who was sitting on my left, sporting an
outsize Stetson.

We were on the plane going back to London from Paris Orly,
where I had bumped into Patrick and Bailey on their way home

from this party thrown by the Patinos in Mexico. Since I knew Patrick well by this time it seemed natural that we should all sit together on the plane home. I later found out Bailey had raced Patrick down the aeroplane aisle to grab the seat next to me. But at the time I had no idea of that. I was just trying not to say anything stupid to the great photographer after my Fred Astaire comment. But sometimes when we think we've said the wrong thing we actually couldn't have said anything more right.

About six months later, when I moved in with Bailey, I realised Fred Astaire was one of his ultimate heroes. When a musical with dancing in it came on television he was always glued to the screen. He could do all the moves to the song 'All I Need Is the Girl' from *Gypsy*, except the sailing out of the window bit at the end. If Bailey could come back as anyone, it would be either Pablo Picasso or Fred Astaire.

After that brief aeroplane encounter Bailey and I didn't see one another again for a few months. I moved into a hotel in New York and started to think about living in Manhattan again, in fact, until I was booked to do the Paris collections for British *Vogue*. Barry Lategan was the photographer and the other model, for the doubles, was someone I was very fond of: Eva Malmström (who, later, with her husband Sonu Shivdasani went on create Soneva Fushi in the Maldives, and a worldwide luxury hotel chain too).

Beatrix Miller caught me in *Vogue*'s studio in Paris and said she had an idea that I should do a photo shoot with a Brazil theme: the photographer was going to be Bailey. She suggested I fly over to London especially to see him – so, even though I was meant to be going back to New York, I took that life-changing detour.

When I entered the studio I saw him sitting on the floor, studying a magazine layout, a cigarette hanging out of his mouth. He browsed through my portfolio in a very offhand manner, as if it bored him intensely. My heart fell. 'Yeah, I've heard of you. I've heard of every model who's any good. And I can see you've worked with the best,' he said flatly. 'See you around.'

It's strange when in hindsight you find out how these things come about. Unbeknownst to me, Grace Coddington, the then fashion editor of *Vogue*, had cannily engineered our meeting. She was always trying to keep Bailey's restless creative mind occupied with something new, and had intuited that my Hawaiian genesis would intrigue him.

All I knew was that after that meeting, Eileen Green was on the phone to me. 'OK, Marie my love, you're booked on a job with Bailey. This could be great for your portfolio. But please, by Mary, Jesus and all the saints, don't sleep with him. I'm telling you, my dear – keep your knickers on. You'd be the first and probably the last. Good luck now, angel.'

Bailey's status as arch-seducer was legendary. There were lots of wild stories about Bailey. For example, according to legend, one evening at La Coupole, the restaurant in Paris, Bailey bet Roman Polanski the cost of the meal that he could seduce one of the women in the restaurant, then and there. He picked out a fashion editor among the diners, she proved willing to be hauled off to his Rolls-Royce – and the consequence was Polanski paid the bill. Another story had it that one night at Mr Chow's with David Puttnam and Terry Donovan, Bailey thought a beautiful woman opposite him in the restaurant was flirting with him. Urged on by his companions, he went over to chat her up. She seemed to know his name; he asked her if they'd met before – and she had to remind him that they had in fact once been married. It was his first wife Rosemary Bramble. 'She'd changed her hairstyle or something,' said Bailey weakly.

I knew these stories before I met Bailey – but what I didn't yet know was that they were all true. Bailey subsequently confirmed them with many wicked chuckles of laughter.

Duly warned, I turned up for our *Vogue* shoot early in the morning, my stomach eaten away with nerves. This was my first cover shoot, an exotic 'holiday getaway' photographic story about Brazil that was actually shot in a chilly studio in Parsons Green. Bailey had been to Brazil, and brought back photographs that we used as front projections: a jungle scene with a hyacinth macaw in the background, a colonial church, and the boardwalk of Ipanema, which I posed in front of wearing beachwear, blossoms in my hair. Afterwards when they saw the pictures people always asked me how I enjoyed my trip to Brazil.

On the first day of the shoot, Bailey and I barely spoke. I was supposed to be portraying Yemanjá the Brazilian goddess of the sea, and my hair was allowed to go wavy and unbridled, and my eyes dramatically made-up. But come the second day, Barbara Daly the make-up artist (who wasn't using Caran d'Ache this time) was off sick, and Bailey came to me, waving the Polaroids from the previous day at me and asking if I could possibly recreate the look. I reassured him I would be able to, and I think he was quite impressed with the results. It would have been a different story a few years before but by now I was an experienced model. I was ready to paint my own face, and also, in many ways, I was ready for Bailey.

I had worked with so many different photographers, and with each of them I had tried out different techniques. With Patrick Demarchelier I had leaped around the studio, so he could catch me mid-air for dynamic shots that were fresh, young and athletic. He was inspired by Avedon and it showed. But with Barbieri the work was entirely opposite: static, motionless tableaux in homage to iconic cinema directors, from Bergman to Visconti. There was even, uniquely, a full-length mirror beside the camera in Barbieri's studio so we models could perfect our poses. By contrast other photographers did everything they could to avoid making us self-conscious. With Arthur Elgort, for example, I had to unlearn everything I knew because he wanted every movement to be as natural as possible. He would shoot me out on the street, hailing a taxi cab, wind in my hair and my coat flapping everywhere – a total commitment to naturalism. Even something as simple as sitting down was different depending on which photographer you were with. 'Sit down' from Barbieri meant 'drape yourself over the chair'. 'Sit down' from Arthur Elgort meant 'flop across the chair. No, really sit on the chair. Like a real person, not a model!'

It was like starting all over again with each photographer. In these pre-motorised days, even their cameras worked differently, each with its own rhythm: Hasselblads with their slow ker-click, ker-click.

Nikons with the chick-un, chick-un, Pentax with their quick tick, tick, tick shutter sound – and the timing of your movements has to change accordingly. I was working with the best international photographers, but essentially I was here, there and everywhere, a 'jobbing' high-fashion model. Altogether it meant that I could never achieve a working relationship of any real depth.

When a model and a photographer work exclusively with one another, the results can be outstanding. Like an artist and a muse, it becomes a working partnership – you grow to be in sync with one another. I learned to read Bailey so well I knew instinctively what he wanted me to do, how he wanted me to move. He didn't even need to speak. All it would take was a look, a hand motion, rather like a conductor to a first violinist. It wasn't unique to me and Bailey: Janice Dickinson and Mike Reinhardt, Anjelica Huston and Bob Richardson, Oliverio Toscani and Kirsti, Kate Moss and Mario Sorrenti – they all had intense photographic relationships. And yes, they were sexual relationships as well.

So how did Bailey and I fall in love? That day the shoot went well – supplementary to his regular 'stay like that, pussycat!' I even got the odd 'fantastic!' – and he offered to drive me home, to the Portobello Hotel where I was staying in the cheapest, tiniest room. As we drove through the cold London streets the sky was white; there was the hopeful air of something about to happen. Finally I said quietly, 'I think it's going to snow tomorrow.'

Bailey glanced at me sideways from the driver's seat. It was that look again. The sideways stink-eye, the *maka-ele-ele* look. I was beginning to like that look.

When we got to the hotel he took me for a glass of wine in the bar. I knew that he had a live-in girlfriend, the inheritor to Penelope Tree, but I had also heard wicked rumours about how Bailey had won her as a bet one night, when he thrashed her boyfriend at poker. I didn't question if this was true, or anything about her. It was very much a case of what you don't want to know you don't ask. Bailey and I said, 'Goodbye, see you soon,' quite innocently.

But when I got up to my room I felt strangely elated. I had no reason to – there was nothing going on between us. But I had a presentiment that something was beginning. Something good. Out of the window, snow was starting to fall on the West London streets.

After that first job he quickly began to book me all the time: two or three times a week. I delayed going back to New York ... Eileen Green became very keen to know what was going on. Every time I went to the agency I could see her eyes flashing at me, part-proud, part-concerned. The second shoot we did was – *quelle surprise* – in his own bedroom. Photographers can be cheeky but Bailey made an art form of it. That was one of the things I loved about him: his outrageous nerve.

His house in Primrose Hill was chaotic and bohemian, a mixture of Bailey's style and Penelope Tree's. Outside it was painted sky blue and overrun by ivy; inside the decor had the high drama of the late sixties. The walls were all black, there was the obligatory 'purple room', a spare bedroom complete with hand-painted pink minarets. There was even a den-like room stuffed with velvet sofas that had six TVs mounted on one wall. All through the house there was a jumble of books and paintings and carvings and *objets trouvés*. A huge aeroplane propeller hung in the hall (a detail the film director Antonioni, who visited Bailey's home when he was researching *Blow-Up*, stole wholesale: David Hemmings as the bad boy photographer has one in his studio too). And the noise in this house was incredible. There were seventy parrots in the basement and hangers-on making themselves cups of tea in the kitchen. Rock music was blaring and everyone was chattering. But upstairs in his bedroom we shot the photos in comparative seclusion. Unlike most of the top photographers, Bailey doesn't allow a big crew on to his set and never has. Only his most essential staff were allowed. The atmosphere in the bedroom that day was heightened, and intimate.

It was another cover story for *Vogue*, and the pictures were extremely sexy. Bailey and Grace Coddington thought up the look together – they really were an inspired team. Every photographer needs a good fashion editor and vice versa. They put black satin sheets on Bailey's wooden Jacobean four-poster bed, and I reclined across it wearing long black satin evening gloves, stockings with a suspender belt and black patent high heels. In one of the pictures I am caressing one of the heels – very Bailey, that idea. My hair was straightened and glossed so it shone like black lacquer.

It still felt like work, doing this shoot, though having said that, there was an attraction there that I had never felt with another photographer. He was so different to anyone I'd ever met: constantly teasing, flirtatious then gruff so you never quite knew where you were with him. That was very sexy to me. By that time I was established as a model and I had begun to feel settled with who I was. Unlike anyone else, Bailey totally threw me.

I knew we were creating photos that were, for their day, very risqué. In one of them I am biting the tip of the evening glove; in another a nipple is exposed. It was editorial work for *Vogue*, but it was at the same time highly erotically charged. To get the two together was practically unheard of at that time. But I was ready to do that kind of work, to push boundaries. I was uninhibited, at ease with my body – I had grown up in a bikini, after all. I had also done, as we know, that nude family photo album with Shinoyama-san, and I was familiar with nudity being very accepted, prestigious even in Japanese photography. 'Take your clothes off' meant something very different to me than it did to, say, a country vicar's daughter like Jean Shrimpton.

So I needed Bailey – and if I can be bold enough to say it, he needed me. We very quickly found our photographic groove together. And as for our sex life, well . . . I wasn't ready to take up residence in that great Jacobean bed for another four months at least. Shortly after that shoot he asked me out on a date, and came to collect me from Gunter Grove where I was then staying with Grace Coddington and her husband the photographer Willie Christie. Bailey and I sat awkwardly across the room from each other like nervous teenagers on a prom date. Grace Coddington's walls were hung with grey cashmere (well, she was the fashion editor of *Vogue*, of course her home was stylish) and I remember we both commented on how soft, how sensual they were. Then it turned out that Bailey had arranged a double date for us that evening, with Beatrix Miller and Barney

Wan, the art director of British *Vogue*. I was a little disappointed initially that it wasn't going to be a romantic night *à deux*, but as it turned out we four gelled really well. That night we dropped Beatrix off and went back to Barney's and every time he went into the kitchen to get more drinks we started kissing and fumbling. I was ecstatic inside with lust, lust and more lust.

> 'She wears red feathers and a huly huly skirt.
> She lives on just cocy-nuts and fish from the sea,
> A rose in her hair, a gleam in her eyes,
> And love in her heart for me . . .'

Bailey would put his arm round me and sing this little ditty.

'What is that song? I've never heard it before!' I'd protest. I thought he'd made it up until I heard it on the TV one day. Our courtship moved onwards, lightly, gradually. I was attracted to him and we slept together really quickly, but I held back in other ways. I wouldn't consider moving in with him, say, nor would I even stay the night at his house. The mysterious and unwanted girlfriend had by now moved out of his home, but I felt the bed was still warm.

Something in me made me refuse to slot pliantly into his life. When I see photos of myself from that time, I think I look really young, childlike, even, but I also look very self-confident. Maybe I was a hard nut to crack.

Bailey and I would work together in the daytime and then spend the evenings out at San Lorenzo or Mr Chow's, bantering about the idiocies of the fashion world – what a gift to find a soulmate who was in the same industry as me – and taking the mickey out of people we knew. Nobody was spared: I was often told I should have stayed up in those coconut trees. Staying with Grace and Willie was perfect. They adored Bailey, which made everything feel more comfortable, and helped me trust my own judgement about him. It also allowed me to begin to see his closely guarded softer side, to realise that the swaggering, bullish photographer was a public caricature.

As Bailey and I spent more and more time together, my friends warned me not to give my heart to him. I would become just another name on his infamously long list of conquests, they said. But I knew it was more than that. And when Bailey invited me for a weekend away in Paris, what could I say?

*

'I see you got her first.'

It was a familiar voice, that London drawl. I turned around and realised it was Mick Jagger wearing a fur Parka and shades and verbally slapping Bailey on the back. We were in the lobby of L'Hôtel in Paris, where Bailey and I were staying in a suite. Mick, being Mick, had the penthouse. They were major players, those men; kingpins, cocks-of-the-walk. They drank deeply from the heady sixties brew of new social freedoms, the pill and ubiquitous sexual experimentation. Women were throwing themselves at their feet at that time, and naturally they saw sex as a free-for-all, not a thing of many colours and consequences as women do. That Mick and Bailey should banter about me in front of me like that enrages the feminist in me now. But at the time it was habitual, this careless arrogance. Men often spoke about women as if they weren't there. I just stood there like a lemon – a sour lemon – while Bailey grinned at Mick and put his arm round me, saying, 'Yeah, tough luck.'

I had worked in Paris many times, but I had never been whisked there by a man. In fact I had never been whisked anywhere by a man. Being treated with chivalry was a novelty, and a beguiling one. To most it would have been called a dirty weekend in Paris but to me it was a romantic weekend. Bailey and I walked out from L'Hôtel down the narrow streets to the Saint-Germain des Prés Café de Flore (where once Picasso and Chagall drank and de Beauvoir and her philosophical soulmate Sartre wrote). We went on to eat at Brasserie Lipp, with Mick (who asked me if I knew that the Hawaiian flag had a Union Jack in one corner? I certainly did, but I was impressed by his knowledge) and from there Bailey and I went on to La Coupole, the cavernous restaurant set under a dome of mirrored gilt that was open twenty-four hours a day and eternally popular with the fashion crowd. Everyone was here, drinking champagne, pushing food round their plates, waving at each other across the banquettes. It was where Pat Cleveland made her first entry on to the Paris scene in a gossamer Karl Lagerfeld dress with her arms held aloft *à la* Isadora Duncan. It was where countless naughty things had happened underneath the table – or, in Bailey's case, outside in the Rolls-Royce. But tonight we were content simply with each other.

He pointed at a table where many models were sitting. 'See her? The dark one? I've had her. And the blonde as well. And fuck me, the brunette too. Had her against a wall, actually.' He spoke not boastfully but with mock-surprise at his own success. I couldn't help laughing. His bravado was silly and yet I found it strangely charming. If anything I found his openness about his conquests refreshing – reassuring even. It wasn't a sordid secret – this was just how it was for him. I knew I was with someone special and different, and I knew that meant I would have to accept unacceptable behaviour from him.

He told me about what life was like when he started out as a assistant to the photographer John French, when the awfully posh older women at *Vogue* used to pat him on the head – literally. He made it sound as if they patronised him thoroughly: 'Say something again in your funny cockney voice, do! Oh, say it again . . .' But at that same time these women would have gone to bed with him given half the chance, his cheeky-chappie style was so glamorous and fresh. He was really spoiled.

He was great company as always, regaling me with stories about his friends: Sir Howard Acton, George Melly, Helmut Berger, Roman Polanski . . . 'So then George took a great big salmon that he had just caught, and do you know where he put it?'

While Bailey was in full flow I noticed across the restaurant someone I knew from *Vogue*, a fashion assistant. Her eyes widened as she saw Bailey and me alone together. I felt a frisson of pride as I realised we were an item in the public's eyes.

On our return to London the press, too, had got hold of the idea that I was Bailey's 'squeeze' and used to swoop on us for a shot as we left San Lorenzo or Mr Chow. They were sometimes a pain but I always bore in mind the fact that they were just doing their job –

and some of them were friendly. I began to know a few by name, like Richard Young, one of the first British paparazzi, who would go on to be the main photographer for Bailey's newspaper *Ritz*.

Fame sat comfortably on my shoulders, possibly because it was something I was used to after Tokyo. It seemed natural to me. It was not that I felt it necessarily deserved: it just was. Bailey was – and is – wise about so many things, including fame. Because he had been through it himself – he had become famous very quickly in a way he hadn't looked or asked for – he was good at explaining to me how to handle fame, how to stay in control. When the press shouted stupid questions at me like, 'So is there a ring on your finger then?' he would tell me to protect myself and ignore them. 'Don't rise to it.'

I sure rose to it, though, totally by accident, when a journalist asked me the secret for great skin, and I replied: 'Sleep, water, vitamins and lots of sex.' I wasn't allowed to forget that for years after. I just said it off the top of my head – it was a very passionate time for me and Bailey, after all.

Bailey viewed fame not emotionally but coolly, intellectually. He encouraged me to ask myself 'What can I get out of this?' and 'What responsibilities does this bring?' And he always maintained: 'If you're successful, you have to become a nicer person, because if you don't there's something very, very wrong with you.' Fame, I began to understand, brought privileges, but obligations too.

As my thinking evolved so did my 'look'. I find it funny and flattering to read now that make-up artists like Charlotte Tilbury and Mary Greenwell sometimes use looks inspired by me – but I always knew that look was my own. Ninety per cent of the time, I'd hazard, I did my own make-up rather than work with an artist.

It all started with those pictures in Bailey's bed. He had scoffed at the pastel-coloured paints a lot of make-up artists used on me, and preferred it when I darkened my eyes with kohl instead. The effect was seductive and womanly, and fashion editors loved it. So that was it; the girlish petal-blossom face was gone for ever. At first I just rubbed on sooty black eyeliner like boot polish ('Just squint and give it a good rub!' said Tina) but then my technique became more intricate. Inspired by Serge Lutyens, then the chief make-up designer at Dior, Barbara Daly and Heidi Morawetz, who is now at Chanel, I learned to paint on three layers of eyeshadow, then eyeliner – and a beauty spot. I painted this over a little freckle I already had, otherwise it would have shifted every time. I liked the way this harked back to screen sirens of the fifties – my favourite Hollywood era – but I also liked experimenting with asymmetry.

Jaw

I realised that my jaw was infinitesimally lop-sided: this gets picked up on film, because, as I see it, the camera always lies. From the left, my jaw is more angular and defined; from the right the gradation is softer, more curved. In my business these tiny fractions mean everything. I saw that I wasn't perfect – but perfection, I told myself, often doesn't work in photographs. The camera is the devil in disguise. I guess that means retouchers do the devil's work!

Sometimes I think my entire career was based on my left jaw. I instinctively turn to expose it in photos. Most photographers notice that's my best side, consciously or unconsciously, because nine times out of ten they will ask me to display my left. I think a lot of people presume that models are perfect physical specimens – it's just not true. Models have cellulite; models have acne and fat ankles. The best models are the ones who know how to work it, how to be clever about their defects, whether it's standing *en pointe* to disguise bad ankles, or painting on a beauty spot to counterbalance a weaker jaw.

*

For a model, looking in the mirror isn't narcissism – it's your livelihood. If things go wrong on a shoot – bad lighting, bad hair, bad make-up – it may not be your fault, but it will be *seen* as your fault. It's your image, and therefore your responsibility. One of the unfair facts about modelling is that if everything works in a shoot, the general response is always, 'Wow, isn't David Bailey a great photographer?' while if something goes wrong, people just say, 'Jeez, she looks terrible.'

I noticed that people described me as 'enigmatic'. Attaining this look was easy for me. I simply hollowed out my mind to be absolutely vacant, so people could ascribe to me whatever mysteries they wanted, while I thought about my dry cleaning, or whether I should stop at the fishmongers for some shrimp.

Bailey helped develop my look. He insisted on stockings, and high heels too: if he came to collect me in the evening and saw I was wearing flats he would sulk in the car until I put heels on. 'They make you look like Minnie Mouse!' he'd holler. I found a certain pleasure in acquiescing to what he wanted. I must have been falling in love with him.

It had become increasingly unnatural for us to live apart, and going away together on a working trip to Italy (in his Range Rover: he drove, I navigated) showed us how blissful it would be to spend all our time together. 'That's it,' he said, shortly afterwards. 'You're moving in with me.'

He didn't give me any say in the matter, you notice. Typical Bailey. But the truth was I had also started to like being told what to do. It was a relief. I could relax because someone else was calling the shots. I loved it. It meant I could enjoy the inverse power of being cosseted. And more to the point I could be blissfully lazy. I was a laid-back island girl, after all. People thought I suffered under some kind of tyranny from Bailey, who was routinely referred to as my 'Svengali'. But on the contrary, I enjoyed being passive, especially over decisions I didn't care about. He was always asking me, 'Where shall we go tonight, Marie? What shall we do? Make a decision, girl!' I found it joyful. I knew exactly what I was doing and, being strong enough to play at being weak, I consciously chose – much to the irritation of friends and the press – to submit to his will. There was certainly an element of sexual power play there too.

Moving into his house, I was self-conscious about what Bailey's friends would think of me, and keen not to come across as a presumptuous new chatelaine. On my first night at Bailey's an Italian friend of his came to visit; I refused to leave the bedroom. The next day, Bailey was out on a shoot, but I was so keen for his assistants and Cezar the housekeeper not to think I was waltzing around the house as if it were mine that I spent the whole day hiding out in the bathroom and bedroom.

As I mooched around the bedroom I leafed through a book of George Sand's letters, only to notice it had Penelope Tree's name in it. In the bathroom, I discovered a few pots of women's cosmetics that I suspected were hers; they freaked me out, these things. But only temporarily. I soon grew to really like the sound of Penelope from stories Cezar told me about her, and when Bailey and I got married, she sent a very warm telegram.

Later when we met we got on like a house on fire, and when it turned out she wanted some of the things she'd left behind at Bailey's, I sent them back to her in a package. But her Old English Sheepdog, Stokely Carmichael (named in honour of the black activist who refused military service, declaring 'If I'm gonna do any fighting, it's going to be right here at home') and Merlin (a French Briard) stayed with me and Bailey, and became ours.

Apart from these few faltering first incidents, I took to life in Primrose Hill with ease. Bailey and I were in love, and that gave me all the confidence I needed. It was one of those times in life when you are carried forwards on a tide of certainty: you can do anything, because you feel secure and loved.

So I began to feel his home was my home too. Cezar, the black Brazilian cook, housekeeper and all-round 'major domo' was welcoming and he and I were soon discussing the cooking over coffee in the kitchen. I moved in my belongings and joined Bailey's household. Yet here in Primrose Hill I felt out on a limb, cut off from the rest of London that I knew. The house was on Gloucester Avenue, near Camden Town and the railway tracks: apparently, so the story goes, Catherine Deneuve (his second wife) had arrived, took one look at it and headed straight back to the place Saint-Sulpice.

I grew to love the area but my taxi bills were enormous, since going to see friends meant jumping in a cab. I might be dashing off to see Sabrina Guinness – she who later went on to date Prince Charles, though she was always disappointingly discreet about him. Sabrina once worked as a nanny and I remember seeing her with a small snotty child in tow, who went by the name of Tatum O'Neal. Ryan O'Neal was over here filming *Barry Lyndon* at the time. And, speaking of which, I had finally met my idol Marisa Berenson. Bailey and I went to a party for her given by Martin and Nona Summers, where she was wearing a gorgeous YSL silk stole, though not for long, as it dramatically burst into flames when she sat too close to the fire. (She was fine. It was the silk stole that died.)

When Bailey and I went out to dinner he would drive us across town in the Rolls to Mr Chow's in Knightsbridge or San Lorenzo in Chelsea. He would never drink and drive, and I always had to lug along in my handbag a six-pack of Tab, the caffeinated diet drink to which he was addicted.

At Mr Chow's I used to hang out with Tina, who by now had married Michael Chow, after they met in Japan (isn't it fantastic when two people you care about fall in love?). Naomi my sister remembers being embarrassed when Tina and I broke loudly into song in the restaurant once. The song, she reminds me, was the Oreo cookie song – we were both Americans exiled in Britain, after all.

One night I saw Lana Turner there, with Russell Harty (she had just appeared on his show). Though in old age by this time she was elegant in a silk cheongsam. And she was so tiny, even with enormous high heels. I remember watching her tottering down the staircase and being aghast she might trip at any moment. She was so dinky, I could have caught her in one hand, like Superwoman.

At San Lorenzo we would be guaranteed to see someone we knew, from Bianca Jagger, in a chic Tommy Nutter suit, to Sean Connery and Donald Sutherland having dinner with Lesley-Anne Down, still the most beautiful girl in London. Bailey and I would always be invited to join someone's table; I still feel comfortable enough there to go in on my own in the evening for a plate of pasta. It's like a second home.

Bailey would always give me the menu to read to him. 'What are the specials tonight, me old toe-rag?' (I don't know what that word means, and I still don't want to know.) I began to realise, gradually, that Bailey was dyslexic. His talent and intelligence are visual, not literary. But he knew how to direct my reading, and under his guidance I discovered Woolf, Flaubert, Greene, García Marquez . . . I had always been a voracious reader and now I was hitting my stride. Bailey was proud of me, asking me about everything I'd read and then telling our friends, 'Marie EATS books!'

Under his guidance I began to mature intellectually. I had a lot to learn about culture, religion, art and literature, and Bailey was so knowledgeable. We talked about paintings for hours: what was this pop art sculpture in the hall? Where had he bought this banjo decorated by a Scottish naïve artist? Should he buy another Lichtenstein? A Belloq or a Cartier-Bresson print?

After so many years of living out of a suitcase I had come to rest at last, and it was a pleasure to share small everyday things with someone I loved. Our relationship was very playful. Bailey had terrible domestic habits, and I teased him for them. At night when he took off his smelly shoes and socks I might throw them out of the window. He would rush down to retrieve the shoes, but if I'd thrown out just the socks, he wouldn't bother.

Of an evening he might slump in front of a cop show like *Kojak* or *Starsky & Hutch* on the television, munching on apples, while I would sit behind him reading a book and smoking a joint. He hated it when I smoked joints. 'Fucking hell, Marie, put the fucking thing fucking out! You're not a fucking hippie chick any more, you know.' (I'd never heard anyone swear as much as Bailey and unfortunately it rubbed off: I still catch myself using the worst expletives while shopping in Marks and Spencer: 'What do you mean you don't have any Santorini fucking tomatoes?' much to everyone's horror.) In turn, I would reproach him for slinging apple cores over his shoulder. I made a point of refusing to pick them up for him; thank goodness we had Cezar.

Housekeeping was not my strong point. I bought all my groceries at Harrods. It was simply the only place I knew to get good fresh food at the time. (Bailey never knew – he'd have been furious.) When we went over to Paul and Linda McCartney's in St John's Wood she would effortlessly whip something up in the kitchen: a delicious spinach salad with vegetarian bacon and cheese would appear as if out of nowhere. I loved going over there – it was so comfortable and boho, with toys everywhere for little Stella and Mary. Linda's father represented Willem de Kooning and there would be a really famous painting of his on the wall and their children's drawings would be pinned up next to it. Linda was naturally an excellent cook and she'd even have her guests in the kitchen while she was cooking, it came so easily and gracefully to her.

When Paul and Linda came round to Primrose Hill it was another story. I would retreat into the kitchen with Cezar and not let anyone come near. One time Cezar and I planned a vegetarian moussaka, which I had high hopes for. But when he served it up at the table it was swimming in oil. As a great gloopy tablespoonful landed on Linda's plate and sat in a puddle of orange-coloured goo, Bailey and I exchanged dismayed glances. Linda and Paul bravely tried to eat it – but put it this way, no one asked for seconds.

Domestic glitches like that never came between me and Bailey. We were simply, sweetly happy. He made me feel beautiful and loved. 'The geezer upstairs stamps out a perfect body every now and then, and Marie's is the closest I've come to perfection,' he has told his biographer Martin Harrison. It astonishes me even today that he should say this; back then when I was so immature and young it was unfathomable. I was used to looking in the mirror more out of anxiety than vanity. With Bailey I began to believe, for the first time in my life, that I was beautiful.

This brought its own pressure too. You can never have an off day when you are living with a photographer. He had a camera with him at all times. On my side of the bed I had a stack of books; on his, there were cameras of all types, all loaded, all ready for action. It wasn't so much that he wanted to photograph me in the throes of passion (for that we used the Polaroid – didn't everyone?), rather, he would get separation anxiety if he was far from a camera for long.

The last thing he would see at night wasn't me, it was the camera.

I might be shaving my legs in the bath and he would be there snapping away. That would annoy anyone! But I got to know that the creative artist never switches off – and, by extension, neither can his model and partner. It was just another thing that bound us together. Generally, I served the artist with pleasure. I've always looked at my working relationships in that way.

A few years later when I accompanied Bailey to an Olympus photographers' workshop in Antibes, at the Hôtel du Cap, I met Jacques Henri Lartigue for the first time – a great honour. As we walked up the steep, elegant private steps that lead from the sea to the hotel, he took both my hands and told me I reminded him of Renée, one of his former muses. Later, in the pool, I posed for Jacques, at his request. The result is one of my favourite photographs, in which I am floating in the emerald seawater of the pool, my head tipped back like a kind of sea nymph, in a shimmering state of watery rapture. The photo has a timeless quality, and it's very erotic too, for all that it was taken by a photographer in his eighties. It's different to Bailey's work in that it's very feminine, very delicate – a response to its subject rather than a vision of what he wants her to be.

Lartigue also took an extraordinary picture of me and Bailey, part portrait, part subtle optical illusion (if you flip it you see our same image, reflected in the bonnet of the car).

That weekend we all went on a sailing excursion to the Ile Saint-Honorat, about a mile off the coast and inhabited only by monks. They offer hospitality to visitors in a restaurant in the monastery that serves only bouillabaisse, and we drank plenty of wine on the outdoor terrace while waiting for our food to arrive. We waited for about two hours, in fact, until two waiters proceeded in holding a huge vat of the fish soup. As they came towards the table, though, one tripped, the vat fell and – *voilà* – bouillabaisse everywhere. 'Hell, I'm not waiting another two hours,' said Helmut and began picking prawns out of the mess on the ground. I, too, grabbed chunks of fish, I was so hungry. On the boat on the way back, we were fooling around for John Swannell's camera and Helmut, being Helmut, tied me to the mast. In the picture, I'm camping it up, making a face like Joan of Arc bound to the stake, while Helmut's standing next to me, his eyes wide. That picture is now in the National Portrait Gallery's permanent collection.

I've never thought of myself as a great model in the sense of a Shrimpton, an Evangelista or a Moss. But I happened to be around at the right time, with Bailey, the right artist, and I helped him make some of the defining images of that period – no more, no less.

Bailey and I were shooting together so much that when I worked with other *Vogue* photographers too, such as Eric Boman, Willie Christie and Arthur Elgort, Beatrix Miller had to put her foot down. She had received complaints from readers that I was on every page. Apparently one thought the many different looks I modelled for *Vogue* were simply a way of fooling the readers: 'You can try and disguise her with a blonde wig (page 60) but we can still tell it's her.' So I made the decision to work exclusively with Bailey. At the time others were critical of this thinking ('You'll lose out! Your profile will drop') but I was certain it was the right thing to do. It was a no-brainer. Work with a different snapper every day? Or develop an intense, almost telepathic working bond with the most gifted photographer of his generation, who happens to be your lover? It meant I missed out on fantastic jobs and opportunities and certainly lost out financially, but for the creative fulfilment, and the pleasure of working with someone I loved, I wouldn't have done it any other way.

The first trip I took abroad with Bailey for British *Vogue* was to Australia, for my third cover shoot. Bailey went away first, and I had two weeks at home alone. During this period I taught myself how to play chess properly, by consulting the *Encyclopaedia Britannica*. Bailey was fanatical about chess and took a portable set everywhere he went. It was automated so he could play alone if necessary – but I rather wanted to provide an alternative to that.

En route to Australia, I grabbed a week at home in Hawaii – it was bliss to see my family, though there was a moment of culture clash when Grace Coddington arrived at Honolulu airport collecting me on a Qantas flight to Sydney. My little sisters and mother all worked at threading leis for her, using blossom from the plumeria tree in our garden, and, as was customary, garlanded her when she arrived at the airport. She was delighted, which naturally pleased them all, but when she went into the airport shop and bought lots of plastic leis my family were horrified. They didn't understand why their real, scented, hand-made leis weren't good enough. But as it turned out she had her own reasons: when we got to Australia her fresh lei was wilted and brown, and for the shoot we used the plastic leis, which were perfect. The result was that well-known shot in which I am reclining on the beach, leis round my neck, and a great inflatable Disney turtle (which Bailey found in a moment of inspiration in Woolworth's in Cairns) is coming after me, looking for a hug.

From Cairns we took a trip out in a tourist boat to see the Great Barrier Reef. As entertainment the crew hung a sheep's carcass over-board – and we daytrippers all screamed in horror as a monstrous prehistoric-looking fish, an enormous grouper, leaped out of the water and devoured the sheep in one ferocious bite. 'How terrifying!' every-one said, and then, to my amazement, they all jumped in the water to go snorkelling. I wasn't swimming anywhere near that grouper, and Bailey wasn't swimming, period. So the two of us were left sitting alone on deck. Bailey got out his portable chess set: my big moment had arrived. 'I'll play,' I said very coolly. And to his surprise I beat him. All those afternoons with the *Encyclopaedia* had paid off.

It was in Queensland I discovered how grungy working trips for fashion magazines, even British *Vogue*, could be in those days. Bailey and I were expected to share a tiny bedsit with the fashion editor and travel writer; to get some privacy, we ended up sleeping in the kitchen. This is fairly typical of working life: once, in Paris, Bailey and I were put in the basement of such a hot, dingy hotel that I woke up panting from the heat in the middle of the night and found he had disappeared. 'Bailey?' He grunted in response. He was lying on the floor with his nose rammed up against the crack under the door where fresh air was coming in. I went and joined him, prostrate in front of this tiny gap. It was a good job they knocked first before they brought our *café complet* in the morning, otherwise we'd both have broken noses. An air-conditioned suite at a top hotel? Not on *Vogue*'s budget, back in those days. It didn't matter to us, though, as we were so wrapped up in each other and our blossoming relationship we barely noticed.

At the weekends we would take trips into the countryside. It was important to Bailey to show me his England – he took me to Worthing, Blackpool, Somerset, Whitby, Yorkshire, Oxfordshire. Without him, I would not have seen the country at all. After work he might say, 'Let's go for fish and chips!' and we would motor all the way to Brighton for it. I would hold the warm parcel of chips in my lap while we drove on to Beachy Head, to sit and look at the view and eat in contented silence.

We also went together to Patrick Lichfield's wedding to Leonora Grosvenor. I guess it was one of our first big public dates; we drove up to Chester together in the Rolls. I wore a tight brown jersey dress with batwing sleeves and a tiny waist. The designer, Yuki, had made it for me – he was very hot at the time though he went on to become Mrs Thatcher's favourite designer (how fickle is fashion). I also wore a hat – the first time I ever did so outside a studio shoot.

The wedding was a very grand affair in Chester cathedral, attended by the Queen. Joanna Lumley was there, wearing morning dress, just like a man. At the time I thought it rather odd but now I look back and think, How fabulous, how totally original. As one of Patrick's ex-girlfriends I think she was playing the usher. It was my first grand English society wedding, but it was one of the last of its kind. It was now 1975 and the 'them and us' mentality of the English aristocracy had been fading since the sixties (as Bailey and Patrick's friendship went to show) and big society functions were changing. Bailey always described this movement into the upper classes as 'infiltration' – they absorbed him, not he them. I saw another sign that the old England had disappeared when many years later I went to the wedding of my dear friend Imran Khan to Jemima Goldsmith – a truly cross-cultural union. And finally, just recently, when I went to the Dent-Brocklehurst wedding at Sudeley Castle the atmosphere was totally different and a million times more relaxed and fun. And that wasn't simply because I was sitting next to Hugh Grant.

Bailey and I were beginning to feel like a proper couple. It wasn't always easy, though. Early on in our relationship there was a silly blip that was nearly fatal. Bailey was away shooting in Italy and I went out with Grace to a party at the Rainbow Room at Biba – which was now based in the Derry and Tom's building on Kensington High Street, a far cry from the little boutique where I bought those suede boots. There, under the Art Deco curves, I noticed a man with that familiar gorgeous dark brow: it was Bruce Robinson. We were delighted to see each other and I told him all about my love affair with Bailey, and how happy I was. We carried on chatting through the evening and afterwards he insisted on giving me a lift home. On the way he thought I should just pop in to see his new apartment – so, naïvely, I did. We talked for a bit and then he tried to kiss me. Horrified, I made my excuses immediately. He sweetly put me in a taxi without any rancour – he meant me and Bailey no harm. I had been stupid, but what I did next was even more stupid.

I always used to collect Bailey from the airport, so I drove out to Heathrow with his secretary Jilly in the Rolls-Royce. After throwing our arms round each other we walked back to the car. 'What's our girl been up to then?' he asked, and straight away I opened up about everything, told him how I saw Bruce at the Rainbow Room, and what happened next. A woman would have spared her lover the pathetic story, but I was still in many ways a child. We drove home in silence, Bailey practically emitting steam from his ears. When we got home he shouted at me so furiously I assumed I had blown it. I rang my mom in floods of tears. 'I think it's over,' I sobbed. 'That's it. I screwed up.' Mom clucked her sympathy down the line to me. She'd not met Bailey yet, but she knew instinctively how important he was to me.

That evening there was a happy reconciliation. I had realised how much he meant to me, through confronting what it would be like to lose him. Bruce and I had been young lovers, having lots of fun.

Jerry Hall and I had just done a fashion show for Antony Price at Olympia. Mick and Bailey came with my sister Naomi and our good friends Brian and Liz Clarke. We had opened the show wearing motorcycle helmets covering our hair and faces, and sitting astride two enormous revved-up Harley Davidsons.

This photograph is part of the National Portrait Gallery's permanent collection! I'm thrilled to be there with my dear friend Helmut Newton. We were on our way to Hotel du Cap at Eden Rock and camping it up like crazy to avoid being seasick. It didn't work in my case!! John Swannell took the photograph.

My first location cover-shoot for *Vogue*. We travelled all around Queensland and the Great Barrier Reef. Bailey found Jiminy Cricket at the local Woolworth's in Cairns.

opposite page This is the same trip and now we are on Dunk Island. The reason my eyes are so large and piercing is because the sun was so incredibly bright that I had to close my eyes between each shot. I still have a small brown spot on my right eye, and I'm sure I got it from getting my eyeballs fried!

We had all gone to have lunch at Yves St Laurent's amazing house, full of the most beautiful art and treasures. Diana Vreeland happened to be in town, so Bailey and I were looking after her, which was great fun. She had amazing energy and a true zest for life. She never wanted to sleep – never! I am in head-to-toe Yves St Laurent, which was a generous and kind gift from him.

This was at the launch of the book *Trouble and Strife* at the Ritz Hotel in London. Isn't it interesting to note that while I appear to be hanging on for dear life, Bailey doesn't touch me at all? He appears more interested in the lollipop.

I was leaving Langan's, where Michael and Shakira Caine had given one of their great parties. I had probably been carried away dancing with someone Bailey did not approve of, so took my shoes off to run after a furious Bailey. I am clutching gold Manolos and running away from the paparazzi!

Monte Carlo during the Grand Prix. Because Bailey was under contract to Olympus Cameras we were always invited to the race as they also sponsored Formula One driver James Hunt. Believe it or not, the swimsuit came from M&S. Helmut Newton and I did a series of photographs in Monte Carlo for *Ritz* newspaper.

Taken at the Habitation LeClerc Hotel in Haiti at the time of Baby Doc Duvalier. The atmosphere on the island was very tense and I was relieved when Bailey decided to shoot around the hotel. We were there with French *Vogue*. The most exciting thing to happen to me on that trip was meeting the real 'Petit Pierre' Aubelin Jolicœur. They confiscated my copy of *The Comedians* at the airport and when I told Aubelin this, he said, 'But cherie, there is a room with thousands of copies in every known language

Shot by the incomparable Lartigue in his own unique style. This was a personal gift to me from Jacques and I treasure it.

Taken by the legendary Lartigue. I adored him and was honoured that he took photographs of me. He used to say I reminded him of René, one of his favourite models and girlfriend from the 20s. He always had a twinkle in his eyes. When I met him, he was in his eighties. This was taken at the pool at the Hotel du Cap in Antibes.

Grace Coddington, the fashion editor on this shoot, shot this for us in the Great Barrier Reef. I always describe it as 'the macho adventurer and his reluctant companion'. Bailey was given the neck-piece by a Papuan from New Guinea. The tan is my own, no fake-tan creams existed then. Imagine my sun damage! We later used this photograph as a Christmas card with the saying 'Mele Kalikimaka' 'Hauoli Makakiki Hou' (Merry Christmas and Happy New Year).

From *Trouble and Strife*. Bailey calls it my passport photograph.

But with Bailey it was something quite other. He was my first true partner.

*

We were in San Lorenzo when Bailey proposed to me. It was Mara's doing: as the owner of the restaurant she took (and still takes) a motherly interest in her regulars, and she ticked off Bailey for taking me there every night for months without making me his wife.

One evening Mara said she was going to stand next to our table until he had written 'Mrs Bailey' in my passport. This he finally did – in pencil. I wasn't having him deface my passport with ink. The idea of marriage wasn't entirely out of the blue – Bailey and I had talked jokingly about it ('So, what if I made an honest woman of you then, sunshine?') but really, we didn't feel the need to get married. The old bourgeois conventions didn't mean as much to us as they had to previous generations. It never occurred to me to want a white wedding, though certain other people of my generation yearned for one. I never carried a veil around with me, put it that way.

The most pressing reason for us to get married was a practical one: it would put an end to all my problems with passports, customs, visa . . . By 1975 I was sick to death of my immigration dramas. I had had enough of being strip-searched, impersonating a student and standing for hours in the 'aliens' queue along with every other nationality under the sun. To cap it all I had had a horrible experience at immigration when an official asked me sternly if I knew what the punishment was for outstaying my work permit. 'No,' I said, bewildered.

He lowered his voice to a blood-curdling whisper: 'Death by hanging. Do you hear?' I practically fainted before my better judgement kicked in and I realised he was just scaring me.

The idea that we were going to be married surprised some people, who regarded me as an insignificant attachment to the master. A new secretary had taken over from Jilly and on the morning of my wedding, when I got back from having my hair straightened at my hairdresser Leonard's, she seemed surprised to hear, I knew, I was getting married, as if she thought I was being done a big favour.

I was determined from the beginning not to take his name. Helvin simply sounded better with Marie than Bailey did. I also didn't want to provoke accusations within the industry that I had acquired airs and graces in becoming 'Mrs Bailey'. My own name was good enough for me.

I didn't want a diamond ring, either. Tina, and later, when I met her, Jerry, said I was crazy; my mother also told me I'd regret it. But there was still a bit of a hippie in me. I thought diamonds were for stuffy older women, and I saw something trashy in a young girl wearing ostentatious jewels. Diamonds were not cool, as far as I was concerned. In fact, forget diamonds, you could have won me with a box of chocolate-covered cherries with brandy in the middle. Chocolate spoke to me. Can someone hit that silly girl I was over the head with a frying pan, please?

Bailey still hadn't met my parents, though I had put him on the phone to Mom and Pop a few times. But my parents' own marriage was by then already fractured; when I was at home on holiday my mother pulled the car over to the side of the road and told me that they were divorcing. It was gut-wrenching to hear. But I was pretty independent by that time. I never doubted I was doing the right thing in marrying Bailey.

It was a small, private civil ceremony at St Pancras register office on 3 November 1975. Our guests included Cathee Dahmen and Michael Roberts and our witnesses were Michael and Tina Chow. Yves Saint Laurent, Karl Lagerfeld and Valentino all sent me dresses for my wedding but, stupidly, I didn't wear any of them. I just wore orchids in my hair, open sandals and a flimsy white silk dress with a light YSL jacket. It was a freezing grey day, and my unseasonal outfit caused some amusement among the guests. As we stood for our wedding snap, taken by Terry Donovan, outside on the steps of the office in the bitterly cold wind, Tina kindly draped her fur cape across my shoulders. I am devotedly anti-fur and it is the only time I have ever worn it – but perhaps a shivering bride on her wedding day can let her conscience slip.

Our wedding dinner was that evening at Mr Chow's, and the guests included Manolo, Grace Coddington and of course Terry Donovan. A few weeks later we flew to Honolulu, where my mother arranged a wedding party for us, a wonderful Hawaiian occasion that mingled pride and high emotion with farce. Bailey looked out of place in the sunshine in his heavy dark jeans (this time he was the one in unsuitable clothes) and he hated his ceremonial lei of scented maile leaves and kept furtively trying to slip it off whenever he thought he could get away with it, but every time he did so a well-meaning Hawaiian friend would put it back round his neck. Paul and Linda McCartney had also been able to come to the party on their way to Australia and, worried they might be bored, I had told my family to make sure they had some fun. Somewhere the wires got crossed. I turned round to find one of my mother's friends – male – happily perched on Paul's knee for a celebrity snap. Wincing, I removed him as fast as possible.

It was a strange time for me because it was the first time I had seen my parents since their divorce. Mom introduced her boyfriend to me which I found really hard to handle – I had never had to confront the idea of her as a sexual being before. Paul picked up on my discomfort and was really supportive about it. 'I've been there, and you just have to deal with it in this way, y'know, Marie . . .' It was a huge relief to me to talk about it with him; it was a delicate situation and he responded with great sensitivity.

We had a month in Hawaii, including a week with Paul and Linda as well as Heather, Linda's daughter by a previous relationship, and little Stella and Mary. I took Heather out shopping for vintage clothes for her mother, selecting about fifty outfits to take back for her to choose from. Bailey could hardly tell Paul and Linda to stop smoking grass, so I could do it with impunity for once, and we all got high and happy together on *pakalolo*. Paul and Linda and I plotted a trip to a concert by the American duo Loggins and Messina, only we had to work hard to persuade Bailey. He hated going to concerts, always maintaining the only music he liked was the Stones.

'Oh please!' we said. 'It'll be great!'

Bailey conceded that OK, he would come, 'So long as it's not two guys playing the bloody guitar.' Paul shot me a look, because we knew that was exactly what it would be. For their part, Paul and Linda wanted to keep the whole thing very private, as they were on vacation and didn't want to be mobbed at the concert, or to upstage Loggins and Messina. But a friend of my mom's, a local TV personality called Lucky Luck, persuaded us that he would sort the whole excursion out. It would be very hush-hush, he said.

When the car he ordered came to pick us up it was a white stretch limo. That would have been bad enough, but this was Hawaii. There was only one white stretch limo on the whole island. Inconspicuous we were not. 'You're going backstage now!' Lucky told us triumphantly. My misgivings turned to horror as we were all shepherded through the wings and into our seats, which were – you couldn't make it up – on the stage itself. We cringed; Bailey rolled his eyes; the evening was a hilarious disaster.

On our way out to the limo, Paul and Linda, whose presence had been efficiently advertised, were surrounded by a throng. One guy, I remember, called out, 'Hey! Paul! Have you read *Helter Skelter*?' This made me anxious, because I'd read it. It was a book by Vincent Bugliosi who was the prosecuting lawyer on the Manson murders, and it detailed how Manson had scrawled the lyrics to Paul's song with that title in blood on the walls of Polanski's home. I was worried that Paul would be devastated if he knew about this and braced myself for his reply. But to my relief he called back jovially, 'I wrote it, man!' and we all piled back into the limo.

When Paul and Linda had flown off to Australia Bailey and I were left on our low-key honeymoon in Hawaii. But I knew that, deep down, he wasn't happy there. He could never lounge around on a beach or body surf. Bailey's idea of sport, I've always said, is playing chess sitting next to an open window. Instead he was always on the move, exploring the island, driving off on his own to visit the bird park so he could do what he liked doing best, taking pictures. Generally, though, he found Hawaiian culture uninspiring, called its Americanisation antiseptic and preferred travelling on the hoof, to wilder, rougher shores where the indigenous culture was stronger.

Such as Tahiti, where we went a few months later. Here we stayed on the island of Rangiroa, on a shoot for Italian *Vogue*, but also keeping an eye out for the Tahitian lorikeet – though more in hope than expectation, since it was supposedly one of the rarest parrots in the world. One day on the trip, Bailey and I visited a deserted motu, out in the Pacific ocean. The fashion editor came along too, but, suffering in the heat, she opted to sit under a parasol while Bailey and I went exploring the jungle.

When our path through the trees divided, Bailey and I took different routes through the vegetation, planning to meet up back at the beach. As I walked alone a bird swooped past my head. It had the deep glossy aquamarine colouring of the elusive lorikeet – could it possibly be . . . ? Then another, and another flew by, till there were hundreds of these birds flying about me. They were definitely the lorikeets. I ran to find Bailey and breathlessly beckoned him to come see. His surprise and delight made me so happy. That paradisal moment is preserved in my memory, perfect.

On our return to London I contemplated writing up the experience for the RSPB magazine (Bailey was a subscriber, of course) but I decided the tiny motu would be better off safe and secret, without hordes of binocular-wielding ornithologists.

Late, panting, we returned from our walk to rejoin the fashion editor and sail back to the mainland in a ten-foot whaler. A Pacific storm brewed out of nowhere and tossed our little boat practically out of the water, the prow pitching and crashing in the enormous waves. Bailey was sitting up in the bows, playing the macho adventurer; the fashion editor was crying with fear. I was petrified, but whenever Bailey turned to look at me, I threw my head back and laughed as if I was carried away by the thrill of the moment. Boy, did I ham it up. Later he said he had known then that he would never regret marrying me. What an actress!

*

'Remember, Ginger Rogers did everything Fred Astaire did, but she did it backwards and in high heels.'

FAITH WHITTLESEY

'Marie! Ssssh!' said Bailey, loudly, dramatically.

'You ssssh!' I giggled softly. It was a Saturday night, and we were hiding behind the heavy purple velvet curtains in the drawing room in Primrose Hill, in the dark. Friends and acquaintances were always coming over uninvited and we just craved some time alone together. The only way we could avoid visitors was by turning the lights off and pretending to be out. Then the doorbell rang again; the parrots downstairs squawked. We both ducked down below the window, stifling our conspiratorial laughter. 'Hellooo?' a voice called through the letter box. We ignored it, whoever it might be, and held each other tight.

Chez Bailey it was always open house so we simply had to resort to these techniques. When Penelope Tree was with him there was a story that someone was living in their guest bedroom for ten days before Bailey said, 'When's your friend going to leave?' and Penelope answered, 'I thought he was YOUR friend!' I had a sense of hospitality instilled into me – Hawaiian culture includes elaborate rituals for looking after your guests, and perhaps I picked up some of that from Japan, too – so, in the early days, I felt duty bound to entertain everyone who came through the door. I was always slicing pineapple for visitors and running up and down stairs with bowls of snacks and mugs of tea. I soon let all this go when it became accepted and not appreciated.

On Sunday mornings while I was at home trying to have a lie-in, the doorbell would be ringing constantly. Bailey's friends were always coming round, like Jerry Schatzberg (who directed Faye Dunaway in the film about a model, *Puzzle of a Downfall Child*), David Puttnam, and Terry Donovan, who was there every Sunday morning without fail. I'd make them a pot of coffee, leave a plate of croissants, a pile of newspapers – and just disappear. There are times when you just want to be alone. Personally I need and crave a good deal of solitude. The roof extension on the seventh floor came in useful because I could sunbathe naked up there with my cat Sheba, and people knew not to come up.

Later in life I would find my own ways of solitude, achieving it by going on Buddhist silent retreats and by living alone: back then, I had to get by without it. During the week Bailey's studio was always crowded, with up to thirty people coming and going; we lived above the shop, so to speak. The constant energy and hubbub was fun but I also found it exhausting: I picked up on all the nervous vibes of his sitters, the frantic assistants, the way everyone was tense, wanting to impress Bailey, or wanting something from him. I found it hard to relax because my antennae for energy are so sensitive. Bailey, more practical by nature than me, didn't know what I was on about. When I said I found it spiritually draining I would get the old *maka-ele-ele* look.

One time I remember answering the phone. 'Hello, can I speak to Malcolm, please?' I didn't recognise the voice on the other end of the line; it sounded like there was a party going on his end.

'Malcolm who?' I asked.

'You what, love?' said the man at the party.

'Malcolm WHO?' I screamed.

'Oh, McLaren, love, McLaren. He's round at David Bailey's isn't he?'

I'd never even met Malcolm McLaren. Neither had Bailey. It was a madhouse.

Then there were the animals. We were so crazy for them we had an account at the pet shop, Palmer's of Camden Town. Cezar was their caretaker and his particular responsibility was the dogs – which I wouldn't have anything to do with after they bit me on the ass so I needed tetanus shots. Bailey adored animals and, despite being a no-nonsense East End pragmatist at heart, he always said that an animal could clear the inner atmosphere of a creaky old house. First he bought me a rabbit, and then another one to keep it company. Next he bought me some cats: Marilyn, Fluffy, Inky. Then he got me Sheba, an elegant Birman who came all the way from Tring. She always walked with a slight limp – and perhaps that was why I chose her, because her beauty was stunning but it was her vulnerability that made her lovable. I was saving Sheba to breed with another purebred cat but one day she was raped by a one-eared, one-eyed, no-tailed tom cat who mounted our balcony. And so along came her kitten Susu, who lived with me for all her life too.

I had read that on the first night with a new pet you have to keep them close, so close they can hear your heart beat, so I spent the whole night on the bathroom floor with all our animals, starting with Sheba. She later displayed her loyalty to me by shitting on Bailey's pillow. By this time the two rabbits had multiplied into about seventy and I had to give them away to a local school. Next I acquired snakes (but not for long; they went back to Palmer's), guinea pigs, goldfish, terrapins and a large tortoise whom I never saw again after he disappeared under the floorboards. Apparently he waddled out ten years later and surprised Bailey's new wife Catherine.

Amongst all this chaos of bird feed and rabbit doo-doo, there were often belongings left behind by visitors. Greg Allman of the Allman Brothers came with his wife Cher when she was being photographed by Bailey and forgot his gorgeous, ruby-coloured, gold-stitched velvet jacket. It hung in our hall cupboard for months, emitting a seductive stink of grass. Bailey still banned me from dope at home but when I wanted a hit, I knew what to do. Every couple of weeks, I would creep into the dressing-room closet and bury my face in the fragrant folds of that jacket. Mmmm! It was so impregnated with dope that just one deep breath would take me there . . .

One Saturday morning Harrison Ford arrived to be photographed by Bailey. They created a fantastic portrait and Harrison, who was charming and laid-back, left in a taxi for Heathrow to go off to film the first Indiana Jones movie. Bailey and I began planning what we would do with our day. Maybe he wanted to go and photograph a rare parrot he'd heard about; perhaps I should make a picnic for us to take . . . Then the doorbell rang. Guess who ran down to answer it?

It was Harrison standing on the doorstep.

'Uh, I'm sorry. I got halfway to the airport and then I, uh, realised I forgot my shit.'

Being a smoker myself I immediately understood what he meant and invited him in to look for it. We went up to the dressing room: no sign. In the studio, we searched on hands and knees: no sign. Finally, Harrison leaped up. 'I got it!' He was holding a little brown lump he had found behind the door. 'Great,' I said, though inwardly I was thinking to myself: That ain't your shit, that's an old dried-up poop left behind by Stokely or Merlin . . . I had to say something.

'Harrison, are you sure? We have lots of dogs, you know, and it looks like a piece of doo-doo . . .'

He shrugged and stepped out of the front door to where his taxi was waiting, and said with a handsome grin, 'Well, I'll find out when I smoke it.'

Though I hated the constant hubbub in the house I have to admit I loved the infinite variety of people who visited: Kirk Douglas (Bailey really captured his masculinity – he responded to other macho men well); Sting (I missed him! Devastated!); Dizzy Gillespie, Cher, Sir Laurence Olivier, Racquel Welch, Dustin Hoffman . . . The Kray brothers, even, had sat for Bailey before I knew him (Ronnie always sent Bailey a Christmas card from prison, scrupulously formal and polite, in very childish handwriting).

Once, Anna Wintour, then fashion editor of *Viva* magazine, knocked on my bedroom door. 'Marie, darling,' she said. 'Bob Marley's downstairs on a shoot and he wants to say hello to you.' I went down, of course, though he was my sister's idol, not mine. In a flash of inspiration I asked him nicely if I could possibly get two tickets to his gig that evening, so when Suzon and her boyfriend Jesse, who were visiting us from Jamaica at the time, got home that afternoon I presented them with their dream tickets and backstage passes. I remember Su heading out, so excited, wearing her Rasta beret in yellow, green and red. 'We're so irie, man,' she told me as she walked out of the door. I had no idea what she meant! I was so happy, later, that I had been able to give her that treat.

Another time, when my sister Naomi was staying with us, Bailey had an appointment to photograph James Herriot the writer and vet in North Yorkshire. So we three piled into the Range Rover and drove up there to his farm. Naomi and I were horrified to see him thrust his arm into a cow's backside, all the way to his elbow! His grumpy approach to us didn't help, either. We drove on to Whitby, where Naomi and I wanted to see Dracula's supposed grave. Bailey clearly thought we were daft. At the end of a long day we stayed in a B & B where the landlady gave us two exotic choices: 'scampi in a basket' or 'chicken in a basket'. Naomi and I watched and laughed while Bailey ate them both.

Catherine Deneuve and Bailey remained close after their divorce, and she often came to see us at Primrose Hill. One visit was fraught, because I had pneumonia. Every time I moved I was in agony from the pleurisy that had developed, and I had been too sick to leave our oak four-poster for weeks. The bedside table was crowded with my medicine bottles; I was so sick even the cats wouldn't come near me. When Catherine arrived I was at the height of the illness. Of course I wanted to get up and see her – I had got to know her quite well by this time, and she came with a new boyfriend and I was curious to see him – but I was feverish and crying and sick: I could barely drag myself out of bed let alone make myself presentable for Catherine. I begged Bailey not to let her come in to see me, but he did. I guess she insisted. I remember seeing her and the new boyfriend coming in through a haze of codeine. The boyfriend was so handsome he made my teeth rattle – or was that the fever? Catherine sat on the edge of my bed like some kind of blonde visiting angel. The next day I was taken to hospital and put in an oxygen tent.

Cezar was still turning out highly calorific suppers. He was a good cook (he had once cooked for Arthur Schlesinger, JFK's special adviser and author of *A Thousand Days*) and could not be dissuaded from his heavy, old-fashioned gourmet style. His food was so rich that Mick Jagger began to worry about Bailey's cholesterol. After another dinner dripping with butter, Mick actually asked me, 'Is Cezar trying to kill Bailey?' Thenceforth I tried to instigate a new diet regime.

I practically put chains on the fridge to stop Bailey snacking. I chopped up a great mountain of raw veg for him to eat for supper in the evenings ('Here's your vegetable Vesuvius!') which he ate, grumbling. The diet I put him on made him totally miserable.

When a certain Irish cream liqueur was launched, he joked that it was named in his honour: 'Baileys: once tasted never forgotten' became a catchphrase for a while, and he bought me a bottle in the hope I would drink it instead of smoking dope. We glugged our way through the whole thing before I realised that it was weight-gain in a bottle and banned it from the house.

My efforts paid off: Bailey lost thirty pounds in six months. It's a double-edged sword, when your husband starts to look more gorgeous. Women were always throwing themselves at him. Of course they were – he was David Bailey. Was he faithful to me? Of course not, but for me, love and monogamy aren't inseparable. My attitudes to sex are very much those of my generation: I don't believe that fidelity is true proof of a man's love. I didn't think about who he was screwing, because I knew his heart was mine.

*

Every Friday Bailey and I would go for dinner at Beatrix Miller's. As it was rather like a salon, you could predict who would be there. Bailey and Tony Snowdon would be looking daggers at one another (there wasn't much love lost between them) and I was often seated by the great comedian Peter Sellers, whom I found a gloomy, intense presence.

'Am I going to be next to Peter Sellers again?' I'd complain to Bailey in the car on the way there.

He was quick to chide me.

'Marie, there are thousands of people who would love to sit next to that man.'

So I persevered with him, and eventually we found some common ground to discuss: hallucinogenic drugs. Perhaps he got something else out of our conversations too – there's a silly photo in which I am beaming at him and he's ogling my cleavage.

At one of these dinners I inadvertently put a dampener on things when the conversation turned to love and relationships.

'Do you believe marriage is for life, Marie?' Drusilla Beyfus asked me.

Without thinking I replied, 'No – it's a finite arrangement that lasts as long as it serves its purpose.' As the words came out of my mouth I looked across the table at the hopeful, loved-up faces of Gayle Hunnicutt and Simon Jenkins, who had just become engaged. I hadn't meant to offend them, but there was no going back on my strong pronouncement. Perhaps I was wrong, anyway – because they're still happily married today.

Once one of the dinners guests was Cecil Beaton. Though he was entering old age – or, as Hugo Vickers, Cecil's biographer so elegantly puts it, he was coming close to the cashmere cardigan phase of life – he was still very dapper in a white cravat and a suit three sizes too tight for him. I was always a great admirer of his work (and subsequently bought some of his prints at auction) and I was privileged to meet him. He seemed to make the same mistake many people of his generation did in confusing me with someone else I looked ethnically similar to – Tina Chow, in fact. 'Darling, those photos we did were simply splendid.' I accepted the compliment, since to correct him would have been ungracious. I assumed it was an elderly man's error, though Hugo Vickers later told me it was just as likely to be simply one of the games Beaton liked to play.

After dinner we all walked along the King's Road – at a pace that suited the oldest member of our party – to the Chelsea Cinema, where Ossie Clark's fashion show was about to begin.

It was the first fashion show I'd ever been to in a theatre and the show was glam, glam, glam – there was a screen on stage where you could see the models getting changed in silhouette. The models included the stunning Amanda Lear and Patti Boyd; it was a great show and it was, as it turned out, his last great hurrah of the seventies.

I went on to work with Ossie a great deal and to become one of his muses in the early eighties when he was having a brief renaissance, riding on the wave of the New Romantic mood in fashion. I promoted his work for free in Japan and modelled some of his creations, like a gold leather bustier, and my favourite, a green satin and lace corseted dress, which was like nothing I'd ever worn before. It was so restrictive and sexy, especially when paired with a glossy Anna Mae Wong wig. Bailey insisted I remove the dress gradually in a saucy sequence of Polaroid SX70 photos we shot for British *Vogue* of me playing strip poker with Sandy Lieberson the prominent film producer (Bailey usually preferred using 'real' men, not anodyne male models).

I used to visit Ossie in his studio on the Fulham Road, where I was always astounded to see him cutting directly on to the cloth, without using patterns like other designers. Once, as we were working away at the design table, a grimy grungy figure with long blond hair walked in off the street in a big old baggy coat. She turned to me and I saw her face was hauntingly beautiful, though ravaged by hard living: it was Marianne Faithfull. At that time she was using heroin and her complexion gave the lie to what Diana Vreeland always said: 'Heroin does wonders for a girl's skin ... Look at Edie Sedgwick.' Marianne looked at me intently. 'Got any spare cigarettes, darling?' she said huskily. I reached into my bag immediately but I realised things were really going wrong in her life when she followed with another question: 'Got any change too?'

She was, Ossie explained to me, living rough in Soho. These were Marianne's drug-addled wilderness years, and it was heartbreaking to see someone who had once been an icon of the sixties reduced to such desperation. Later, thank God, she made a stunning recovery and went on to become a great recording artist, author and actress.

When Ossie and I flew to New York for a fashion show sponsored by the British Council we sat by each other on the plane and he told me how sad he was because he wanted to take his sons to Greece, but didn't have the money. Later I managed to lend him some. Then as we settled down to sleep he wrote his diary, a huge volume that he filled with tiny tiny handwriting and detailed little sketches.

'Jeez, Ossie, that's incredible!' I said as he showed it to me. But the secrets of his diary remained unknown to me because his handwriting was too small for me to decipher. (It was at that moment, actually, that I realised I needed reading glasses.) I later encouraged Ossie to publish his diaries in facsimile form because they were so beautiful, and introduced him to my then publishers, Michael Joseph (for whom I wrote my memoir *Catwalk*). They didn't go for it, and it fell to another publisher to print one volume, years later after his death, transcribed from the original. I guess the real diaries with their tiny tortured handwriting and intricate, extraordinary sketches are now languishing in an archive.

Ossie's fashion show was held at the Pierre and everyone came, including Diana Vreeland (of whom more later), and Andy Warhol. During our days in New York Ossie and I went to Andy's Factory many times. My first impression was how many cute male assistants he had working on his canvases. It was very glam, the Factory, spacious and elegant, with high ceilings, but it had a real workshop feel – a true precursor to artists today like Damien Hirst who have huge numbers of staff working for them. We sat with Jay and Jed Johnson (the brothers, one was a model and one an interior decorator). Peter Schlesinger, David Hockney's boyfriend; Briget Polk, the artist whose breast paintings caused such a stir; and Andy and Fred Hughes and a few others at Andy's long polished Biedermeier table, while one of his 'boys' was sent out to get some food – salad, fries, chicken, bread, fruit – nothing fancy, but accompanied by excellent wine.

Fred, Andy's business partner and right-hand man, smilingly suggested that I might like to sit for Andy. But I already knew what the deal would be. To be painted by Andy would cost about $75,000. Fred was famous for going to this or that princess or oil magnate and saying: We'll make you a Warhol, just sign here... Nevertheless I was tempted. For a Warhol portrait, it was a snip at the price, if you asked me. When I rang Bailey that night I asked what he thought. 'Are you nuts? We could buy a palace in Jaipur for that money.'

In New York Bailey and I were invited to a dinner in the World Trade Center, given by the Robert Capa institute to celebrate the photographic work of Bernice Abbott. The party was in the Windows on the World restaurant and Bailey and I walked into the lift, only to be followed in by Jackie Onassis and her bodyguards. As it moved slowly up the dizzying height of the building my ears popped and I began to feel queasy. Lifts have never agreed with me. To my mortification, my stomach turned, my head reeled at the thought of how high up we were, and I was quite suddenly sick in my little YSL evening bag. I tried to do it discreetly, crouching at the back of the lift, but everyone in there must have known. Bailey edged away from me, and Jackie O., surrounded by her bodyguards, threw glances over her shoulder in puzzlement.

When the lift doors opened the paparazzi were waiting outside, but the attention was on Jackie O., thankfully, and I ran to the ladies, dumped my heart-shaped velvet YSL bag in the bin (mortifying!) and put a brave face on for the party.

Later that evening when I was introduced to her she was very gracious and pretended not to have noticed my nauseous faux pas in the lift. It was a star-studded evening and Bailey and I were having fun with Tina and Michael – and yet I couldn't wait to leave. After the dinner I simply didn't want to stay for the dancing. I didn't feel at ease there. I was hanging on to the wall all the way down in the lift.

Years later she rang me to discuss Fred Astaire for a book she was writing. 'Hello, it's Jackie Onassis,' came the very breathy, gentle, girlish voice. I cried for days when she died. She was a Princess Diana figure to my generation. I sat on my father's shoulders to wave at her when I was a child. She was part of my psyche somehow. She was the most regal woman I have ever met – the only woman, in fact, to whom I felt I should curtsey.

Around that time in New York I went to a party for Bianca Jagger's birthday. It was one of those events where, to make things more intimate, groups of about ten guests split off and go to someone's house for dinner, and then everyone meets up afterwards at the party itself. I ended up at Ahmet Ertegun's house, sitting at a little card table in some social discomfort. To my left was Lee Radziwill, Jackie Onassis's sister, who wasn't at all impressed with me, perhaps because I wasn't eating anything – it was red meat, so I thought it easier just to push it round my plate than to make a scene and ask for vegetarian, but she looked askance at me as if I had very poor manners. On my right was Alexander Cockburn, the British journalist turned New York intellectual, who was far too serious for me, and opposite was Bill Paley, the head of CBS, who had an ear trumpet and kept bellowing 'What? WHAT?' whenever I tried to make conversation. It was a relief when a stretch limo arrived and took us all off to Studio 54.

Was it that night that Bianca Jagger so famously rode into the nightclub on the back of a white horse? Try as I may, I can't remember. Was I too stoned? Perhaps history has exaggerated the whole event anyway. Bianca to this day maintains she never made her entry to the club on the horse, and that she simply posed on the horse for a few photos. But now when my godchildren ask if I was there the night it happened I can almost feel myself imagining it for their benefit. Memory can be a frangible, fugitive thing. To quote the psychoanalyst Darian Leader: 'We all rewrite our histories without knowing it, often weaving in the memories of others into our own narratives.'

*

When Bailey took me home to meet his mother Gladys in Leytonstone, he told her I grew up in a coconut tree. She looked at me. She looked at him. She whistled. 'Well, how about that then? Now you're here, love, you'd better have a cuppa tea.'

Gladys was called 'Glad' by everyone including Bailey and his sister Thelma. ('How lovely you call her this happy name,' Catherine Deneuve once said.) I always found it odd that Bailey and Thelma called their mother 'Glad', just as they always called their father 'Burt'. Though Burt was dead by the time I came along I had the feeling things had been difficult between him and Bailey – he was a macho East End tailor and Bailey's photography and his love of parrots hadn't gone down too well. But Bailey and Glad were really close and he was a good son to her.

One year Michael Caine insisted we bring Glad with us to his annual Fourth of July dinner at Langan's, so she could sit next to his mother and they could keep each other company. Bailey was dubious about it but we picked Glad up in the Rolls and brought her along. Mrs Bailey and Mrs Micklewhite (Caine is not his birth name) took one look at each other and developed an instant dislike. They refused to sit by one another. Glad spent the whole evening at Bailey's side tutting about things and asking the same question again and again. Meanwhile the celebrity whirl carried on around us: the Million Dollar Man mingling with Prince Andrew and Joan Kennedy with Roger Moore. But Glad only wanted to keep Bailey next to her.

Round at her house, we would sit in a room off the kitchen. The front room was 'only for special occasions' – but no occasion when I was there was ever special enough. The toilet, according to East End tradition, was in an outhouse, with newspaper for loo roll. I'd never seen anything like this. I didn't understand why Bailey didn't move her into better accommodation with an indoor toilet; eventually I persuaded him to buy her a place, but it was wrong of me. She was never happy there.

I loved the food Glad served: exotic bread-and-butter pudding and the strange delicacy known as 'spotted dick'. It was my childhood dream of eating Dickensian food come true.

'Would you like a lemon barley water, love?' Glad would say in the summer. I always accepted, imagining this cocktail was some kind of fresh cordial she made herself overnight crushing barley and squeezing lemons. Only later did I discover it came from the corner shop in a bottle.

Christmas, round at Bailey's sister Thelma's, meant paper hats, crackers, *Morecambe and Wise* on the telly. One year, worried Glad was lonely, I gave her a Yorkshire terrier. We ate mountains of food, the plates piled high like Everest with great slabs of turkey, at least three different veg and roast potatoes, then pickles – pickled onions, piccalilli, pickled gherkins – and all topped off with rich gravy and chopped beetroot. After the first year I passed on the pickles but I always finished everything on the whole plate, starting at the top and working downwards. Was I very greedy then, or were plates just smaller in those days?

When we left, Gladys would wave after us: 'Mind how you go, love!' I was fond of her – and of our Christmas feasts. 'Delicious!' I wrote nostalgically in my diary last year. 'Miss it terribly!'

SIX

SMALL WORLD

'I wish I'd known more people. I would of loved 'em all.
If I'd a knowed more, I woulda loved more.'

TONI MORRISON, *Song of Solomon*

I first saw Jerry Hall backstage at the Kenzo ready-to-wear show in Paris in 1976. Her head was full of pink foam curlers and she gave me a big toothy smile. Kenzo had asked me specially to look after her because she was, like me, an American, and it was her first time in Paris. What a bore, I thought. Little did I realise I'd just met my future partner-in-crime, confidante and so-called 'terrible twin'. I sighed and introduced her to all the other models I knew: Tina and maybe a few others, and she shook hands with them sweetly, gawkily.

There were crates upon crates of champagne backstage, and a real buzz in the air. It was a landmark show for Kenzo, because he was breaking with convention and using editorial models for the catwalk. Kenzo, whose boutique Jungle Jap was a wild success, was a young, hot, taboo-breaking designer and always fun to work for – he was one of the few whose clothes were not made for grandes dames and that I might consider wearing myself. As we were waiting in the wings I looked behind me and saw Jerry – transformed. Her hair was now cascading like Lady Godiva's down past her butt. She was breathtaking, and she stole the show.

I gave her my number, told her to call me if she ever came to London, wished her luck and didn't give her another thought.

I always went to Milan for the ready-to-wear shows – a very intense experience. In his exposé of the fashion industry *Model* the investigative reporter Michael Gross wrote of late seventies Milan: 'However bad the rest of modelling is, Milan is worse. Milan is to modelling what Cheyenne was to the American West, an untamed, lawless frontier.' And it was true. I saw it all: the Latin tempers; the young skinny models wearing the gold Rolex that betokened a playboy boyfriend; the long tables of millionaires' sons or chancers posing as millionaires' sons, eager to get what they could take for slapping a Rolex on your wrist. Even before Bailey, I never got caught up in all that sordid life. I've always had an internal radar that reads 'danger, danger, danger'.

By the late eighties there were huge wodges of cash changing hands in Milan. Models' fees had started to go through the roof and Guy Héron, who handled most of the top models for the shows, claims he was walking around 'with a case containing hundreds of millions of lire' according to Michael Gross's book *Model*. I started carrying my cash home in the safest place I could think of: stuffed flat inside an old packet of Wolford tights.

In Milan, Bailey was furiously jealous. 'So who is this Jeff geezer then? Was he your boyfriend?' My ex, Jeff, now living in Milan, had tried to get in contact with me. But I had learned my lesson from the Bruce Robinson escapade and didn't meet up with him.

In Rome we would do the Collections, working on frenzied photo shoots in ruined palazzos right through the night after waiting for the shows to finish, waiting for the clothes to arrive, waiting, waiting, waiting. Other times, Bailey and I would hang out with the fashion crowd, as well as writers, film directors, artists ... In mainland Europe the demarcations between cultural disciplines were much less defined than in England: everyone mixed along together.

One evening in Rome we went out to dinner and I had Federico Fellini (so charming and open; my number one favourite film director) on my left and Alberto Moravia (brooding and intimidating, he never let you forget he was one of Italy's foremost novelists) on my right. Another night we went over to the huge, dark Palazzo Ruspoli and I smoked opium with Dado Ruspoli, the legendary aristocrat who was a leading figure in the milieu that inspired Fellini's *La Dolce Vita*. He really had the gift of making life seem sweet. At his palazzo I once admired a tiny silver perfume flacon on a table covered with objets d'art. 'Have it!' he said. I still do.

There was a distinctly raffish glamour in Rome. Staying with Helmut Berger I woke up one morning and came down to breakfast only to see that someone in grand clerical Catholic robes sitting at the table. He looked at me rather sheepishly and soon disappeared. I flew home to Bailey saying, 'Guess what? I had breakfast with the Pope!'

I walked into my Milan agency one morning to see Ricardo Guy and they told me there was a friend of mine waiting for me. 'She's called Jerry,' the receptionist told me.

'The name doesn't mean anything to me, I'm afraid,' I said, politely trying to excuse myself.

'Oh, but she's been waiting for hours,' the receptionist said. 'You'd better just go and say hello.'

So I walked through to the office – and there was the gorgeous girl with the hair like Lady Godiva. She told me with a touch of pride that Bryan Ferry was going to put a picture of her painted blue like a mermaid on the cover of his album, *Siren*. I got the feeling from her smile that he might be interested in her for more than just his album cover. We planned to hook up when we were both in London.

Sure enough, I got a phone call several months later, Jerry rang me up to invite me to the home she was now sharing with Bryan Ferry in Holland Park. 'You must bring Bailey with you,' she said, 'It'll be a double date!' So we went round 'for tea', and Jerry offered us cucumber sandwiches and scones, playing at the whole English thing, though of course none of us touched the tea and all we drank was champagne. Jerry played the gracious hostess, showing us proudly round the house, which used to belong to John Cleese. She and I giggled a lot, being silly and American together, while Bailey and Bryan refused to bond: the double date thing didn't entirely work out.

Jerry was unlike anyone I'd met in London. She was a breath of fresh Texan air. Like me, she dressed sexy, wearing Manolo stilettos and bright pink lipstick with lashings of gloss. She was tall and beautiful and proud of it, and as all Texan girls are she was very feminine and flirtatious too. The poor British women didn't stand a chance.

But the next time I saw her she was looking rather different. She turned up at San Lorenzo wearing knickerbockers, a high-necked silk blouse with pearls and a tweed jacket with brown velvet patches on the elbows: the archetypal English lady. It looked great but with that long blond hair and Texan voice it was also highly incongruous. 'Bryan's been making me over,' she confided to me.

'I can tell!' I whispered back. The tailoring and style were pure Anthony Price – exquisite – but not true to Jerry at all; clearly, Bryan was aggressively restyling her.

'What's he trying to do to that sexy girl?' Bailey asked me on the way home. 'He should just let her be.'

I agreed. I was growing really fond of the girl. Jerry and I were so lucky to find each other; the timing just worked for us. We were both American, both equally strong, but that strength later came between us. Neither would give in an argument. As we got older our friendship worked less well. But in and of its time, it was made in heaven.

The photographic trend of the time was for doubles, which are more difficult than they sound. The camera has its own idea of who looks good with whom. It defies rational pairings. I found it particularly hard to work with other models because Bailey made it strangely painful for me. 'I'm not going to be nice cos you're my missus, you know,' he would tell me before the session. 'No preferential treatment for the wife. You know you're a star. I have to build the other girls' confidence up instead. That's the only way I'll get the right look from them.' And it was true; he would give the other girls on the shoot loads of encouragement, but never a word to me. I might have been the star, but I still needed reassurance. I didn't say anything at the time, but I always wondered: Why? It's just a job, why not give your wife special treatment? Or just a kind word or even a wink now and again? That would have been enough for me. Instead I ended up looking miserable and hurt in those pictures; that's why there are so few of me posed in a group.

But with Jerry it was another story. We found we were able to do great doubles together. We counterbalanced each other not only in our highly contrasting looks – one so dark, one so blonde – but also in who we were. We both had international careers and we matched each other in confidence and strength of spirit: there was never competitive edge between us. How could there be? We had our own looks and we had our own men: end of story.

We both had the same American vibe, a shared overt sexiness. We even had the same taste: both of us loved the sexy tackiness of Frederick's of Hollywood, and the screen sirens of the 50s. We both secretly aspired to be Vargas girls. All these attributes were unusual in England in those days. I'm not saying that all the English girls were wearing Laura Ashley, but . . . they were different to us.

Jerry and I had such a rapport we could work in sync in front of the camera without even looking at each other. In between shots we would have fun and relax. When she started going out with Mick things clicked further into place. Soon we were inseparable.

*

In the high seventies, the world seemed smaller than it does today. There was a group of about two hundred of us who travelled between New York, Paris, Rome, London and LA – actors, rock stars, designers, models and rich socialites with nothing else to do. We all seemed to be connected or acquainted in some way. These days, now that international travel has increased exponentially, the idea of a 'jet set' seems laughable, but in those days it was simply the truth. Whenever Bailey and I touched down in one of the great capitals, we fell in with friends. This was before networking, before email, before the world became so big.

Bailey and I were always on the move, heading wherever the next big work project took us. We did the Collections in Rome, the couture shows in Paris, the socialite thing in Manhattan, the music scene in LA, the Grand Prix in Monaco, the film scene in Cannes. We ricocheted round the world like ball bearings in a pinball machine. Anjelica calls it 'the butterfly years': 'that moment when you emerge from your chrysalis, as it were. You're young and everything's the first time round and everything has that first-time fascination to it, and you're riding high on your youth and your health and your stamina.' These were my butterfly years.

One weekend we would do the traditional English thing, driving up to stay with Patrick Lichfield at Shugborough, his family seat in Staffordshire; I loved going to Shugborough, after I got over the initial shock of finding, the evening I arrived, that a maid or butler had gone through my shamefully chaotic holdall and done my unpacking for me. Soon, though, I came to find it all very agreeable, especially the way Leonora asked the ladies present, 'What would you like for breakfast? What time?' and filled out a little form for each of us, so we had the treat of breakfast in bed, which was heaven. We used to take walks around the estate looking at the follies, one of which bears Masonic inscriptions and has been linked to the Priory of Sion, the secret organisation described in *The Da Vinci Code*. I was fascinated by this huge, grand folly and its clandestine associations. Sometimes, because the house had National Trust visitors, you would look down a corridor and see tourists on the other side of a rope.

Then we would be off again, out of that privileged environment and over to a studio in New York or a Tamil Tiger checkpoint in Sri Lanka. I saw so many different faces and places. Clint Eastwood, striding into the bar of the Grand Hotel in Rome. Orson Welles tucking into a huge chopped salad at Ma Maison in LA. James Hunt surrounded by blondes in Monaco. Grace Jones getting up to sing in a Paris nightclub and surprising us all with her incredible voice, belting out 'La Vie en Rose' ... Bailey and I drove through the lavender fields of the south of France to Grasse to visit Dirk Bogarde and his partner Tony Forward. They were so welcoming, giving us delicious home-made quiche lorraine and my first ever Kir Royale. I was hooked instantly. Bailey and I drove off in our red Jeep, rattling like a tin can. I said, 'The first thing I'm going to do in Paris is buy a bottle of Crème de Cassis!'

In Paris we visited Mark Rudkin, our friend the frozen food heir, at his house in the 7th arrondissement, rue Monsieur, off rue Babylone. It was Nancy Mitford's former home, with a stunning wild garden, and on the night we were there, two guests arrived, late from the ballet: Rudolph Nureyev, dramatically tossing his Isadora Duncan-style scarf and walking with his toes pointed. He was followed by a tiny, delicate Margot Fonteyn. I can't deal with this, I thought, and tried to duck out of the front door – you have to be in the right mood to pay court – but Mark heard my high heels on the parquet and brought me back so that I could give them a deep salaam.

So many moments from those years stick in my mind; parties, dinners, shows, shoots, a few triumphs and a great many embarrassments ...

'Don't drink so much champagne, dear girl!' Shocked, I sat up straight. You always sat up straight when Diana Vreeland was talking to you. 'The peril of champagne is this.' She tapped herself under the jaw. 'Double chin, darling. Now, I don't have one, do I? My secret is neat vodka. Always vodka, never champagne. Too much champagne and you will find yourself slack-jawed.' I was shocked, as I never drank spirits. But maybe she was right, and I wouldn't have this double chin if I'd stayed off my perpetual champagne. I stayed quiet, though. Her imperiousness didn't invite answering back.

Diana – or 'Diane', as some were privileged to call her – was a legend in New York fashion and had been editor-in-chief of American *Vogue* for eight years. She welcomed Bailey and Jean Shrimpton to New York in the sixties. Although they became a fixture of US *Vogue*, their arrival was fraught. The way Bailey tells it, he had a huge row with Jean outside the Vogue building and made her cry so her make-up ran. When the Vogue lift doors opened on the fuming Bailey and the crumpled Shrimpton, Vreeland threw up her arms and cried, 'The British have arrived!'

When I met her she was the costume consultant at the Metropolitan Museum of Art and very much a grande dame: venerable, imperious, magnificent. Here in her incredible bijou apartment on Park Avenue, where the walls were red lacquer, like a Chinese cabinet, and every wall was crammed with books and objets d'art and portraits of Diana, particularly one enormous Oswald Birley painting of her, larger than life-size, Bailey and I crouched where Truman Capote used to sit, watching her opposite us, perched on her sofa as if on a throne, her strong aquiline nose flung back in a captivatingly haughty expression.

'So is that the elixir of your youth, Diane? The secret of your smouldering sex appeal?'

Bailey was being unbelievably flirtatious with her. His talk was really fruity. Would he get away with it? Her eyes glittered at him menacingly and her smeary red lips pursed. But then to my astonishment she gurgled with laughter.

'Oh Bailey,' she retorted. 'You are a cad! A scoundrel!'

Clearly, she wanted more.

'And if you were ten years younger you know what I'd want from you, Diane . . .' She shrieked with mock-outrage. The two of them were really flirting now. 'I'd see to you good and proper.'

'If I were ten years younger you'd have no choice,' she cried.

It was a fantastic spectacle, seeing the wild-man photographer chatting up the retired Queen of American *Vogue* – and one I never tired of watching.

Diana had lived in London during the inter-war years and been friends with Cecil Beaton, Cole Porter and Evelyn Waugh. Her voice was unmistakably of that era. She could describe a pancake and make it sound like Picasso had painted it – 'The depth, my dear! The texture!' – and she accompanied every sentence with dramatic hand gestures. She was captivating to watch, and utterly formidable too.

So much so that once, when Bailey and I were invited over for dinner with Elsa Peretti the Tiffany jewellery designer and a few others, we didn't dare say anything when the maid served the table shepherd's pie, even though we were both strict vegetarians then. I gave him a horrified look as the smell of meat wafted off the plates, and cleared my throat to explain we couldn't eat it but Bailey shot me a glance that said 'Don't!' so I had to pretend to chew a mouthful or two and then discreetly disgorge it from the side of my mouth into my napkin. I was sitting on the banquette next to Diana and I could feel her Gorgon stare on me. She must have thought I had the most terrible table manners. Bailey just pushed his meat around his plate; I tried to sneak off to the ladies with my napkin in my hand but again I could feel her beady eye on me so I gave up, and simply left the napkin guiltily behind me when we left. Bailey, ever the charmer: 'Diane, that was a fabulous dinner.'

Not long after, Diana and I met in Rome, at Franco Rossellini's home, and after dinner we returned to the Grand Hotel together. When I walked her up to her room she told me: 'You have the most wonderful manners.' I guess she'd forgotten about the regurgitated shepherd's pie debacle.

Bailey never wanted to linger in New York; he had been there, done that and filmed a documentary in bed with Andy Warhol in the sixties. But I loved staying there with Jerry and Mick at their apartment in the Dakota building, overlooking Central Park. During the day I might go to a go-see for work, although by now my agency was Elite (Wilhelmina had died and her agency had changed hands) and they would send me round town in a limo, which was a treat compared with hailing cabs all the time.

One evening I went to Madame Pearl's with Jerry, for dinner with Andy Warhol, Fred Hughes, Charlie Watts, Paloma Picasso, Mick and a few others. I was next to Andy and all he wanted to do was bitch, as usual. Trivialities were very important to him. He confided to me that he didn't like Jerry. I was horrified, especially as she was sitting right opposite us. 'She has BO,' he told me. (Like you don't, I thought to myself.) 'Really, she does. I'm sticking with Bianca. She's my friend, not Jerry.' It was just childish talk, so I didn't take offence on behalf of Jerry. I just kept on smiling vacantly. Jerry wouldn't have cared, anyway, as she adored Andy, and he came to love her too. Andy's gossipy tongue could turn on anyone. I dread to think what he said about me in private, though he was nice enough in his diary: 'Got a call from Tina Chow inviting me to a party for David Bailey and his wife Marie. It turned out it was actually a big party. Marie is really beautiful, she had on one of those slit dresses. Eric Boman and Peter Schlesinger were there. I told everybody how I was a male model now, I was trying to hustle work.'

I used to meet up with Andy for tea, either on my own or with Tina. We'd have champagne cocktails, which Tina loved, though he'd just move his glass around, barely sipping it. We liked each other. I'm sure it helped that I was married to Bailey and I was a *Vogue* cover girl. Andy was openly obsessed with status. He loved talking about Penelope Tree, and how her father was Sir Ronald Tree. With his international social-climbing instincts, he was 'Euro' before the term existed.

What did we talk about? It could have been anything from tweezers to Peggy Guggenheim in Venice to the Marchesa Casati's pet leopard. He was either very mundane or very esoteric. He also seemed to want to have 'girl talk' with me: 'Gee, Marie, don't your feet hurt from wearing those high heels all day long?' It wasn't really my thing, but I valued my time with him. His vision of the world was unique. If the job of an artist is to change the world through art, he was a true artist, and his legacy is still all around us.

Staying at Mick and Jerry's was fun: there was often a crowd there, and dinner guests might be Pete Townsend, Jack Nicholson and Anjelica Huston (who were by now a long-standing item), Robin Williams and various Stones. We'd start with cocktails (one evening Mick was in the kitchen for hours using the blender to make white peach juice for Bellinis) and then we'd have dinner. Late at night, sometimes Jerry would get out her jewellery box and show her gems off to the girls, like the Sharon Stone character in *Casino*. 'Look at my emerald bracelet … It used to belong to a Maharani …' I still didn't feel the need to acquire my own jewellery collection: more fool me.

They were happy then, though, during their early tempestuous days. Mick's mother Eva used to ring me when they split up, asking me to persuade Jerry to get back together with him. I grew fond of his parents, and once, after Mick's mother died, when we all went to San Lorenzo, his father gave twinkly looks across the table to my mother Linda, though nothing ever came of it.

One evening when I was staying with Mick and Jerry I went along with them to a Stones concert in Meadowlands, New Jersey. 'After the show, don't expect to have a conversation with Mick,' Jerry warned me, and I was glad she had when, after the last encore to their two-hour show, all the Stones left the stage door in towelling robes and each got into a separate waiting limo. Mick staggered into our limo sweating and panting as if he had just run a marathon. This was totally different to the chilled-out Mick who would appear an hour or two later at the after party. I had never seen this Mick before. I sat quietly alarmed in the front as he lay in the back, unable to move, panting like a fish out of water the whole way back to the Dakota building. Jerry smiled at me reassuringly: this was normal. He was literally out of breath for half an hour. He even had an oxygen canister beside him in case he needed it. The concert-goers sure got their money's worth out of him.

That night I also saw first-hand how the Stones fans treated Jerry: with jealous hatred. These women would push her out of the way, spit at her – I even saw them throwing lit matches in her hair. We had to sit in the lighting rig at the Meadowlands concert to be safe from them. I could empathise, in my way – I was used to models literally elbowing me aside to get to Bailey, clambering over me so as to sit next to him. And every time I went home there would be stacks of models' calling cards and portfolios waiting for him to peruse. They were delivered every single day, these photographs of beautiful women who wanted to work with my husband, and I couldn't help but be slightly pleased inside when he threw them away with barely a glance.

*

In Paris I was still working a lot for Yves Saint Laurent, at his new atelier in avenue Marceau, along with Iman and Mounia. We were all so-called 'exotics', representing Somalia, Martinique and Hawaii. 'It was unusual for such a prominent couturier to work with so many African and Asian models,' wrote Alice Rawsthorn in her biography of Yves Saint Laurent. 'But Yves relished the clash of cultures, which reminded him of his childhood in cosmopolitan Oran.' If he relished working with us, the feeling was mutual. I loved watching his creations progress and change. The run-up to the show took about two weeks, and every day we would go into his atelier and sit waiting for him in a plain white shift, like a nurse's uniform. When it was my turn to be called in, he would dress me in a toile (a version of the final design made in cotton) check it, change it, rip it, cut it and finally approve it. During the next stage of fittings, he worked on the finished dress, constantly tweaking, making sure the fit was perfect on me, changing the proportions of a bow here, the layers of gathering there. The final fitting, for accessories, might go on late into the night, ending in a perfect Polaroid of how the look should be, including make-up and hair. The next day, at the Hotel Intercontinental, the dressers would replicate the Polaroid, and send me to Yves for a final check-over and to Loulou de la Falaise for accessories. Yves would always be the last person you would see before stepping out on stage.

Once I nearly made Yves faint. He was presenting a ready-to-wear collection with a Moroccan theme and I was about to go on to the catwalk. When he checked me over for the last time, he decided my turban needed an extra jewel, and gingerly stuck a hat pin through the fabric. I didn't feel it, but this must have grazed my scalp because a tiny trickle of blood came down my forehead. Yves made as if to swoon and two big security guards came over and propped him up. Yves is a delicate man.

If he was happy with the way the toile was working out he would be beaming and so would the whole studio; if it wasn't going so well he would focus on the problem as if nothing else in the world existed. I am so pleased I had the chance to be part of Yves's creations.

Working with intensely original people is like standing in the path of a tornado. When you come into the presence of genius, whether that of a designer or photographer or any other artist, it is like being touched by fire.

I was thrilled to be invited to the American Embassy in Paris by our ambassador Pamela Harriman Churchill, for a reception in Yves's honour. 'Her Excellency' was charming and showed me round her collection of art – Miró, Picasso, Chagall. She was gorgeous, proud, and cultured. How clever of Big Bad Bill Clinton to have made her ambassador – to me, she excelled at the job.

One of the jobs I did without Bailey was a disaster. I was asked by Chanel to star in their advertising campaign photographed by François Lamy, and it was too prestigious and well paid a job to turn down, as Bailey reluctantly conceded. And Lamy never worked for British *Vogue*, so he didn't really tread on Bailey's toes, as it were. It was to be a three-day shoot in Monaco, and I checked into the Hermitage Hotel near the casino, where I had a magnificent suite. The first day went well and in the evening the artistic director of Chanel, Jacques Helleu, took us out on the town. I tried my first ever oyster – disaster! I spent the next day throwing up. Whenever Lamy changed rolls I ran off set and vomited. It was excruciating, being sick on the pavement and gardens of Monte Carlo, the cleanest and prettiest city in the world. Chanel has never employed me since.

Iman and I were both in Yves's famous couture collection inspired by Picasso's designs for the ballet *Parade*. Here as usual he was breaking with convention by using star editorial models on the catwalk. We wore diamond-patterned suits based on Picasso's harlequin figures, and ballgowns in the *Parade* palette of orange, yellow and black. When the bride made her entrance for the finale Paloma Picasso was so moved by Yves's interpretation of her father's work she burst into tears in a blaze of camera flashes. Bailey, always obsessed by Picasso, adored the show as well.

Soon after, Jerry and Bailey and I were out at La Coupole having tea, when Bailey nudged me. 'That's only him and her,' he said, indicating an elderly couple seated side by side on a banquette, surveying the room.

'Who?' I said.

'Sartre and de Beauvoir. Who else?'

I looked again at the couple, who were surveying the room with great interest. They smiled graciously at us, inclining towards the empty chairs in front of them.

'Let's say hello!' said Jerry and the three of us went over to pay our respects to the grand old couple of French literature. Though neither Bailey nor I had much French, Jerry's was pretty good and we managed to make ourselves understood, and we all had coffee together. Whenever any of us saw them in La Coupole afterwards they greeted us with a wave and a nod. Impossible to say if they remembered who we were.

I loved the way that in Paris, too, all cultural disciplines mingled freely. Fashion has always had a place in the arts there, from Poiret's designs for Diaghilev's Ballets Russes to Josephine Baker's style impact, to the links between Yves Saint Laurent and Zizi Jeanmaire (who appeared at his retrospective show at the Lido on the Champs-Elysées) or Catherine Deneuve (it was Bailey, in fact, who had sent Catherine to him back in the sixties). It was common, at La Coupole, for art, literature, film and fashion crowds to rub shoulders. We were likely to dine there with Françoise Sagan one night and Yves Saint Laurent the next. One evening we had dinner at the home of Jean Camus, the son of Albert. Only in France would the foremost philosopher (Bernard-Henri Lévy) be married to the glamorous actress said to have the tiniest waist in Paris (Arielle Dombasle).

Every country places a different emphasis on fashion. In Italy it's about structure and architecture; in England it's to do with innovation and music; in America it's sportswear: the perfect jeans, the ultimate sneaker. In France it is art and philosophy, the headiest combination of all.

As I began to know Yves a little better, I would be invited to the celebratory lunch after his collections with all his intimates, from Pierre Bergé to his mother. He was fiercely protected by this coterie

Designed by Ossie Clark, this was an incredible gold leather bustier made long before corsets became fashionable. Ossie was way ahead of his time and is the only designer I know of that was capable of cutting directly on to cloth.

A sexy lingerie shot for *Ritz* newspaper, which Bailey and David Lichfield started in 80s. It lasted briefly and today copies are collectors items.

opposite page Modelling with Manolo Blahnik for *Vogue* – yes, our legs are that long! Trick photography actually.

This is my all-time favourite photograph. I look at it now and marvel that I once had a body like that. It was taken in Hawaii and I find the whole image thought-provoking and provocative. By the way, that is Bailey's shadow.

opposite page I did a series of ads for Olympus Cameras. We were always trying to think of new places we could put the small (at the time) 'trip' camera.

This was taken at the old Malabar Hotel in Cochin, Kerala. Although I look relaxed and languid I was actually suffering from terrible dysentery. The paleness of my face is due to the illness. As I've always said, when you live with a photographer you never have days off.

opposite page Bailey and I were shooting for French *Vogue* in Haiti during the time of Baby Doc Duvalier, son of 'Papa Doc'. The atmosphere around the island was extremely tense and I was relieved when he decided to shoot around the grounds and gardens of the Habitation LeClerc.

This is by far one my very favourite headshots from British *Vogue* in the 80s. It defines the look of the 80s, – thick brows, big hair, strong make up.

Happy days with Mick and Jerry and me all glammed up at a *Vanity Fair* party.

of friends and admirers, known as the court of Yves. In the midst of them all the man himself was charming, gentle and always laughing. His English was broken but droll; once, offering me a fluffy beignet known as 'the sigh of the nun' he quipped: 'Or should it be called "the fart of the nun"?' Everyone round him tittered appreciatively.

At the end of a long day of fitting sessions at Yves's atelier, Loulou would fix Yves, Pierre and herself the habitual whisky and soda. She began asking me if I'd care for one too. It wasn't usual for models to be included in this whisky ritual, and, flattered, I said 'Merci bien'. I hated drinking the stuff but I knew it was an honour, a sign I was a step nearer Yves's inner sanctum.

Of course my insecurities told me it was simply because I was now married to Bailey. But I knew that Yves seemed genuinely interested in how I chose to put together my outfits. Would I wear this with jeans? he asked. Would I sling this belt over this shirt? I began to feel Yves liked me in my own right, and, most flatteringly of all, that he thought I had style. Was I afforded preferential treatment because I was a star? No. But maybe being married to Bailey changed things subtly. I noticed that Karl, who wandered round with a huge bottle of Evian, wouldn't offer a swig to any other models but me.

Karl Lagerfeld, then at Chloé, was also fantastic to work with. The extrovert yin to Yves's introverted yang, he was always great fun, thrived on company and couldn't stop talking. His shows were insanely chaotic. He'd hire the top models in the world, but we'd never have our own designated rails of clothes. That would be far too organised. Instead we'd all be standing there in our panties, covering our breasts, some with shoes, some without, with no clue what we were going to wear until he'd shout: 'You! Pat! Take the satin dress. Now!' 'You! Marie! The puffball skirt! Go!' Miraculously, it worked. He must have known what he was doing, because every-thing always worked brilliantly for Karl. He used chaos theory to propagate perfection.

Once, just as I was waiting in the wings, Karl's boyfriend perched a parrot on my hand. I walked down the catwalk in a flowing eighteenth-century gown with silk stockings and court shoes, this huge green Amazon parrot biting my fingers. Knowing that parrots' brains are guided by their ears, I purred at it gently which made it stop nibbling me – for a moment. It was a nightmare having this bird on my wrist but evidently the effect was fantastic – and it can't have been entirely a coincidence, anyway. Karl had visited me and Bailey in London, so he knew all about our menagerie.

No one else worked quite like Karl. Valentino by contrast was very methodical, with painstaking care. We would be fully made up by his hair and make-up artists for every fitting, and each girl was given an individual full dress rehearsal, recreating the 'passage' down the catwalk for Valentino, who would be sitting in state like a pasha at the end of the runway, issuing instructions ('Walk tall!') or tweaking the look at the last minute ('Lose the jacket!').

The major designers today – McQueen, Galliano, Westwood – tack instructions to the wall backstage to explain the theme of the show. They want a uniform look from the models, rather than the individuality that was encouraged in my day. 'NO SMILING – GIVE ME ANGER!' the directions might say. Or 'SEXY AND SMILING'. Or even (allegedly) for a particular Galliano show: 'PRETEND YOU ARE BEING HUNTED BY 20 COS-SACKS ON HORSEBACK'. Sure enough, Kate Moss raced down the catwalk looking terrified.

No matter how tired I was after work, Paris nightclubs were too seductive to pass on. At number 7 on the rue Saint-Anne was the famous club Le Sept, a red Deco den where people went to see, be seen and see themselves in the act of being seen.

It was the natural place for us to go of an evening. After Charlotte Rampling's wedding to Jean Michel Jarre, where we watched fire-works set to classical music (which I found breathtaking) Bruce Oldfield, Bailey and I went out to Le Sept. I had a delicious salad of black truffles. The door code was, according to one former DJ there, quite simple: 'You didn't have to be rich or famous . . . you had to be beautiful.' I started to go there dancing with Yves, Pierre Bergé and Loulou; Antonio Lopez, the prominent fashion illustrator, was always there with Jerry and Grace Jones, and maybe Tina Chow too.

Other nights the company might be the Japanese designer Kenzo, and a beautiful male model. Sometimes I trekked out with Loulou and Karl Lagerfeld to the Algerian dance club in the suburbs called La Main Bleue. But never in all of my days or nights in Paris did I see Yves and Karl in the same room together. By the time I came on the scene they had fallen out irreparably.

Once Bailey and I were invited to Yves's birthday party at Maxim's. It was the first time I'd ever been there and I loved its dark, plush, old-fashioned *belle époque* style and kept thinking of the scene set there in *Gigi*. We turned up with Diana Vreeland, but as soon as we arrived we realised we'd been wrong to bring her along, as Yves's group was too tight to admit any but the chosen few who'd been invited. He was already beginning to withdraw from social frivolities. He was a thinker, profound and introspective: the party scene was not for him. Loulou greeted us looking fabulous as ever and sporting an entirely original fashion innovation. She had two huge fresh Stargazer lilies worn, like earrings, from the lobes of her ears; kissing her hello, you were overpowered by their fresh, heady scent.

And perhaps she was surprised to see what I was wearing, too. It was one of Yves's trademark transparent blouses – one that he had given me after a show, in fact – of black chiffon, off-the-shoulder and studded with gold dots. I noticed him do a double take when he saw what I was wearing. I had decided to reproduce the catwalk look and was wearing the chiffon over my bare flesh, as I had done in his show. My breasts were absolutely visible, though draped in chiffon. I liked the sexy look but Yves was shocked, I think. He intended the look for the catwalk but not necessarily for the night-club. But as the evening progressed I saw him pointing me out to people admiringly and I relaxed as I realised he was rather impressed by my nerve.

It was said that later in life Yves retreated into himself, got hooked on drugs and became totally reclusive. Not strictly true. I saw him quite by accident in Morocco at the Mamounia. I was there having tea when I saw him come in, walking with a stick, accompanied by a manservant and Moujick's inheritor, a third-generation pug. I thought twice about whether I should go over, given the reports about him. But I did, and he was lovely and warm and friendly and remembered me. That said, three months later when we did a tribute fashion show to him at the Savoy, he didn't turn up.

In Paris Bailey and I used to stay at the Hôtel de Bourgogne, because it was near to French *Vogue*, until someone mentioned that there was a one-bedroom apartment available in the former mayoral offices of Chirac, on the place du Palais Bourbon. It was only a pied-à-terre, a little flat with a huge bed and a tiny kitchen, but it suited us fine as all we wanted was a small space of our own. When my great friend the designer Ninivah Khomo came to stay she was surprised that Bailey and I didn't have anywhere more grand, but we didn't care about that kind of thing. It was basic but it was all we wanted: a bolthole.

Here, I kept my portable lightbox and my personal magnifier (my 'loupe'), for it was often in Paris that Bailey and I had to turn around jobs for French *Vogue* quickly, and sometimes, if time was tight, he would trust me to go through the contact sheets selecting the final shortlist of shots. That he allowed me to do that showed he must have had great confidence and trust in my eye.

If he was pressed for time I would also pick out the best shots from other models' work with him too, choosing the best six or ten shots out of perhaps five pages of contact sheets. I don't think any of the magazines ever knew the shots were of my choosing; to them, Bailey was the master.

Breasts

'What . . .' said Yves, 'are THOSE?' He was pointing at my breasts. For couture, a bosom was considered a real hindrance. It wasn't at all the done thing to be a B-cup. After all those years of puffing into the blow-up bra, my bosom had finally expanded of its own accord. Genes will out – my mother's built like Jayne Mansfield – and also being on the pill had given me more shape too, as had eating more, which comes with happiness.

They were always surprising me, my tits. When I first arrived in London permanently I did a shoot with Harri Peccinotti for *Nova* magazine, possibly for their very last issue. I thought it was a standard kind of shoot, but when I saw the results I was amazed to see my erect nipples were the focal point of the pictures. I'd been wearing tight thermal T-shirts and no bra, framed from my waist upwards, so perhaps I should have realised before. From that moment I started to think carefully about each photographer's agenda. I was surprised but not cross – *Nova* was a really cool magazine and I loved those pictures. I wish I could find them.

I briefly became a Bunny Girl – only for a one-off shoot Bailey and I did for the cover of the *Sunday Times* magazine. At my costume fitting at the Playboy HQ on Park Lane – like a mini Vegas show palace – I found my costume was really loose around the bust. 'Go down the corridor,' the Head Bunny Girl advised me, 'And open that cupboard ...' When I did so a bundle of white toilet rolls practically fell in my face. The cupboard was stacked with them. Toilet paper was evidently a Bunny Girl's best friend. Boy did I stuff my costume out, filling the breast pockets for a full Wonderbra effect. I looked very curvy on the *Times* cover – an unnatural Double D.

Out one night in Rome at Jackie O's, the club where everyone used to hang out, from the *jeunesse dorée* to artists and writers, there was a real party mood, with me, Loulou and Dado Ruspoli all dancing round on top of the world and Bailey looking contentedly on. Perhaps this was because our mood had been enhanced by the languorous high of the opium Dado and I had smoked earlier at his palazzo. Suddenly I felt some hands creep across my chest, beginning to massage my breasts, which were, as usual, free from a bra in a stretchy chiffon top. It was Loulou. I could smell her perfume and hear her murmuring as she massaged me. Bailey was watching. Everyone was: Dado, Gil, the man who owned Jackie O's ... I was frozen. I wanted to get out of her embrace but Bailey was enjoying the sight, I could tell. So I let her carry on for a while, before wriggling away and leaping on to the dance floor.

That night Bailey, Loulou and I all flitted back to the Grand Hotel, but when she came up to our room, I knew what I was going to have to do. I lay down on the bed and pretended I had passed out. Loulou and Bailey were tapping me on my arm – I think he would have loved us to do a little party for him, the two of us getting it on with each other while he watched. But I just snored deeply. I've had maybe one or two gay experiences – obligatory for someone of my generation – but I knew it wasn't for me, however much I adored and admired Loulou.

So my breasts sometimes got me into trouble. And perhaps they still will. I sometimes wonder what pictures of me are still in Bailey's archive. Even if my face isn't in some of them, I've been told I'm identifiable by just my nipples. I guess I'll take that as a compliment.

*

'The meeting of two personalities is like the contact of two chemical substances; if there is any reaction, both are transformed.'

JUNG

'Bailey!'

'It's only bloody David Bailey! Here! This way! Over here!'

Bailey and I had been out to a trendy restaurant in LA with Anjelica Huston and Jack Nicholson and the paparazzi were waiting outside. But the only person they seemed to be interested in was Bailey. Of course, they were fellow photographers, so it made sense that they should respond to Bailey. But it was funny to see Jack Nicholson being ignored. He could have danced the lambada for them and they would still have had eyes only for Bailey. Bailey didn't seem to care – it wasn't his style to even notice something like that. But I realised in that moment that Americans, too, had heard of Bailey.

This was a period when LA was welcoming all kinds of European talent, from Polanski to Isabelle Adjani to Helmut Berger. At that time there was a growing appetite for European art-house films, and it was a time of great cultural exchange and energy, of fashion, film and art worlds colliding, and it attracted Bailey. Bailey had a big vision. Every New Year's Eve Bailey sent a Telex to Howard Hughes at the Inn on the Park, asking to photograph him. Hughes never replied, but Bailey sent the Telex persistently for a decade. He also pursued Castro with the same unrewarded energy. He never stood still or allowed himself to stagnate. His vision was always wider than fashion, than London, than photography. So he decided we should try living in LA for a while.

We took a suite at the Chateau Marmont. Unlike the luxury hotels where anyone could find you, such as the Beverly Hills or the Beverly Wilshire, the Chateau felt private, decaying and a little sepulchral. There was something eerie about the atmosphere of this place, where John Belushi had died a year earlier. We would park in the underground lot and take the lift straight up to our floor; it was like an apartment block and you never knew what was going on in the rooms around you. As Tom Stoppard said in his play *Night and Day*, 'hotel rooms constitute a separate moral universe'. There could be an orgy or a murder, I once whispered to Bailey in the gloomy mock-gothic corridor. 'Or both,' he replied. Sting was staying on the floor above us for the whole three months we were there and I never saw him – though not through lack of looking out on my part. I was a huge fan.

Daytimes, Bailey was busy working. He was inundated with offers; once he asked me if he should do Tom Waits's album cover, but I said, 'Who's he?' and he turned the job down. Jack Nicholson wanted Bailey to work as the cinematographer on his directorial debut *Goin' South* but after much deliberation Bailey decided cinematography was too specialised a discipline for a one-off project. I had a quieter time – there was no fashion community in LA and I never worked there much. Instead I might hang out with Anjelica, at the gorgeous villa with the pool out the back that Jack had bought her, which she filled with her father John Huston's Irish heirlooms and her late mother's Italian treasures. I thought it was heaven but Anjelica, a true Cancerian homemaker, yearned to live with Jack. 'Why has he bought me my own separate place?' To my mind, she had the perfect set-up.

I loved doing my own thing during the day while Bailey worked. I looked up Jackie Collins, whom I had met through Shakira Caine, and I went to her ladies' lunches where, after we'd all had masses of champagne to drink, she would put her tiny tape recorder down in the middle of the table and say, 'OK, girls, start talking!' Sometimes it wouldn't work and we'd clam up; other times the chatter would really flow: indiscretions, affairs, tales of fabulous wealth and extravagance. They were some of the naughtiest stories I'd ever heard.

One night Bailey and I were both late back to the Chateau – me from a modelling job, he from a shoot with Jamie Lee Curtis. 'She made a huge play for me, that little vixen,' he told me. My shock turned to amusement as he detailed how she had done it, making it into a comedy turn. I wasn't threatened at all, and saved my jealousy for other times.

It was a time of great sexual licence, and people were doing it everywhere you looked. One night particularly sticks in my memory as LA at its most debauched.

The warm sunlit evening began with Bailey and me meeting Alana Hamilton, who had divorced George and was dating Rod Stewart, and Helmut Berger, the Austrian actor known as 'the most beautiful man in the world'. Alana wanted to take us for drinks and supper at a little private club that looked very unprepossessing: no lights, no signs, just a little hatch that opened up – and revealed a pair of eyes I found thrillingly familiar: they belonged to the Fugitive! I nearly swooned as I realised it was my childhood hero the actor David Janssen. I kept nudging Bailey and saying 'It's the Fugitive!' through discreetly gritted teeth – but Bailey, of course, had been raised on different TV programmes and had no idea what I was on about. Inside the club there were plenty of other recognisable faces, like Frank Sinatra – but I only had eyes for the Fugitive.

Next we four headed up to Sammy Davis Jr.'s house in Beverly Hills, which, like all the stars' homes, was behind huge security gates staffed by armed guards. Inside there was quite a party going on with about fifteen Oakland Raiders from the famous American football team, all surrounded by sexy women. There was something unsettling about the way the men were evidently guests, and the women had been 'laid on' for them. As background entertainment a huge television screen set in a sunken area in the living room was playing Sam Peckinpah's most violent movie, *The Wild Bunch*.

Sammy Davis Jr. welcomed us in. 'I must show you people my collection.' This turned out to consist of pornography through the ages: ancient phalluses, explicit Japanese sketches, priapic Greek figurines . . . There was even a naughty sculpture in his shower. His wife Altovise, who had been around at the beginning of the tour, had split by this time. She'd seen it all before. I was surprised, but amused.

When we returned to the living room, the atmosphere was rowdier and I could see that down in the sunken area some of the girls were on their knees in front of a few reclining Oakland Raiders. Clearly, they were giving blow jobs. Then one of the sexy girls circulating with drinks started chatting Bailey up. He flirted with her in return, and I suddenly lost it.

In those days, instead of expressing how I felt and confronting Bailey, my reaction was simply to walk out. I headed straight out of the party into the cool LA night. The door slammed behind me and I was left looking at the ranks of smart cars in the private parking lot. I remembered we'd come in Alana's Rolls-Royce Corniche so I found what I thought was her car and got into it. I was sitting, angry and unhappy, in the front seat and before I knew what was happening two huge guys got into the car on either side of me, one on my left, another on my right. One of them was a football manager – who came from a famous Hollywood family – and they were both in high spirits. Immediately, the risk siren went off in my head. They were teasing and prodding me, messing around with this pretty girl they'd found in the car. I sensed danger: I had to get out of that situation pronto. The men just laughed at me. Desperate, I crawled right over one of them to get through the door – they wouldn't move to let me pass. There was no chivalry here.

Once I made it out of the car I ran to the huge wooden panelled doors of the house, panicky and tear-stained, and was about to ring the bell when the security guard with the gun appeared and asked me what I was doing. He was very suspicious of me, evidently assuming that I was some kind of hooker. 'Once you're out of the house, you're out,' he told me menacingly.

All I could do was sit and wait on the stone steps feeling intensely vulnerable and frightened. It felt like ages until Alana, Helmut and Bailey came through the door saying, 'There you are! We'd been wondering where you'd got to.'

I look back and think it must have been hard for Bailey to handle this young wife of his who was always walking out on him when she was unhappy. As a response it was incredibly detrimental to our relationship; it would have been much more adult to tell him what was bothering me. Another of the reasons I didn't speak was because I had learned I could never win an argument or a disagreement with Bailey because he would always have the last word or simply back down absolutely so there was nothing left to argue against. Bailey was still ahead of me intellectually and I had to run to stand still with him. He was very good at shutting down arguments. The morning after the Sammy Davis Jr. party I could have sulked in silence for eternity.

But one of Bailey's great qualities is that he doesn't bear grudges. He made the first overture of reconciliation. 'Come on now, let's not be bad friends.' It was big of him to take the initiative. But having said that, the fact that he decided the argument was over – *c'est tout*, we're friends now – meant I never could express why I had been cross with him. Instead, the voiceless sadness and resentment festered deep down within me. There was never time to explore these feelings. The way we all lived was too fast for that. It was always on to the next city, next person, next photo shoot. Next! Next! Next!

*

'Where does a dream go after you've dreamt it? There are people living in a dream world, and people living in the real world, and people who don't know the difference.'

Bailey and I still shared great happiness, particularly when we were heading off abroad together. Our holidays were always working – Bailey's camera was omnipresent – but they were great adventures too. We would drive to Rome in his Range Rover (he ditched the Rolls-Royce Corniche after it got smashed and scratched by vandals one too many times – it was a magnet for anger, that car) with a picnic made to last us two days. We barely stopped driving the whole way there, with Bailey at the wheel eating Cezar's spicy chicken drumsticks (deep fried, of course) flinging the bones out of the window as we went.

Exploring further afield we kept on the move as well. On a trip to Sri Lanka we explored the whole island, stopping at twelve different guesthouses over a period of a month, travelling like snails with all our belongings on our backs. For him, that meant photographic equipment; for me, just a drip-dry dress and sandals. We immersed ourselves in the local culture, visiting every shrine and temple on the map until we got to the checkpoints of the newly formed Tamil Tiger guerrilla group and couldn't go any further. Here we had the time to be free, to be ourselves, at peace with the world and with each other. We started to become alive to our surroundings, to notice things in enhanced detail, the way you do on holiday. The daily monsoon was a revelation. You have no idea what one is like until you experience it. The rain is so heavy and dense there's not enough room to breathe. In these torrents, an umbrella is all but ridiculous.

At the reclining Buddha of Polonnaruwa Bailey threw his cigarette butt into the water and a huge black fish surfaced and gulped it down. In the evening at dinner we thought we'd try something new on the menu, and were presented with a plate bearing a huge black fish.

'That looks horribly familiar,' he said. I gasped: 'Cut it open and it'll have a cigarette butt inside it!'

Neither of us dared to taste the fish. That night we sat quietly amongst the mosquitoes on the ramshackle terrace of our hotel, playing gin rummy together in perfect contentment. Though we seemed so different, Bailey and I were very much alike in temperament.

Bailey was seduced by India, though I never learned to be comfortable with the poverty there. We travelled to Delhi, Calcutta, Bombay. We saw Christian tokens in Goa (including the reliquary for a piece of St Francis Xavier, which is only displayed once a year); in India the Hindu teacher Sai Baba made Vibuthi magic happen before our eyes, crumbling ash into Bailey's palm that apparently alchemically transformed into a solid silver coin. Even Bailey, Mr Sceptical, was amazed. In Calcutta Bailey forged a close bond with Mother Teresa, working with her for free on her brochures for fund-raising initiatives. He knew how to cope with her, but I didn't. I found her a tiny terrifying powerhouse of a woman. In an instant she knew who would do her bidding and who wouldn't and I guess she knew I wouldn't.

Another trip took us to Haiti on a fashion story for French *Vogue*. When Bailey asked who we should bring along as a double to work with me in some of the shots, I suggested Janice Dickinson. She was guaranteed fun, as I had learnt backstage at a Kenzo show when, just before stepping on to the catwalk, she tipped a whole bottle of champagne over her head. She shook herself off like a wild animal, spraying the assembled models, and then freewheeled on to the stage like a true performer. Kenzo loved it; when you booked Janice you knew you were bound to get her crazy antics.

But at the airport, instead of Janice, a beautiful young girl breezed up to us, clutching a huge bag of pistachios and saying, 'Hey! I'm Debbie Dickinson!'

On the aeroplane Bailey kept looking at me questioningly. What was going on? There had possibly been a mix-up or perhaps Mike Reinhardt, Janice's photographer partner, simply hadn't been keen on the idea of her shooting with Bailey. Either way, it didn't matter. Debbie turned out to be a great model, and a lot of fun too. She was a keen gymnast, which came in useful as it was a swimwear shoot. There were shots of her in very high heels with her hands touching the floor, her body arched in an athletic oblique.

Haiti was a world apart. As soon as we arrived at the airport the customs men confiscated my copy of Graham Greene's *The*

Comedians, his novel set in Haiti. What were we letting ourselves in for here?

But how languid the atmosphere was, and how sensual. The whole vibe in Haiti was sex and voodoo – and baseballs. We were escorted round the republic on what turned out to be a tour of almost exclusively baseball factories. As far as I could see it was the only thing the country produced: baseball after baseball after baseball. When we discovered the local art, especially painting and sculpture in Port au Prince, it was a great thrill after all those baseball factories.

Bailey was also keen to photograph the all-powerful president Baby Doc Duvalier (son of Papa Doc). The former Tonton Macoute, the Duvaliers' armed guards, were a menacing presence everywhere we went. Even though they were now in civilian jobs, working at hotels or driving cabs, you could still tell by their formidable build and sinister black Ray-Bans that they were fighting men. They'd be serving you breakfast and you'd feel they were about to slit your throat. Far more simpatico was Aubelin Jolicoeur, the man who inspired the character Petit Pierre in *The Comedians*: a tiny, immaculately dressed black man carrying a cane who was charming and clearly made it his business to meet everyone who came to the country.

Bailey and I stayed at an annexe down the road from the hotel, which was a private residence: L'Habitation LeClerc. This was the former home of Pauline Bonaparte, the naughty sister Napoleon banished to Haiti. We were locked in here behind gigantic wooden doors. We soon found out why, however, when all through the night people chanted and banged on those doors: some kind of voodoo shit was going down. I didn't feel at ease at all. The final straw came when we were informed, via the travel editor of French *Vogue*, that we were not fit to be admitted into the presence of the Duvaliers because we had not brought the correct attire with us. Madame Duvalier would not meet me unless I was wearing long white gloves apparently, and Bailey likewise had to wear morning dress. The woman from *Vogue*, who was frankly a bourgeois nightmare, seemed to think we had committed a grave oversight in forgetting to bring this formal dress. But Bailey and I weren't going to pander to the whims of a petty dictator, so we flew home again without even meeting him. A few years later Baby Doc was deposed.

Japan was another story. We went there with Serge Gainsbourg and Jane Birkin, and had a fantastic time. I loved them both: Serge for his frankness (he simply said whatever he was feeling) while Jane was utterly adorable and a raving beauty. Renoma, the French men's clothing company, was using Serge and Jane Birkin in their Japanese advertising campaign and Bailey's photographs of them were plastered on billboards all over Tokyo, Renoma also insisted that Serge and Jane gave a performance of their infamous song 'Je T'Aime ... Moi Non Plus', and they reluctantly agreed to do it. We all had a stiff sake together and then Serge and Jane got up in front of a packed crowd in a nightclub and lip-synced and did heavy breathing to badly piped background music. Bailey and I sat cringing on their behalf in the audience.

Afterwards we four were taken out to a gourmet Chinese restaurant where the signature dish seemed to be cruelty. Everything we tried to eat turned out to be alive. We were offered prawns but we found they jumped around when you put them in your mouth. Jane and I were horrified; Serge loved it. Another dish was simply a bowl of eyeballs, which seemed to be gently swivelling. Lastly they served a soft-shelled turtle, which tried to crawl away before the waiters slit its throat and mixed its blood with sake. Bailey, Jane and I were all practically retching at the table, and couldn't bear to watch. Serge quaffed the warm red drink with relish.

Years later I was flying back home from Paris when I saw Jane was getting on the aeroplane too. Great! I thought, looking forward to her company. Then I noticed that as well as carrying her trademark wicker basket, she was also wearing a baggy pair of men's pyjamas. But Jane is a free spirit, so I assumed she just had a pyjama thing going on. Then I caught sight of her face, which was swollen as if she'd been sobbing for hours. 'Oh Marie,' she said when she saw me. '*C'est tragique.*' She always mixed her French and English charmingly.

'I've just left Serge. *C'est pourquoi* I'm still in his pyjamas.' She had grabbed a few belongings and was heading home to her mother's in Kensington. I consoled her as best I could. We had a bond, in a way, because both of us had married the big beasts of the sixties jungle, both fascinating, both difficult, both ultimately untameable.

Books, portraits, TV commercials, adverts: there was always a project or several on the go with Bailey. He completed ten books during the ten years of our marriage. The most ambitious plan was perhaps the film he planned to direct, called *Paperback*. He had written the script as well, some kind of brooding *ménage à trois* scenario reminiscent of Polanski's *Knife in the Water*. He persuaded everyone he knew to take part. Helmut Berger would be the lead, I would play his wife, and other stars would include Giancarlo Giannini and Georgina Hale. Filming would take place in Nice at Les Studios de la Victorine, where Truffaut shot *Day for Night*; Yves would provide the clothes (as a favour to me); and we would take a huge villa for the summer by the sea, so we could save on hotels and put the stars up in our guest rooms. But those guest rooms were fated to remain sadly empty.

Funding this film turned out to be harder than anyone expected, despite the fact we had two top British producers and the Victorine studios on board. One time Bailey even had to resort to using my modelling earnings to pay the crew and art directors and assistants. I flew in from doing a show and shoot for Yves in Paris and they were practically standing on the tarmac waiting for me and my bundle of cash to arrive. Bailey distributed the notes and kissed me on the forehead. 'You're a lifesaver! The movie will go on!' But after months of pre-production the whole project ground to a halt. 'You should get an Oscar just for managing to make a bloody movie!' Bailey fumed. Years later he would finally make his own feature film, *The Intruder*, starring Nastassia Kinski. But I was relieved this one folded, to be honest. I was happy to get home to my cats. And perhaps I wasn't cut out for acting anyway. It was just another entry on the long list of noble failures.

*

It amuses me to consider, briefly, all those near misses, all those 'brilliant' creative schemes that came out stillborn, starting from the Japanese romantic comedies I was invited to star in and finishing up with the reality shows I turned down because I didn't fancy eating kangaroo testicles on TV or being shouted at by a talented but volatile chef.

In between there were so many parts I was up for and never got. David Puttnam told me I should be in a James Bond film with Roger Moore; apparently Cubby Broccoli wanted to meet me and I was invited to a James Bond premiere. Bailey masterminded the whole thing: he thought I should attend the premiere dressed to kill. In those days designers didn't lend out dresses for occasions like that and, anyway, I had a vintage gown I wanted to wear. When I arrived at the premiere someone stepped on the back of the gown; the fabric was so ancient that a whole segment ripped away with a sickening tearing noise. I never heard from Cubby Broccoli.

I was up for a part in *Day of the Dolphin*, by Mike Nichols. Roger Donaldson invited me to audition for the role of the girl that Fletcher falls in love with in *Bounty* with Mel Gibson. J.P. Donleavy's son took me to lunch three times to discuss the film of *The Ginger Man*. A director asked me if I would understudy Jerry Hall in *Bus Stop* (no thank you!). I was nearly in so many films, but to name a few of them: *Shanghai Surprise* with Madonna, *The Prince and I* with Michael York, and *Apollo 13*, and *High Road to China* (starring Tom Selleck), and, least suitable of all (I've never been a singer) the Broadway musical *Nine*. Though that didn't work out I took singing lessons with Mary Hammond for six months which was one of the best things I have ever done. I learned so much about projection and breath control – and confidence. By the end of the lessons I even managed to rise to the challenge of singing in front of the star of *Miss Saigon*. It also helped me get a handle on the slight lisp that I've had since childhood. But when I was ready to go, the musical folded, needless to say.

Jerry and I had parts in a film called *Diana and Me*, starring Toni Collette, but we were evidently so miscast we ended up on the cutting-room floor. Most embarrassingly, an agent insisted we still had star billing, even though we didn't actually appear in the film.

After *Trouble and Strife* came out, people evidently thought I was up for doing nude scenes, and Just Jaeckin, the man who directed the Emmanuelle movies (and whom Bailey always sardonically referred to as 'Just Jerkin') invited me to appear in his erotic film *Madam Claude*. Bruce Robinson asked me to appear naked in his film *How to Get Ahead in Advertising*. Thanks, but no thanks.

One evening late at night when I knew Mick was away I rang up Jerry, really excited about a book I'd just finished: the autobiography of Henrietta Moraes. Jerry, who knew Henrietta a little, went straight out the next day to buy it, and she loved it too. 'Wouldn't it make a great movie?' we said.

Jerry and I founded a production company, Hel-Hall. If Mick could have his own film company, why shouldn't we? Our project suddenly appeared on page three of the *Sunday Times*, which was something of a shock. But by now we had bought the rights to the book and the project was taking shape. At a party at Mick and Jerry's house one night we saw our leading lady.

'Look,' I said, nudging Jerry. 'It's Henrietta.'

'So it is,' sighed Jerry.

It was the young actress Rachel Weisz, fresh from her first feature film, who was there with her friend the director Sean Mathias. She would have been perfect, and when we sent her the book she said she was keen to play the role. Tom Stoppard kindly agreed to polish our script, and recommended Frederic Raphael as our writer. But Raphael wasn't interested. And besides, Jerry and I started to disagree over the nature of the film. I felt strongly that Henrietta herself should have no input into the film, conceiving of it as a general portrait of the period and Moraes's milieu; Jerry thought it should be more like a biopic. (She even got Henrietta herself involved, bringing her along to the launch of my book *Bodypure*.) When our rights to the story of her life expired, we let them go. Our year's work on the project came to nothing.

I can still see the movie it could have been: the music, the art, the

culture and, at the centre of it all, Francis Bacon's incredible muse
... If I win the Lottery, I'm making that film.

Next Jerry and I were meant to write a book, with Peter Mayle,
about the so-called high life: where to shop, where to party, how to
dress. The project folded because Jerry's agent, Irving 'Swifty' Lazar,
wanted her to complete a simpler solo project: *Tall Tales*, her autobiography, which came out in paperback around the same time I
published *Catwalk*. And Peter Mayle went straight off and wrote *A
Year in Provence*, so it all worked out for the best for him.

When *Ab Fab* was a hit, Jerry and I were approached by Kathy
Lette to star in a similar sitcom. After doing a fashion show together
in Paris I asked Jerry and Lizzie her daughter (my goddaughter) out
for tea and I showed Jerry the script. 'WHY have they made ME
the anal one?' cried Jerry. I didn't know. It was just a silly script.

In the end, I believe one should always concede gracefully to one's
destiny. None of these projects was meant to be.

*

'Ouch! You're hurting me!' Jerry and I were up to all sorts of mischief
under the table at Elaine's restaurant in New York. Kicking each
other, giggling, fooling around: nothing serious, of course, but
enough to cause a bit of a stir. It was just a double act, a game that
led people to ask, gullibly, if we were having an affair. Certainly not!
Although a photo exists of us outside Langan's kissing on the lips, it
was only the briefest of clinches. We just loved provoking a reaction,
especially when we were around Mick or Bailey or stuffy old men. It
was a bid to attract attention, a way to get a response. Together we
had some kind of power.

In fact, together we could be a nightmare. At the shows in Paris we
always insisted on doing our hair and make-up our own way. After all,
we were hired to look like ourselves: we both had definite looks and
neither of us was like, say, Linda Evangelista, who was the ultimate
model's model, because she was a complete chameleon. Not us.

Backstage we used to hide out under the stairs or in a cupboard,
waiting while we heard the hairdressers and make-up artists calling
our names. Sometimes it didn't work and we'd be discovered ('HERE

they are!'); sometimes we'd saunter out at the last minute so no one had time to try and mess with our hair or our look.

By this time I certainly thought of myself as a star model. I made sure I got exactly what I wanted. Every top model had stipulations and these were mine. I wouldn't do go-sees any more; all castings I went to had to be one-to-one, so I could go straight in and straight out; I had a choice of hairdresser and make-up artist; I had copy approval; I didn't do lingerie or swimwear shoots with anyone apart from Bailey; I only did doubles with models I approved; I wouldn't wear fur, period; and, finally, I didn't take any jobs on a location where there was snow. I wasn't going anywhere cold.

No wonder the Terrible Twins was now our moniker. As Ann Leslie wrote in 1977, 'Helvin and Hall were known as the "terrible twins" for the terrible fees they charged. For Helvin is a girl who can if the fancy takes her pick up £1,000 for the job ...' As inflation soared in the late seventies so did our fees; soon it was more like £2,500–£3,000 per job. In a sense, Jerry and I paved the way for Linda Evangelista's famous comment about not getting out of bed for less than $10,000. She was given hell for that comment (which has been described as the 'let them eat cake' of the 1990s) but frankly, it was not a huge amount of money in our world. International campaigns were phenomenally well paid and they subsidised the more prestigious jobs, like editorial work for *Vogue*. The flat day rate for modelling for British *Vogue* used to be twenty pounds. Now it's fifty.

Generally, I found it was fun to play with people's preconceptions of how much we were earning. When Clive James came to Paris in 1981 to make a film about the Collections, Jerry and I took him out dancing at the Palace, which was by then the place to go. 'The best thing that happened to me in Paris was going shopping for diamonds with Jerry Hall and going dancing with Marie Helvin,' said Clive James, to camera. Then he turned to me and said, 'So what are you going to do now?'

I said, 'I'm going to go home and count all my money.'

He then turned to Jerry and said, 'And how do you feel?'

To which she replied, 'Rich!'

So there we terrible ones were, Jerry and I, being naughty at Elaine's, having dinner with Michael and Shakira Caine, Michael's publicist and Mia Farrow. Shakira, our friend, was lovely as ever but Mia made it clear she was totally uninterested in talking to me and Jerry. For our part we felt we had met quite enough Hollywood actresses not to be impressed by her. Giggling, we played up our closeness to irritate her a little, perhaps. She sat there under her long blond hair looking very po-faced, and only came to life when Mick Jagger walked into the restaurant and joined us. Mia seemed thrilled to meet him. In fact, as I watched them talking I had a suspicion she was playing footsie with him under the table. Wanting to protect Jerry from this I distracted her with some silly conversation about how a tom cat's penis has barbs on it so when he withdraws from a female cat she screams.

'Only *you* would know that!' said Jerry.

Then Michael Caine interrupted Mick and Mia – 'Excuse me, my dear, I think there's someone you should meet' – and took her across the restaurant to where Woody Allen was sitting, at his usual table right by the restrooms. Jerry and I weren't really interested in Woody Allen – and by the look of it neither was Mia. She seemed to boomerang straight back to Mick's side.

That was my take on the evening, anyway. To read Michael Caine's account of the evening Woody met Mia is to read a totally different story. (He didn't even mention that Jerry and I were there, I might add.) But all of us naturally attach widely varying significance to the same events. What we would all agree on, though, was that at that time there was a dizzying sense of sexual possibility. A chance introduction might easily lead to a scandalous break-up or a ten-year marriage. Everywhere there were random flings and accidental affairs. They say 'the seventies' didn't really begin till 1975 – and by that rationale, that night in 1979 when we all dined at Elaine's, the decade had just gotten into its stride.

Where was Bailey that evening? Off on some far-flung photo shoot, in all probability. We often spent time apart – and felt the corrosive effects of absence on our relationship. Combine absence with the heady sexual atmosphere of the seventies and it was not surprising that we both suffered from sudden and paralysing fits of jealousy.

Bailey was sweet and generous with me, in his way. He just didn't buy me jewellery often. Remember, I was the idiot that didn't want diamonds. (For my entire marriage I didn't have a credit card or a joint account with him. I rarely got paid for any of the work I did with him, and if I needed money, I had to ask him for it.) Sometimes, if I took a job independently from him, I might take my cash from the shoot and buy him something I knew he wanted. When I went on a shoot in Japan I came back having spent all my earnings on a new Contax camera for him; another time I went to Garrard the Queen's jewellers on Regent Street, to buy him the new digital Pulsar watch. There were raised eyebrows in that stuffy jeweller's when I said I wanted to pay cash and I was escorted upstairs where I counted out my five hundred pounds in a combination of dollars, francs and pounds sterling. Bailey reciprocated and bought me a treat: a gorgeous Tiffany necklace and bracelet designed by Elsa Peretti.

The first time I wore them was when we went out to dinner with Nicholas Roeg, the great film director, and his then girlfriend Candy Clark, whom he'd recently directed in *The Man Who Fell to Earth*. She was a very sexy redhead and Bailey started flirting outrageously with her. I was so mad I would have done anything to get at Bailey. Then my opportunity came. 'Oh, I like your bracelet,' she told me.

'Do you?' Bailey said. 'I'll buy you one.'

'Don't bother,' I said with a glassy smile. 'Have this one. Go on. Take it. It's nothing to me.'

I put the bracelet in her hand and walked straight out of the restaurant, accompanied by my friend who was also dining with us. In another act of rebellion against Bailey, we went and got stoned on Primrose Hill together. Again, I had failed to face up to a problem in my marriage; instead, I had simply run away. I had no voice to tell Bailey how I felt. I found it easier to punish him – and Candy, though she wasn't to blame – with an act of twisted generosity. What a mess.

Candy Clark rang me the next day to say she couldn't possibly take my bracelet, but I insisted she keep it. It was tainted for me by that time.

Bailey's jealousy had a different character, being very vocal. He could be harsh and frightening, but at least he didn't simply walk out on me – he gave me something to respond to. The angriest he has even been with me was one night in Paris when my sister Naomi and I went out with Mick and Jerry and Johnny Pigozzi. We dined at La Coupole and then we piled back to Jerry and Mick's room at the George V, had a few drinks, then Naomi and I went chastely home to our hotel and by midnight we were tucked up in bed, chatting. The phone went. It was Bailey, in a furious rage. Where had I been? What had I been doing with Mick? Was I fooling around with him?

Nothing I could say would persuade him he was being irrational. No matter how many times I explained that Jerry had been out with us too, he wouldn't let it go. I even put Naomi on to him, but nothing would pacify him. Around three a.m. I hung up; he rang back; I hung up. When he rang again Naomi hissed, 'Don't answer it!' but I did. I desperately wanted to placate my husband. When Naomi and I flew back to London early the next morning as planned my eyes were puffed up from crying.

The strange thing was that Bailey had nothing to worry about from Mick. He never made a move on me, and I wouldn't have fooled around with him for the world. It was a classic case of misplaced anxiety. The person Bailey really should have worried about was another of his best friends: Jack Nicholson.

I was always surprised by the way he pursued me, because I assumed men were like women in that loyalty would – in most cases – prevent them making a play for their best friend's partner. But evidently not. Jack (who, by this time, had split with Anjelica, who was now going out with Ryan O'Neal) was a great friend to me and Bailey, but when Bailey was away he would raise the stakes a little, taking me out for dinner *à deux* at Langan's, San Lorenzo, Mr Chow's. He was an incorrigible flirt, and I admit I found his attention flattering. Round at the home of our mutual friends, Martin and Nona Summers, he would tell the table, 'You have no idea how crazy I am about Marie!' Everyone would just laugh it off, but he would continue: 'Ab-so-lute-ly craaazy!' Perhaps he was just doing it for dramatic effect; perhaps the fact that he knew I would never go behind Bailey's back with him meant that I was the perfect flirting material – always out of reach. These incidents threw me a little, even though I always had a lot of fun with Jack. By this time, 1980, I had discovered cocaine. Halfway through dinner I would be handed a neat little vial of powder and I'd disappear to the ladies for a hedonistic hit. Wow! What a stimulant. But I didn't know how to handle it. Instead of washing out my nostrils like a pro I would wake up in the morning with my nose blocked solid, and go straight to my driving lesson where I'd pretend to have a cold.

'Oh dear, are you bunged up again then?' my geeky driving instructor would solicitously enquire, and then go back to trying to rid me of my sloppy Hawaiian driving habits.

When Jack started filming *The Shining* I used to go and visit him on set at Elstree. As they filmed the famous scene of Jack typing nonsense in the huge lobby of the hotel, I was standing silently behind Stanley Kubrick, trying not to even breathe. It was great going on set but I was always very careful not to distract anyone.

The next day Jack persuaded me to take a screen test for the film. I stood leaning at the ghostly hotel bar and exchanged some lines of dialogue with Kubrick. Bearded, inscrutable and totally absorbed in looking into the camera, Kubrick simply nodded and said, 'Thank you.' I didn't get the job – but when I saw the film, I noticed that there was no part that seemed to correspond with the one I'd auditioned for. In fact, there were barely any women in the film; I decided the role I must have been up for was the beautiful woman in the bath, who turns into a hideous old hag before your eyes. It had been a close escape.

Jack said Kubrick wanted to keep me on his files for a possible future project that was going to be very sexy. I did have a call back from his office about ten years later but it was for a semi-nude role so I turned it down. I can only imagine he was referring to *Eyes Wide Shut*. I think I had another near escape there too.

But the dynamic on the set of *The Shining* made me uncomfortable, because Jack and Stanley Kubrick seemed to be so hostile to Jack's onscreen wife, Shelley Duvall. They were forever excluding her on set. She was so miserable she bought herself a little Bichon Frisé to keep her company. My heart went out to her and I tried to be really friendly to her. Little did I realise that it was all part of Kubrick's directorial plan. It worked, sure enough – she gave a riveting, terrifying performance in the role, so different to her previous comedic work – but still, I always felt this method approach to directing was a little cruel.

Jack never took *The Shining* home with him and threw fabulous dinners in his temporary house on the Chelsea Embankment, where his great cook would entertain crowds of different people, from the theatre producer Michael White (who had produced everything from *Oh! Calcutta!* to *The Rocky Horror Show* to *Ain't Misbehavin'*) to the dazzling Michael Crichton (far too handsome to be a writer) to the tall, cold Sigourney Weaver (who was wearing a jumpsuit and brimming over with tales about some freaky horror film she was working on, which turned out to be *Alien*). All the prettiest girls in London would come, and sometimes the prettiest girls in Paris too. But at the same time he was also desperately trying to get back with Anjelica.

'Why won't Toots come over?' he would complain (he always called her Toots).

'You don't think it could possibly be because she knows what's going on here?' I retorted.

A conversation that sticks in my mind was a debate about the book *Being There*, by Jerzy Kosinski, who was an author Bailey and I adored and had met in New York. I argued for it; Jack was against.

'It's unfilmable,' he declared. It went on to be Peter Sellers's last great filmic achievement, directed by Hal Ashby.

Going round to Jack's was a pleasure, and he was always charming, especially to me. I admit I fantasised about having a fling with him. I believe such fantasies are healthy, in their way. I would never have gone there, though, because as far as I was concerned he was always, first of all, a friend of my husband. Bailey was still the one and only man in my life.

One year for Bailey's birthday I plotted a secret party. I took over the top floor of Mr Chow's and filled it with his friends. They assembled there at eight-thirty; at nine p.m. I arrived with Bailey for what he thought was a quiet supper *à deux*. As we clambered up the stairs to the top floor, all we heard was a muffled attempt at silence and the intriguing sound of someone whistling the 'Colonel Bogey' (like all his male friends, Bailey loved the movie *The Bridge on the River Kwai*). 'What's going on?' said Bailey, and rounded the corner to see Terry Donovan's big beautiful face whistling and all his friends clapping him. I love surprising people: not telling my mom I'm coming home and then turning up out of the blue; things like that. And I particularly loved surprising Bailey. Like many men who are always in control, he enjoyed having that control wrested away from him. I took a risk that night, but it sure paid off.

Womb

'MAYBE WE NEEDED A BABY – Model Marie Speaks Out'. That headline in the *News of the World*, printed the year we split up, appals and amuses me in equal measure.

I have never felt a strong maternal impulse; kids have never been what I wanted or needed. I prize independence, solitude and adult conversation too much. When people ask if all the pets Bailey and I had at Primrose Hill were child substitutes I always scoff at their amateur psychology. We just loved animals. If I see that sweet, trusting expression of love and tail wagging furiously, I'm lost.

I never felt any pressure to have children; my parents never hinted that they wanted grandchildren; in fact, none of my siblings ever started a family. We tend to prefer cats. My sister Suzon was so determined she would never want children she even went so far as to voluntarily have her tubes tied. She was convinced she would adopt a huge brood, and went to great lengths to convince the doctors at Berkeley University in California that she was a good candidate for the operation. My mom even had to sign papers for her because she was then just in her early twenties. The culture – and possibly the genetic inheritance – in my family is simply not conducive to children.

But there was a brief moment in the late seventies when Bailey and I did consider having a baby. Crazy as it sounds, this was more to please Jerry than for any deeper reason.

'Marie, darling, we'll have babies together and it'll be so much fun!' She persuaded me, with her great force of character, that we should both get pregnant at the same time. It was sweet and genuine, this idea, and it would have been lovely if only I'd shared her opinion that a life without babies was only half a life. It was also a little like a variation on our favourite American pastime, double dating.

I decided to put the matter in the hands of fate, and came off the pill for six months, strictly no more and no less. During that time my period was late and I must admit that when I told him, Bailey was very excited. He never told me he wanted a child though; given that he went on to have three gorgeous kids of his own, he must have been broody, deep down. But my late period was only a false alarm, and when the six months were up I was, truth be told, tremendously relieved that I hadn't become pregnant. I went straight back on the pill.

Jerry made me godmother to her first-born, Elizabeth Scarlett, who was without question the most beautiful baby I have ever seen (and has now become a dazzling model). But after holding her I was always delighted to head home and be alone again. I worry about the safety and welfare of those close to me, and if I had kids my worry-o-meter would have gone off the scale. I would have been one of those moms who are constantly waiting up late and phoning and texting. I've never been easy with babies, their mess and their smelly burps and gurgles, and I stayed pretty hands-off as a godmother until she was about six. In fact I haven't always been a perfect godparent. There is a rumour that at the christening of one of my goddaughters, Evi-Elli LaValle, at the Brompton Oratory I tried to light up a cigarette, which sounds dangerously true to me. Perhaps I can just blame my father's militant atheism, which meant I forgot for the briefest of moments that smoking is not customarily permitted when you're sitting in the front pew in church ...

They say that all female emotions are centred in your womb, and perhaps it was a sign of an underlying deep unhappiness that I began to have real trouble there. I was in and out of the Portland Hospital for Women all the time.

Perhaps I was now paying the price now for some damage done to me when I had the abortion in Japan. Having it was absolutely the right thing to do and I have no regrets about it – but I do wonder if the operation wasn't bungled in some way. 'If you're going to have children, you'd better do it soon,' my doctor told me. I looked deep inside myself, but nope. I couldn't find any maternal urges.

I love my single life and the fact that I can conserve all my energy for me. When I tell journalists this they frequently misunderstand. 'I have no children. I'm not married. I don't have anyone living with me, so I have less stress,' I once said, explaining why I had fewer wrinkles than might be expected in someone my age. Allison Pearson in the *Evening Standard* said that while this was 'dangerously enviable' it was also 'the saddest declaration of independence' that she'd ever heard. But Barbara Ellen of the *Observer* took the opposite view. She 'got it', in fact: 'A little while ago Marie Helvin became my new favourite celebrity by dint of a gloriously frank interview she gave about the importance of women grabbing back some "me" time and refusing to spend their entire lives pandering to the needs of their men, their children ... Bad Marie. Naughty Marie. Selfish Marie. But Feminist Marie, too. The best kind of feminist: a woman who is happy.'

*

Over time, I began to become familiar with the concept of the English eccentric. In Hawaii the only eccentric I had ever met was a photographer for *Young Hawaii* magazine who never, ever took his Ray-Bans off and called himself Cosmo Propellor. Later in England I had the pleasure of meeting Stephen Tennant, one of the original Bright Young Things and now in his eighties and living in decaying splendour in his family seat in Wiltshire. I went along when Nicky Haslam our great friend and the then social editor of *Ritz* magazine and Bailey called in at Wilsford Manor to interview and photograph him for the magazine. We found the aged aesthete lying fully dressed on an unmade bed, wearing bright blue eyeshadow, rouge and powder and baggy khaki shorts, the better to display his famously beautiful legs.

I could see he had painted his legs with brown pancake make-up, which had come off on the sheets, so I told him how he should use designated body make-up for his legs instead – a suggestion he seemed delighted by. We chatted about make-up some more and then he showed me his diaries, full of beautiful handwriting and tiny sketches, including a lovely one of Josephine Baker that he said he had drawn from life in her dressing room. Bailey persuaded him to pose on the landing so he walked there, with a little difficult, and reclined gracefully on a rackety armchair pointing his toes for Bailey.

Meanwhile I had popped into the bathroom, where I found the sink and bath full of shells in coloured water. Stephen liked preserving their colour that way (and had in fact shown Gertrude Stein how to do it in 1937). It was delightfully impractical, his bathroom, more of a fairy grotto than a place to wash.

On our way to Wilsford Manor we had stopped off to have lunch at Reddish House with Cecil Beaton, now more infirm after a stroke. Cecil and I sat in the sun in his conservatory, surrounded by open African lilies and their overpowering smell, he in his wheelchair, me dying in the heat and trying to make conversation. Out of the blue he asked, 'Have you ever heard of Patti Smith, my dear?'

I said, 'Yes, indeed, I've read she thinks she is reincarnated from the poet Arthur Rimbaud.'

Bailey arrived in the conservatory at this moment and overheard the last words of the conversation. 'Only Marie could sit with Cecil Beaton and try and talk to him about the Rambo movies.' Cecil looked at him disdainfully, giving him the old *maka-ele-ele* look, Beaton-style.

In the early seventies I often worked with Zandra Rhodes, whose hot pink hair, heavy Egyptian eye make-up and three eyebrows meant she was often referred to as an eccentric. However in person I always found her steady and kind, not obviously wacky at all. Though all her signature pink was a vivid statement, she wasn't a far-out designer either. Erroneously bracketed with the punk movement, in reality she was a lot more tame. People were uncomfortable with real punk anarchists like Vivienne Westwood and Malcolm McLaren and she was a much more convenient, acceptable 'punk'. When Bailey and I did a shoot we had to write 'Vive La Punk' on my chest to tell the story – the clothes alone didn't really do it. But whenever we met she was charming and gentle, picking me up in her Mini to take me to jobs for her. I even went with her to Yugoslavia.

It was a surreal trip. I didn't know I needed a visa for the Eastern bloc and was detained at the airport for about four or five hours. The guards were very glum and cross with me until they received a phone call, and suddenly became all smiles. Word had evidently come through from the top that I could pass through security: 'Marshal Tito says you are an honoured guest,' said one with a deep bow.

The show took place in an enormous hall – God knows what the communist audience made of Zandra's bright pink kaftans – and afterwards we were ferried in a convoy of buses through the darkened streets of Belgrade (no such thing as street lights here) to attend a state banquet. Marshal Tito sat at one end of an impossibly long table, and his wife at the other. Somewhere in the middle I sat opposite Zandra and next to Paco Rabanne, the French avant-garde designer who also became a top perfumier. Just as Paco and I were sipping the thick powdery soup and chatting about space men (his work then as now had an intergalactic theme) her face just collapsed and she sank head-down into her soup. It was weirdly graceful, like a dying swan. Everyone flew into a panic around her and Alex her silkscreen printer and companion was instantly at her side, helping her up and wiping her down. Within minutes she was back to normal, as if nothing had happened, chatting away to the astonished person on her left.

It emerged that she had simply fallen asleep at the dinner table; she was suffering from a mild form of narcolepsy. It never seemed to affect her or her work and I continued modelling for her for years. But after that incident I somehow always thought of an excuse when she came to pick me up in her Mini.

Five or so years after our trip Tito died of a heart attack, and then Yugoslavia split up into its constituent countries. Our fashion trip was a glimpse into a regime now vanished.

I had an experience of the Soviet bloc proper when I went to Berlin on a shoot with Pat Cleveland and Mounia, the black model from Martinique whom Yves Saint Laurent adored. After our fashion show in West Berlin, I came up with an idea. 'Let's go across the border, girls!' I felt we should grab the opportunity as we would probably never get another chance. At the American side of Checkpoint Charlie they were friendly and let us through, but on the Russian side they took issue with our handbags. They went through everything: all our cosmetics, our compacts, our lipsticks, books and magazines and temporarily confiscated them. They gave Mounia an especially hard time. She fought back and told them they were being racist; they didn't understand what she was saying. Already our little excursion into Soviet territory was turning into a drama.

When we finally got through to the other side, it was like going into a dark room. It was only three p.m. and we were in the heart of the city, but there seemed to be no lights; the buildings were blacked out and very high. We walked past the Brandenburg Gate and down the wide boulevard of Unter den Linden. It was totally deserted: no cars, no people. We passed a couple of shops that were closed up. I started to get nervous we would lose our way. Finally in this total greyness we saw a light – a coffee shop. We walked in and the noisy hubbub inside died. The café went completely silent. Everyone stared at us. We must have looked like a strange trio, I'll admit. Gradually, however, people began to approach us and were friendly. They wanted whatever we had in our handbags, but because of the officious customs men at the border we had nothing to give them, only cigarettes.

Hastening to get home before nightfall, we crept away back to the side of the world that we knew. I wanted to send a memory of our crazy Berlin trip home to my father, and I knew he loved black rye bread, so I sent him a huge loaf in a care package. Months later, he said to me on the phone: 'Marie, a big hunk of mould has just arrived with a Berlin postmark on it. Could it be from you, honey?'

SEVEN

SUZON

'Who looks outside, dreams; who looks inside, awakes.'

JUNG

*O*n the surface everything was just wonderful. I lived in a bubble of perfection. I was happy, successful and known in all the fashion capitals. I was 'the girl everyone wanted to look like', according to the *Sunday Mirror* in 1977 – not that I was particularly interested in what they wrote. My marriage had its ups and downs but there were more of the former than the latter; we shared a sweet intimacy and simple contentment. I didn't think about Bailey's infidelities, determined that what I didn't know wouldn't hurt me. I supported pioneering anti-vivisection charities; the 'Beauty Without Cruelty' campaign; and I worked with Linda McCartney on the anti-fur movement; I worked for Amnesty on women's abortion rights issues; and I helped to launch a charity called WomanKind with Jane Lapotaire. I was forever parading in front of the House of Commons with animal rights petitions. ('This is not a sentimental issue,' I earnestly told the press. 'The issue is about our humanity and morality.') I used my profile to publicise worthy causes; I had creative fulfilment and professional recognition. I felt as if I was in a really good place. Then something happened that was so terrible it forced me to reassess everything, from my marriage to my spirituality. The gilded bubble of my life burst.

For a while, I had been a little worried about my sister Suzon. She had fallen in love with a guy called Jesse and the two of them had been doing the hippie trail together between Bali, Jamaica and Goa. Su and I wrote to each other often and I would be excited to spot her mail, which I knew by the postmark, the distinctive turquoise ink and the cute way she turned her dots into flowers. Then a letter arrived from her that seemed a little groggy. She repeatedly wrote that she was ill, really ill. I wrote straight back asking her to call me collect from the post office in Bali or wherever she was. I felt convinced something wasn't right with her.

Su brought out all my protectiveness. Her nature was so sweet and gentle that people often took advantage of her or were mean to her. Once when we were shopping in the mall as a family we noticed a terrible commotion. Su was being chased by a furious security guard. She was only eight years old or so but she was evidently about to be sent to jail. Why? In her little fist she was holding a tiny terrapin, as big as a fifty-pence piece. She was sobbing her heart out and Pop shouted at the security guard for scaring her so much. You always just wanted to put your arms round Su and make her safe.

Later when she started school the local tough girls called *tiidas* bullied her because she was so pretty and trusting. I – always the streetwise elder sister – bribed them off with True cigarettes I'd stolen from my parents.

Soon enough Su came to stay with me and Bailey in London. She was her usual bright self, gorgeous and blonde and tanned, running round the house asking everyone, 'Would you like a cuppa tea?' When I asked her why she'd been feeling ill she laughed. She said she'd discovered she had been dosed up on tranquillizers. Suzon was, true to family form, a health nut who always took a lot of vitamin supplements, but someone had exchanged her ginseng and her vitamins for these tablets, downers that were meant to make you feel sexy and mellow. 'That explains why I had a peacock tattoo done coming out of my pussy!'

I laughed with her, but I also tried to tell her to take care. I knew she was young and carefree and I didn't want to spoil her fun but I have always felt, as the eldest, a sense of responsibility towards my siblings. Caring for them had been instilled in me from an early age. I felt like Bailey's mother Glad when I waved her off at the airport. 'Mind how you go, Su!' It breaks my heart to remember this was the last time I saw her.

A few months later, out to dinner after a French *Vogue* shoot in Paris, Bailey and I had a terrible fight. I don't even remember what it was about. I just felt nothing was right. We left the restaurant without eating and went home to the apartment in the place du Palais Bourbon, where I felt a most unusual urge: I wanted to get drunk. To drink myself into oblivion. There wasn't any alcohol in the flat except ornamental bottles of vodka we'd been given, which had fruit pickled inside them. I took one with me into the bathroom and drank till I was sick. I never drank spirits; this was very out of character for me. I spent the night on the bathroom floor.

Late the next afternoon we flew back to London, Bailey taciturn and angry with me for getting drunk, me washed out and hungover. At Primrose Hill I went through my mail – and my heart leaped when I saw a package with a Jamaican postmark. I thought it would be something from Su. I opened it up, and inside there was a pair of worn old brown boots. They looked like Suzon's kind of style, but there was no letter or anything with them ... They remain, in fact, a mystery to this day. As I considered these boots, the lights in the room flickered out and the house fell into darkness. A fuse had blown. Bailey tramped downstairs to the basement to switch the trip back on, while I sat there in the dark with the boots. I tried them on; they were a perfect fit. They must belong to Suzon, I decided, as we had almost the same size feet. I was still sitting in the gloom wearing the boots when the phone rang.

It was the call you never forget, the call you dread more than anything. It was Jesse, Suzon's boyfriend. He was hysterical. 'Suzon's dead. Suzon's dead,' he kept repeating. I couldn't take it in. I wanted it not to be true so much that I said, 'You mean Susanna Moore?' I feel so guilty for saying that now, because Susanna Moore, the author, was a dear friend of mine, but I was clutching at straws, hoping that it wouldn't be my little sister he was talking about.

'No, Suzon, Suzon,' he said. 'She fell over a cliff. She's dead.'

After he put the phone down I wanted to collapse into hysteria but I had to control myself. I needed to make the hardest phone calls of my life: I had to ring both my parents – separately, because they were living apart at the time – and my sister Naomi and tell them that Suzon was dead.

I don't know how I got through the night. I verged between hysteria and total blankness – almost catatonia. Bailey gave me a sleeping pill, but I don't know if it was the real thing. Concerned he was taking too many his doctor and I had recently sneakily exchanged some of his pills for placebos. The period that followed is vivid yet blurry in my memory. Time, which had seemed to go on slowly while Bailey stomped down the stairs to the fuse box, now raced. There were so many phone calls. My poor parents were too shocked, and grief-stricken to be able to do anything so it fell to me to organise everything. How was I to deal with this situation, which was, to put it bluntly, a dead body in a foreign land? I didn't know. How could we get Suzon's body back from Jamaica to Honolulu? We became mired in red tape and maddening official proscriptions from the Jamaican government. No one would let us transport the body. In despair I turned to Bailey's good friend John Pringle, a white Jamaican (who had been equerry to the Duke of Windsor and was related to Chris Blackwell who founded Island Records). He was a godsend and contacted his cousin Frank Pringle, the mayor of Montego Bay, who helped us coordinate the tortuous procedure of identification and cremation. Naomi arrived the next day from Morocco, where she was living with her husband, the French political attaché; everything after that was tickets and planes and grief, heart-wrenching grief. Our golden sister had died at the age of twenty-three.

I look back upon this period with so much regret and self-reproach. We were told that Suzon, who was living in a hippie commune with Jesse in Negril, had been out cycling, that her bicycle had skidded and that she had gone over a cliff, a drop of about fifteen feet. She had suffered head injuries, and lain there for hours before being found by Jesse. She was airlifted to Montego Bay – there being no hospital in Negril – and was declared brain dead on arrival. In our blind grief we accepted the whole story without demur. We never stopped to ask if there should be an inquest or investigation. We never thought that she might be an easy target – I am haunted now to think of how conspicuous she must have looked wearing that turquoise velvet Yves Saint Laurent skirt I gave her, and those gold Manolos. She would have really stuck out in Negril. We were all really fond of Suzon's boyfriend Jesse, and we accepted his account of the events unquestioningly. But we didn't push things. We believed her death was accidental. The mayor of Montego Bay and also the American Consul General personally assured me in a phone call that this was the truth, and accepting it was the right thing to do. That I gave in so easily is a great source of guilt to me now, but at the time I had enough to do just trying to get through a phone call without bursting into tears.

Naomi and I spent what felt like days on the long flights from London to Hawaii, talking about Suzon and crying. Suzon had been cremated in Jamaica and my mother and father and I had to go and collect her ashes from Honolulu airport. We drove in my father's Lincoln Continental, the same model that Elvis had owned, which was painted gold with diamond studs on the windows, so people always watched us as we went by. This time everyone in the car was sobbing. It used to give me a thrill to ride in, but that day it was just a car.

Grief makes you hypersensitive: as the man at the airport banged the box containing the urn roughly down in front of me I felt it jarring deep within my soul. Cradling the urn in the car on the way home my crying was out of control. But when we arrived at home no one else in my family could bear to deal with the urn. It fell to me to carry it into the house, but there I could find nowhere to put it. The hall was too casual, the bookcase too exposed, the kitchen table grotesque. Death did not fit in our house.

To spare my parents the agony of seeing the urn, I took it with me into my bedroom. Here I put it on my dressing table. But I couldn't stop looking at it, so, in desperation I searched for somewhere safe to put it ... Where? I am ashamed to say I put it in my closet and closed the shuttered doors. Tragedy, as they say, is always a step away from farce.

The funeral was packed: we had put a notice in the newspaper and about two hundred of her friends turned up. Because of my father's strict atheism it was a non-religious service; the only reading was a poem I chose from *The Prophet* by Kahlil Gibran, which I knew Su loved.

We scattered her ashes from a small boat on a stretch of ocean near Moanalua Bay. Here, farce punctured the grief again: I squabbled with my brother Steve when he refused to wear the plumeria lei I'd had made for him. He was a teenager; he hated everything. I should have let it go but under such circumstances one's grief and anger get transferred on to loved ones. Finally at the crucial moment of the boat trip, when the ashes were meant to be scattered, my mother couldn't get the container open. An urn doesn't come with instructions. To open it she started banging it against the side of the boat, without success.

'What am I to do?' she wailed.

One of us said, 'Throw it over!'

Another said, 'Scatter them!'

And our tears turned to laughter for a moment, and then the pain returned even more sharply as her spirit soared across the waves. It was the first time I had ever seen my father cry.

I think of Suzon every time I drive past the bay where her ashes lie – we all do. I know that this is where I will come to rest and join her one day in the future. This thought gives me great comfort. It makes me feel safe – it's the one thing that can't be taken away from me.

When we got home everyone who had attended the service was waiting on our *lanai*, expecting, wanting, needing a wake. It was too much for my father to cope with and he disappeared. My mother, Naomi, Steve and I then began several days of sitting around, crying, talking about Suzon and crying some more. Our friends and neighbours, assuming we'd be too stricken to cook for ourselves, brought round Tupperware tubs of food. But we just wanted to be alone, to share our grief and to talk about our lost girl.

Where was Bailey during all this? He didn't come to the funeral, as he had a job shooting a commercial for Mary Quant cosmetics. Naomi's husband Gérard didn't come either, but he hadn't even met Suzon. Bailey, on the other hand, had got to know her quite well over the years. Much as his absence hurt me, I also felt relieved in a sense that he wasn't there for our long days of intimate grieving at home. He wouldn't have known what to do with himself. I couldn't see him sitting around with us eating ice-cream, reminiscing about the time Suzon said this or did that.

Of the family, Mom was the last to have seen her. They had got up to all sorts of mischief, going out drinking cocktails together, driving back home tipsy and getting pulled over by the police. Mom had been about to be breathalysed but Suzon had said, 'What do you think you're doing? She's my mom!' Her confidence worked wonders – the police apologised and let them go.

On another occasion during Suzon's last visit she and Mom had got stoned together; it was such strong stuff that Mom took a shower that lasted two hours. Our laughter soon dissolved into tears.

Perhaps Bailey also had his own reasons for staying away. The same tragedy had also hit his previous marriage: Catherine Deneuve lost her sister Françoise Dorléac in a car crash. He must have had a horrible sense of déjà vu. Still, Bailey was fantastic to me in his own way. He quite rightly figured that after the funeral in Honolulu I would need some time away.

I flew to LA and met Bailey; then we flew to Mérida in Mexico where we hired a car and drove, drove, drove, right down to the Yucatán. The landscape was an arid desert and the hotels grew seedier every stop we made. But it gave me space and silence, and that was what I needed and Bailey knew it. Beneath the brash abruptness, he is a very sensitive man; spiritual too, in a sense. He was very patient with me, no matter how angry I was. My grief had passed to that stage at which you lash out at anyone close you, and Bailey was my target. I let the fact that he hadn't come to Suzon's funeral grow out of all proportion, till it became a crime. I must have been a difficult wife to handle: nervy, fractious, on edge, and inwardly deeply grieving. A death puts great strain on a relationship.

We worked on that holiday too – believe it or not. We shot a job for *Harpers & Queen*. Death, a disaster, a tsunami: nothing could come between Bailey and his camera. I pulled myself together and you would never know what state I was in to look at the pictures, though my eyes are shielded, semi-closed.

Finally we came to settle in Chichén Itzá, where we found a beautiful hacienda. Here we were able to relax, and explore the ruins of the Mayan temples, those ancient geometric megaliths that point into the sky. Bailey and I set out to climb the very tallest – it was just unfortunate that we got to the very top before I realised I suffered from vertigo. The summit of a Mayan monument designed to help you touch the sun is not a good place to make this discovery. 'Help!' I cried feebly, my head spinning, but Bailey was already racing down the other side ahead of me. I had to grip on for dear life with sweaty palms and take it one step at a time. I descended from that temple backwards as slowly as a sloth. Bailey was waiting for me for what must have seemed like hours. 'Hurry UP!' he called to me. 'It's getting DARK!'

On our way home we flew to LA to see Michael and Tina Chow, who were wonderfully sympathetic with me. They had loved Suzon as well and they were heartbroken too. But already I was beginning to withdraw into myself, into a twilit, depressive state. For the next two years I carried on doing modelling jobs and saw my friends but I had lost all my certainty, my *joie de vivre*. The Marie I once was died along with Suzon. I knew that I would never regain my innocence – that was gone.

*

'The tragedy of a man's life is what dies inside of him while he lives.'

HENRY DAVID THOREAU

'Sadness is not painful, it's trying not to feel sad that hurts.'

What do you do after a death affects you so profoundly? You cope. Or perhaps, especially when it's the first death of a loved one you've ever experienced in your life, you don't cope. Back at home I couldn't bear to go into the spare room where Suzon used to stay. It was so full of her presence that I found it overwhelming. I didn't tell anyone about this, least of all Bailey. My friends tiptoed around me and tried not to mention my family for fear of reminding me about Suzon and upsetting me. They were only doing what they thought best. But what I needed was different: I needed to learn how to let go of her death and remember her life.

Bailey and I never really spoke about Suzon. His instinct too was to shy away from death and to suppress it, though he did once bravely overcome this. I was running down to take him a cup of coffee in his darkroom one evening when, instead of following usual form and sticking his hand round the darkroom door, accepting the coffee and shutting the door again, he emerged out of the room and sat me down. 'Marie, darling,' he said. 'I went into the spare room today. Suzon's spirit is there. But it's good. It's her essence in there and it's all positive. Going in there is a way of keeping close to her.'

I burst into tears, and was very moved by how intuitive he had been in saying this to me. It helped – but I needed more help.

Perhaps I should have sought out a therapist or a bereavement counsellor, but in 1978 these roles weren't widely known about or understood. I chanced upon a book by Elisabeth Kübler-Ross which taught me a lot about the psychological, spiritual and emotional effects of grief. As I read about the different stages of mourning – anger, denial, bargaining, acceptance – I recognised my own experiences. At last, I felt understood. I still really needed to talk about Suzon, yet no one was willing to go there with me. Instead I dwelt on her death in silence, internalising it and brooding on it until my mind began to be affected. I started seeing vivid photographic images of my family, with Suzon missing, or Bailey missing. Sometimes it was I who was missing. I became convinced that I, not Suzon, had been meant to die, and that she had taken my place. As a kind of surrogate parent, as eldest children often are, I felt responsible. I shouldn't have let this happen to her. My image of reality became distorted.

Our brains can provide us with ingenious ways of protecting ourselves from the devastating certainty of death. Rather than accepting that I would never see Suzon again, I started thinking that she had not died, but had merely gone into hiding as part of a witness protection programme. In those days you heard a lot about such schemes in America and I truly believed that one day soon she would contact us. I still sometimes need to check myself from continuing this fantasy. It has been hard for me to keep grounded about her death, to gain perspective on it. I am not fully healed.

My family simply descended into communal denial, trying not to dwell on her because it was too painful. To this day, if her name comes up, my father's face ages by about a thousand years and he leaves the room. My mother and I do talk about her, but not in depth. We say: Oh, I had a dream about her the other day, or Hey, wouldn't Suzon love that film, but it's only ever on the surface, and doesn't go to the heart of her. When my mother dreams about Suzon, she always appears to her as a little girl, but it causes her so much pain to talk about that I try to do it as little as possible. Naomi finds it difficult too. Though I consider myself agnostic, my family is guided by atheist principles and we are not cemetery-goers; we don't have a fixed memorial to her. But her essence remains on the island, and when we drive past the bay we all turn and smile and say our private greetings. She is always with us. Occasionally, when I see a beautiful sky, at dawn or dusk, or a tree's leaves stirring in a certain way, or if I am woken by a bird singing in the middle of the night, I feel touched by her.

Alone in Britain I was left to come to terms with her death in whatever way I could. Over the years I have been to see two mediums.

They usually tell me that her death wasn't an accident, but that nevertheless I still have to let it go. If only they could help me do so. They have been beneficial in their way but I sometimes find the things they say outlandish. I asked one medium why Suzon stopped coming to me in my dreams when she used to appear frequently, giving me such clear advice that I sat up from sleep with her voice echoing in my head. The medium replied that Suzon was spending a lot of time with children at the moment, and that the reason she didn't come into my dreams was that she couldn't find the time. She was really far too busy helping small children cross over. I was either going to laugh or cry. I think you can guess which I did.

Over the years I have also tried contacting Suzon's friends and asking them about her life with Jesse. When Bailey and I went to Bali we looked up one or two of them and reminisced about her. At other times talking about Suzon has not been so happy. Once I was out on a date at the nightclub Tramp with Dodi Fayed when a woman came up to me and said, 'You don't know who I am, but I was an air stewardess for Air Jamaica and I visited the same hippie compound as Suzon …' She started telling me how Su liked to smoke ganja, and I felt more clearly than ever that she had been high when she died, and burst into floods of tears in the middle of Tramp. Dodi was furious with the woman for upsetting me, but I really needed to know everything I could if I was going to lay her to rest.

I was still looking for succour from the pain of Suzon's death in 1999, when I read in the newspaper that the Tibetan Buddhists of Samye Ling had bought Scotland's Holy Island in order to set up an inter-faith centre there. I was instantly attracted. I have much empathy with the Tibetan Buddhist faith and besides, at heart, I'm a girl that belongs on an island, whether it's in the North Sea or the balmy Pacific. I need the ocean and the sky.

So I rang the number advertised for more details, hoping to make a kind of pilgrimage there as part of my ongoing process of coming to terms with Suzon's death. A Buddhist nun called Rinchen Khandro took my call, and I immediately warmed to her calm, gentle voice.

A few days later she sent me some particulars about the island, as well as a note that asked if I was the M. Helvin who was a model and had a sister called Suzon? For she, Rinchen, had lived for a while in the same hippie commune in Negril. Rinchen, before becoming a Buddhist nun had lived a previous life as a hippie; and there she had been friends with Suzon. I was moved and astounded. As a coincidence it was right up there in the premier league. In fact, it went deeper than coincidence – it was one of those moments when you feel you are being guided by a benign force.

Rinchen had a sister called Shirley who also died young, which took our connection deeper still. To top it all off, Rinchen had moved in the same circles as Bailey in Paris in the sixties and vaguely knew him. I planned to visit her on the island with renewed urgency.

I flew to Scotland, and from there to Arran, where I took a small boat with Lama Yeshe who welcomed me to the island. There I met Rinchen finally and fell into her arms. We stayed overnight in a lighthouse keeper's cottage where we dined on vegetable broth and fresh bread, and I slept on the floor in Rinchen's room with two other nuns. In the daytime we went our own ways and meditated in the craggy rocks and unspoilt caves. Tibetan Buddhist philosophy teaches that from the moment we are born we begin to die, and, sitting in front of the wild sea, I learned to feel this as well as know it.

Before we left the island Rinchen and I planted two cherry trees in memory of our sisters. There, where a clear spring bubbles up, we gave them a ceremonial spadeful of seaweed compost and a silent prayer. As the fresh wind blew over the sea I felt a sense of release. 'I swear I just heard Suzon say, *Me ke aloha pumehana*", which is Hawaiian for "Until we meet again",' I confided to Rinchen.

'How strange,' said Rinchen. 'My sister Shirley just said in pure Mancunian, "About blooming time."'

Rinchen and I kept in touch, until she cut her ties with the world and went off on a silent Buddhist retreat. Before Rinchen left I asked her if there was somewhere I could take her for dinner.

'I've always heard the Ivy restaurant is rather good ...' said this remarkably worldly Buddhist nun. When Rinchen walked in, incredibly beautiful with her shaved head and her stunning habit which looked as if it could have been designed by Gaultier, the whole of the Ivy stopped to admire her.

Rinchen was also close to Annie Lennox, and when I bump into Annie we commiserate about losing our favourite spiritual friend. 'She can't be there for many more years, can she?' Come back soon, Rinchen!

Suzon's death is without a doubt the most monumental thing that ever happened to me. Day to day, it still hurts. When people ask me if I have siblings, for example, it's an uncomfortable exchange. Yes, I have a brother in Hawaii and a sister in Bangkok, but I feel I need to say I also had another sister, but she died. To deny her existence, even in small talk, feels so sad and faithless.

Buddhism teaches that every experience has value, but it was many years before I could begin to take anything positive out of her death at all. If I can today it is simply a keen appreciation of how precious life is, and how transient. The death of a loved one changes your brain chemistry for ever. It brings home to you life's cruel impermanence, its fleeting essence.

Before she died I was spoiled. I was famous, I was pretty; in every snap I'm smiling, wearing a glittery dress with a shiny, happy face. I thought I had it all. But gradually, after her death, I realised those things I had were meaningless. I saw I had been skipping through life, winging my way through on charm. Losing Suzon was a jolt, the first jolt I had ever had, the jolt which said, 'This is your life, this moment that you are living in is now.' It woke me up.

Heart

Was I ever the same again after Suzon's death? I lost my innocence in the sense that I became cautious with my heart. It was as if all my trust had been stolen, and I was left with scars.

The tragedy of her death forced me to rethink everything in my life. Increasingly frustrated and bored by the modelling routine, I went into TV instead. I invested a lot of time in children's charities, which I knew Su would have supported. I became a patron of Plan International, which organises sponsorship of children in the developing world. And I had a long hard look at my marriage. Her death contributed to its demise, because it made me recognise that, while I was alive, I didn't want to settle for second best in anything. This, I gradually came to realise, meant I wanted to be on my own. But first there were a few more milestones for me and Bailey.

EIGHT

TROUBLE AND STRIFE

*'Four be the things I'd been better without: Love, curiosity,
freckles, and doubt.'*

DOROTHY PARKER, *Inventory*

I was a difficult job, but someone had to do it. There I was
stretched out on the sun bed by a pool in Hawaii in a white bikini
with my eyes closed, feeling the sun kissing my face while Bailey
hovered over me with a camera. As his shutter clicked I practised my
favourite yogic-style lung-control exercise, which I call 'the Long
Breath'. This entails inhaling so slowly the air reaches every element
of your body; it's so subtle not even a close observer knows you are
doing it. I found this invaluable for keeping me alert yet at rest – the
paradox on which all good modelling poses are founded. For hours,
all of my body had to look 'aah' – as if I had just exhaled. Maybe it
was a difficult job after all, in its own way. There is an art to being
still; you can't just lie there stiffly, you have to attain an almost
meditative state, which, under pressure and in front of photographer,
crew (and sometimes, on location, gawping crowds) is harder than
it sounds.

I wasn't complaining, though. I was always happy to lie down and
close my eyes for a living. It was my favourite pose, that horizontal
one ... I concentrated on floating on that sun lounger, looking
dreamy while Bailey muttered to himself, 'Yesss, that's lovely ...'

That photo, in which Bailey's shadow lies heavy over the tiles in
front of me, and a hosepipe curls provocatively up towards my sun

bed, eventually became one of my all-time favourites. I think it says so much about our relationship: the dominant male shadow (perhaps Jung would have something to say about that), the inviolate female, lying prone, the sexual motif of the hosepipe ... Maybe it's like a witty modern take on the Garden of Eden: Adam and Eve and the rubber snake uncurling beside us. In that picture for once I love the way my body looks. For one moment in time, it was this perfect body in this perfectly composed photograph.

Whenever I see pictures of myself on covers or in magazines, I'm critical. All models are. My immediate reaction is, 'Oh God, I bet there were better ones.' I can't help being negative – it's the corollary of this job that forces you to relinquish all control. For a strong, thinking woman, this job is a nightmare.

Also it's worth bearing in mind that during the era when Bailey and I were married there was minimal retouching. Bailey was all about grainy, true-to-life reportage. That's why he struck such a contrast with Angus McBean and Cecil Beaton and all the flattering, prettifying photographers of the previous era. Bailey's aesthetic was much more raw and I gave myself over to the honesty of his lens. The camera lies; it has its favourites and fancies. But during my era it told barefaced lies, not flattering half-truths whispered in gauze and glycerine and the retoucher's scalpel. Of course now the pendulum has swung the other way again and digital photographs are routinely retouched. That would have made work easier, but I'm proud to look back now and think that what was mine, was mine. Generally I loved the aesthetic of high seventies photography – the louche, spontaneous sexiness. It was raunchy but it was somehow pure too, not artful. For my work with Bailey I usually did my own hair and make-up – the stylised, polished artifice that characterised eighties photography was all to come.

There are maybe two images from my career that I'm totally happy with, and these I cherish. One is that hosepipe photo, the other is 'The Nude of Marie', which Bailey calls my 'passport' photo, in which I'm nude and facing Bailey from sideways on. It's my left jaw I'm displaying, without a doubt. Perhaps he likes this one more than

I do. He prizes it for its honesty, the way I am so barely presented (in every sense); of our photographs I prefer the ones with richer imagery and visual references, the ones that tell stories.

This one, simply a stark nude, I was critical of when it was taken. I didn't think my body was beautiful. Why didn't somebody tell me? Bailey tried to, I guess, and so did others. 'Marie is much better undressed than dressed,' Nicky Haslam said once. 'She's not at all shy of her own beauty. The thing about Marie's looks is that her eyes are so marvellous that you look at them rather than the body even if she's naked.' What a great compliment.

Bailey said lovely things about me, always. But you never appreciate them until it's too late. 'When I made "The Nude of Marie" we'd been married about four years,' he says. This photograph is so straightforward, it's almost a passport picture. All I did was put a bit of wind on it. The ring light hides nothing. What's there is there.'

*

'Between the concept
And the creation
Between the emotion
And the response
Falls the Shadow'
T.S. ELIOT, *The Hollow Men*

Like a moth to a flame, I was drawn to Bailey's creative light. *Trouble and Strife*, a hardback book that was a photographic album of our marriage, was published in 1980, the year John Lennon died, Akira Kurosawa's epic *Kagemusha* was released and Mrs Thatcher declared herself not for turning. I didn't care whether she turned or not. I was trying to protect myself from a barrage of attention that was directed at the scandalous Mrs Bailey who had allowed herself to be photographed wearing silk stockings and no knickers.

How did this outrageous volume come about? Bailey and I created the images over five years of marriage, and, prior to that, a few months of courtship. They were not taken with the express intent of putting them in a book. As Bailey's studio manager Di James con-firms: 'It wasn't that they were going to do a book called *Trouble and Strife* ... It was just shot at odd weekends and afternoons when nothing was going on ... Bailey can never stop taking photos. His camera is an extension of his right arm.'

Some of the pictures were taken for work – the lacy stockings and other props were usually an advertising commission – but the majority were for our own amusement. When he asked me to put a tea towel over my head and come in with the breakfast things, we were just fooling around in our hotel room in Paris. I had no idea the snaps were going to be for public consumption. I did it lightly, in a spirit of fun, or to get him off my back so I could go out with my sister or my friends. If he needed my body parts, I was happy to comply.

Sometimes it was a matter of helping him test out new techniques or newly acquired equipment, like his favourite old-fashioned plate cameras. Once, carried away by the excitement of a new plate camera, I did the silliest thing in the world. As I was posing, Bailey, looking through the viewfinder, muttered, 'Oh, this is great ... You've got to have a look at this,' so I ran round to his side. Well, whaddaya know, there was nothing for me to see. We often laughed as we worked.

Many of the images in *Trouble and Strife* were taken after a shoot wrapped. It was quite normal for Bailey to clear the set – 'Everyone OUT!' – and photograph me in the same studio set-up, but stripped nude. If I was modelling a Jaeger mac, say, he would finish up the session by asking me, in private, to pull it up and flash my butt for a cheeky supplementary shot. It was easy for me, as easy as it had been posing naked on the beach at Molokai for Shino. It was just something I got used to over the years till it felt like the most natural thing in the world. I'm sure it's the same for every other model who's married to a photographer.

For all the casualness, I should probably have figured these pictures would end up in the public domain. After all, Bailey was permanently working on a book. But when he told me, 'They are photographs I take for myself,' I didn't expect that quote to end up, as it did, on the flyleaf of a coffee-table book.

The first I heard about *Trouble and Strife* was when I came into the studio one day and found him sitting in the middle of the floor, surrounded by prints. He was selecting various photos for the book.

One of them was a truly shocking picture of me laid out in the attic at Primrose Hill, covered in newspaper, my arms bound in rope and only my pubic hair was exposed. 'What's this?!' I gasped. I had posed for it – reluctantly – many months before, and had never seen the full impact of the final image. Somehow he had conveniently forgotten to show me the contact sheets.

It's an incredibly sinister image and even as I posed for it I knew it was in questionable taste. Why did I go along with it? Well, he was not only the top photographer of his age, he was my husband. Also I knew that Bailey didn't have a misogynist bone in his body. The photograph was created not out of hatred but a desire to push boundaries. Referring to *Trouble and Strife*, the photo historian Philip Garner describes Bailey as 'working on the edge of risk'. Ditto the great photographer Don McCullin: 'Bailey tests you, tests the public taste. He wants to know how far he can push the boat out towards the edge of Niagara.'

Still, when I saw the finished picture I thought it demeaned me, and by extension women generally. I look at it now and it gives me the shudders – as well as making me think I needed a Brazilian! I suppose it has come to represent for me the darker side of our marriage. I can almost see an invisible thought bubble emanating from my newspaper-covered head: 'Get me out from under here!'

When I protested against that picture going into the final book, Bailey had a ready answer. 'It's not a book of pretty pictures of Marie,' he said. 'It's a photographic essay on marriage. Therefore it's got to be objective and therefore it can't be you, fish face, who goes about choosing what does and doesn't go into it.'

At least I tried. (To give Bailey his due, there were other occasions when he gave in to my demands about where my pictures appeared. When *PhotoMagazine*, at that time the most prestigious photographic periodical in the world, wanted to put my nude 'passport photo' on their cover I kicked up such a fuss – 'The only magazine I do nudes for is *Vogue*.' – that Bailey withdrew the rights.) The reason I didn't fight any harder over the sinister pussy picture at the end of *Trouble and Strife* was my own stupidity. Right up until publication, I could still barely believe the book was going to be printed. These kinds of books are common now, from Helmut Newton to Taschen publishing. But this was 1980. Books like this – candid, nude, artistic – simply didn't exist in the UK. You were either a haughty fashion plate or a David Hamilton soft porn image. This book, in which nudity was shown engaged with heart and mind, was disconcertingly original for its time.

Trouble and Strife was published with a preface by Jacques Henri Lartigue, an introduction by Brian Clarke and quotes on the dust jacket emphasising their intimacy: 'David Bailey is clearly in love, both with taking pictures and the reality and fantasy of his wife . . .'

The preface by Lartigue was more like a poem:

Avoir pour amour une femme aussi belle, jolie, charmante et troublante que Marie, quelle inspiration pour une artiste.

Avoir pour amour une artiste aussi doué et magnifique photographe que David Bailey, quelle chance pour une adorable femme.

Être le livre contenant le résultat de cette merveilleuse rencontre, quelle certitude pour lui d'être superbe.

The launch party was held at the Ritz, and featured all the familiar faces: Manolo, Amanda Lear, Michael Roberts, Michael and Tina Chow . . . The Ritz's exquisite Marie Antoinette room had a fug of cigarette smoke and chatter clouding its delicate gilt walls as the throng grew: Joan Collins came, beautiful and glamorous as ever (if you looked past the hideous fur hat), although she told me with a wry laugh that she was on the dole. Not long afterwards she would win her part in *Dynasty* in a fabulous reversal of fortune; first, though, she had to get through doing *The Stud* (which Bailey, strange as it may seem, was approached to direct). The talk and the smoke got too much for me and I slipped out of the party briefly, and saw two other guests had also quietly absented themselves and were sitting on the ormolu chairs in the corridor. One was Nicky Haslam, so I darted over to kiss him immediately. But who was his companion? She was a tiny elderly lady with skin so pale it made me think of *o mochi*, the pure white Japanese rice cake. She was elegantly attired in quaint forties style with a hat like an upturned lampshade on her head.

'Marie, this is Lady Diana Cooper.'

She stretched out her hand very graciously towards me, and I bowed my head. She seemed so fragile – she was eighty-eight years old, but Nicky told me, 'She knows exactly who you are, darling. She reads *Vogue* avidly.'

Next the reviews of *Trouble and Strife* started to come out. Some were lovely: 'Marie is always elegant, even in the occasional comic poses,' wrote Rupert Martin in the *Photographer's Gallery* magazine. 'The book may be, as Brian Clarke states in his introduction, "a ransom against time", but it is certain that whatever happens to the outward and visible Marie, the elegance and essential sweetness of her nature will remain.' Sir Kenneth Clark, author of the landmark series *Civilisation*, wrote an approving piece in a magazine, in which he said I was timeless, as did Clive James. It's not hard for men to see the best in books of female nudes. But I was bracing myself for an onslaught of feminist criticism. The women's movement was very powerful at that time and I feared their condemnation. It never quite came.

There were some snidey comments – I was so possessed by Bailey, apparently, that every inch of me was his to flaunt and photograph. There were letters to the papers: *Trouble and Strife* consisted of nothing but Ms Helvin photographed in the nude from a number of angles. 'If it was my husband, it would make me wonder what he valued about me most,' huffed Disgusted of Hitchin, Herts. I was a 'subservient, willing young wife', according to some journalists – but generally I was let off the hook by women writers whose attitude might roughly be summed up in the phrase: 'You go, girl!' Emma Soames wrote a full-page editorial in the *Evening Standard* in support of the book with the strapline 'Good Girls Don't, Bad Girls Do, This Girl Does'. The piece concluded that I might never now be a suitable bride for Prince Charles, but that a cool girl like me wouldn't want to marry him anyway. The press coverage generally made me laugh.

But there was one incident with a male journalist that upset me. He came to interview me for *Cosmopolitan* and his first question was: How does it make you feel that men are going to be jerking off over this book? Perhaps he didn't put it quite like that, but that was what he meant. I was so shocked and offended that I struggled to finish the interview. I went to Bailey afterwards practically in tears. Bailey rang him and probably threatened to chop his hands off, or something minor like that. He called to apologise, and all was forgotten. But the question horrified me because it had never occurred to me that the photos would have this effect, or that people would see the book as basically upmarket pornography in hardback. If people got off on it, that was no business of mine; I never think about the effect my work has on people, because that way madness lies. And it was certainly no way to start an interview.

The book was reprinted four times and sold tens of thousands of copies (I never saw any of the dividends, though Bailey did buy me a gold Volkswagen Rabbit Convertible, one of the first in London), but one person who never saw it was my father. I just don't have the kind of relationship with him where I can show him my nude pictures. He was made aware of it, though, when his barber showed him a copy of *Playboy* that included extracts from *Trouble and Strife*. Not that he and I talked about it – I only know because Mom told me.

I started to notice that it was the kind of book women bought for their men. George Harrison was given it by Olivia, Eric Clapton got it from Patti, and Eric Idle from Tania. The idea that these fabulous women were buying it thrilled me. Dizzy Gillespie evidently also saw it because when, soon after it was published, he came round to the house to be photographed, he asked Bailey hopefully, 'Is the missus in?'

On the other hand the book attracted some unwelcome attention, too. I have often felt slightly creeped out when grubby-looking men or over-enthusiastic couples come up to me in the supermarket and tell me it's their favourite book. When I first started using the internet I soon learned not to click on certain websites. *Trouble and Strife* often comes up heartily recommended by men of questionable cyber-reputations. (The first time I went online I was at my friend Brian Clarke's house. I made the mistake of Googling my own name and was immediately asked if I wanted to see myself having sex with a horse, a dog or a llama. I don't think they meant a Buddhist lama.)

Looking at a copy of *Trouble and Strife* used to make me feel uncomfortable. Twenty-odd years later, I have got over that. I have come to accept the book, even to be proud of it. I recognise it now as a work of eroticism in its deepest sense: a celebration of desire.

*

'The fact that an opinion has been widely held is no evidence whatever that it is not utterly absurd.'

BERTRAND RUSSELL, *Marriage and Morals*

It takes two. Two people leave each other, or so Bailey always used to say. And we both did our fair share of wrecking our marriage.

Travelling with Bailey was beginning to be at times, insufferable. Practically back-packing with him from motel to grotty motel, I started to yearn for a hotel where I could flush the toilet and a destination where I would not get dysentery. I wanted a hotel room where the walls weren't splattered with bloody bugs. I wanted a fucking mosquito net. I wanted to go home. I'm a Hawaiian girl: I want to laze the afternoon away by the pool in a hammock with an ice-cold beer. With Bailey travel was sometimes a slog, and his camera, not his wife, always took priority.

I refused to accompany him to Calcutta because I knew I would not be able to handle the poverty. When we went to Bombay he discouraged me from visiting the seedy district of the town where the prostitutes are displayed in 'cages' – the same area which Mary Ellen Mark captured so unflinchingly in her book *Falkland Road*. But one evening I insisted on coming along to a special dance ceremony. There, everyone was smoking *chandoo*, or opium. I tried a few puffs, but it made me feel weak, as if my control were slipping away. Bailey, of course, didn't have a toke.

On one of our trips to Bombay we had a terrible row in the foyer of our hotel. I rushed into the ladies, where as I stood sobbing over the sink I heard a voice cooing kindly behind me. 'Ohhh . . .' I didn't want any sympathy but I thought it was sweet of this woman to offer. Then I realised she wasn't consoling me at all; she was about to ask for my autograph. 'Aren't you Marie Helvin?'

I had begun to realise that my public self was about more than the right make-up and clothes. It was about attitude: poise, bearing, power. I think you can make the effort to turn up the charisma switch, or dim it down, as you please. Susan Strasberg recounts how, as a little girl, she went walking down the street with Marilyn Monroe.

'Why isn't anyone recognising you?' asked Susan, disappointed.

'I haven't turned her on,' replied Marilyn. 'You want me to turn her on?' And – click! – people were falling over themselves for her all down 5th Avenue. Marilyn Monroe was suddenly visible.

I think sometimes I confused or conflated my public and private self: Marie Helvin was 'on' a lot of the time. Once I was out shopping with my sister Naomi and I put on a huge pair of dark glasses in order to disguise myself. 'You don't get it, do you?' said Naomi. 'You just look like Marie Helvin with dark glasses on.'

Increasingly, I decided I wouldn't spend all my holidays trailing after Bailey through sweaty inhospitable climes. His mania for work and rough travel adventure was driving a wedge between us. So for stretches of three or four weeks I'd go back to Hawaii leaving Bailey to – well, I didn't like to think about what he got up to. I think it's different if you have children, but if it's just you and your husband

and you leave him alone for that long, something clicks in his head and he thinks, I'm free! He was also starting to take other models away on long work trips, much to Jerry's horror. Perhaps she brought her own emotional agenda to the situation, because I never let it get to me. I knew he was probably having an affair with Kim, a model who lived on the wild side and one day disappeared off to rehab. But I just let it go.

When I got home to Hawaii the whole place was in uproar because they were filming *Magnum P.I.* there – probably the most exciting production to hit the islands since *Hawaii Five-O*. I found myself really attracted to the star, the gorgeous, dark Tom Selleck. His suave American charm felt like the perfect antidote to Bailey. I stumbled; I fell; I had a fling with Magnum P.I.

I've always been a prodigious sleep-talker, giggling and telling stories all through the night, much to the annoyance of my sisters and other bedfellows. Now this habit got me into trouble. Back at Primrose Hill I was roused in the middle of the night by Bailey growling, 'Who's Tom? Marie, who's this fucking Tom character you keep talking about?'

I played for time by pretending to yawn. 'Oh, you know,' I said, before giving an alibi that even now astounds me with its cheek: 'Tom Thumb.'

Even when we were at home we had started doing different things. I didn't necessarily want to go with him to lectures on daguerrotypes or the lost photos of Margaret Cameron; he didn't want to come with me to parties or premieres. Once I dragged him along to my model booker's party in a pizza place in Mayfair and we spent the evening talking to Marvin Gaye, who, then in the middle of writing 'Sexual Healing', was so smooth and in his own groove. On our way out Bailey said, 'So who the fuck was he?'

Another night we went over to our friends the producer Michael Laughlin and the writer Susanna Moore's home, for a dinner they were giving Roman Polanski. They had taken a huge townhouse in Knightsbridge and after dinner we all moved upstairs to the drawing room to chat, smoke, drink. A post-prandial lull settled over the crowd, as it can do. 'Someone needs to arrive, or something needs to happen,' I confided to Susanna in the bedroom. Somehow we hit upon the idea of exchanging our clothes: I put on her vintage Chinese silk jacket, with a high collar right up to the neck, and she put on my sequinned leopardskin leotard and skirt made specially for me by the Emanuels. We came back into the room very nonchalantly, in costume as each other. The mood changed, all right. Bailey started photographing us and even Roman paid attention for a few minutes. Later when I told someone at *Vogue* about it they commissioned a feature on the theme of a clothes swap and a life swap.

Whenever Bailey was invited to contribute his favourite music to a radio show, he said I knew more about it than him and insisted I choose the tracks for him – such a responsibility! Usually I would choose 'Mountain High' by Ike and Tina Turner and hope the DJ wasn't going to quiz Bailey about why he liked it. We never went on *Desert Island Discs*, which wasn't considered a cool thing to do, back then.

I got a shock when Tom Selleck came to London and contacted me through a mutual friend, Johnny Gold the owner of Tramp. Our affair had been very much a Hawaiian fling until then. We went out for dinner together at Mr Chow's, went back to his hotel – but then when I got home I felt unsettled. It was a holiday affair, and it wasn't going to work in London. The next morning I sent him a letter – by bike, because this felt too urgent to post – about how my marriage was breaking up and we ought to call it off; a week or so later he happened to be taken backstage at the musical *Cats*, where he met his wife-to-be. It all worked out for the best.

Guts

Around this time Bailey came to me, full of excitement. 'It's fucking great, Marie! Guess what Olympus has gone and invented . . .' Bailey was under contract to Olympus (he was even appearing in their adverts: 'Who does he think he is? David Bailey?' which had caught on so much he couldn't go anywhere without a new generation of fans chorusing it at him) and they always approached him with news about their latest innovations. This time it was a fibre-optic camera.

As Bailey gabbled on about how this camera was so small it could be swallowed, or introduced intravenously, it slowly dawned on me that he was asking if he could photograph me from within. It wasn't enough to have my naked belly to photograph, now he wanted an image of my womb to go with it. This was too much for me to stomach (if you'll pardon the pun) and I told him no, point blank. To swallow a fibre-optic camera? To show off my most private areas for public inspection? (I had learned by now that there were no private photographs with Bailey.) I just wasn't going to do it. The whole thing reeked of men taking possession of a woman. 'It would be the ultimate photograph,' Bailey said wistfully. Exactly – and that was why I wanted to withhold it from him. I wanted to keep something back for me.

Secretly, of course I was fascinated. The idea was so novel it appealed to me, but not under those conditions. I knew I would have no say in how it was done or the results and I knew I would get a bum deal, too. I had moved on in my marriage by this time. I had acquired a voice, and the conviction, the sheer guts, to use it to say *no*.

When I married Bailey I was nineteen – an adoring child bride. Well, I was now in my late twenties and I had grown up within the marriage. I was beginning to have a more clear-eyed relationship with Bailey. My hero-worshipping had declined into a jaded kind of equanimity. We had started to get really into one-upmanship, always quarrelling about who was wrong and who was right. It became exhausting, rowing about any topic that came to hand, desperately wanting to be right at any cost.

Bailey was a drinker and smoker: sometimes I'd wake up in the morning and find him and some friends – John Swannell; Brian Clarke; David Litchfield, his partner on *Ritz* newspaper; Olympus MD Barry Taylor – still sprawling, chatting in our living room, surrounded by empty bottles and ash trays piled with Stuyvesant stubs and cigar butts. 'It's never dawn already!' Bailey would exclaim as I drew the purple velvet curtains. He and his friends would head straight off to their jobs, stumbling a little as they walked out of the door perhaps but otherwise, to my astonishment, pretty much together. Bailey never had a drink problem, though there were many incidents, usually at Langan's, where we would live it up with Peter Langan ordering bottle after bottle of Bollinger. There was a real scene there once when after a long bout of drinking, Bailey got into a slanging match with Wonderwoman's husband. Bailey wasn't a fighter, but when it came to verbal fisticuffs he was unbeatable.

Then, quite out of the blue, Bailey stopped drinking and smoking. 'Life's too short to waste on all that,' he told me. I retorted that he would be hell to live with from now on; he replied he would prove me wrong. I said I thought I would be right. He said he knew I would be wrong. We were as bad as the frickin' parrots.

Bailey proceeded to go cold turkey on the alcohol and cigarettes – and he behaved like an angel all the way through it. I had the sneaking feeling he was only being nice to prove me wrong. That was how petty and competitive we had become.

One day Brian Clarke came over after having lunch with C.P. Snow. In the course of his conversation, quoting Snow, he used the word 'acquiesce'. I stopped him to ask what it meant, and ever since it has been my favourite word. I love the way the elegant ease of its sound matches the gracefulness of its meaning. You may have noticed I've used it quite a few times already in this book. I think acquiescing gracefully to someone else can be a beautiful thing, especially when it involves an element of sacrifice and means putting your own considerable strength in abeyance. And perhaps I was particularly drawn to the word at that point in my life when Bailey and I were caught in a struggle of wills. To acquiesce to him was what I yearned to do, yet pride, and a new sense of my own burgeoning independence and maturity, prevented me. When Tina Brown, then editor of *Tatler*, came to interview Bailey I met her and we got on well; in her subsequent piece she described me as 'a sweet toughie'. I was beginning to live up to the title.

*

'We seek the teeth to match our wounds.'

KENNETH TYNAN

We were in the bathroom sitting in positions that had become familiar to us over the years. I was in front of my dressing table; Bailey was perched on the edge of the bathtub. But this time there was an icy silence between us. I had found Bailey's intimate photos of Catherine and since then I had spent my time crying, moping, on the phone to Jerry (who, with her fierce loyalty to me, wound me up still further) and refusing to talk to Bailey. Now it was time for confrontation.

'I guess this means divorce,' I said.

'I guess so.'

'I guess I need a lawyer,' I said.

'I guess I do too.'

The exhausted banality of the conversation masked a lot of pain. Coolly, I powdered my face in the mirror but inside I was devastated. 'Why are you doing this, Marie? You've ignored so many other infidelities before, why make a big deal out of this one?!' a small voice shrieked in my head. But I ignored it and started to darken my beauty spot with a black pencil, very carefully.

'So shall I move out then?'

I couldn't believe he'd said that. But like a fool I did the decent thing. 'No, Bailey, it's your home, you can't possibly!'

Instead, I moved upstairs into the spare bedroom, where the spirit of Suzon still lingered. I never went back to Bailey's bed. I told my agent I would take jobs abroad – anywhere, just to get away from London.

I worked in New York for a bit, but then, happily, an invitation came from Plan International who wanted to send me to Indonesia to visit the child I sponsored, Partini. She was adorable and it was wonderful to be able to help the local community in small but significant ways. I bought the village a hen house, seed and chickens. The trip was mutually beneficial; I needed a break and I managed to do some good at the same time. Later I would also travel to

Kathmandu for Plan International to visit my other foster child, Krishna; Don McCullin came with me to photograph the trip for the *Sunday Telegraph*. After that first trip to Indonesia, a photograph of me and a piece about my trip ended up in the *Daily Mail*. Unbeknownst to me, a man called Mark Shand saw it and cut it out.

Bailey kept his distance from all my do-gooding overseas. Before I left I was studying Indonesian vocabulary for my trip, at which Bailey scoffed. 'All you need to know, if you get kidnapped,' he said, 'are the words for "My husband will not pay".'

Splitting up with Bailey tested my strength. So much of my identity had formed around being wife and appendage to the great artist that I struggled to know who I was without him. It wasn't that he deliberately made me feel that way – it was more to do with the social conditions of the time, and how I internalised my position as his young wife. I remained externally confident and 'up', but inside I felt deeply insecure. I wasn't sure who I was, or if I had any place in the fashion world without Bailey.

I was meant to be writing a book with Peter Mayle, a sort of autobiography, but when Bailey and I split up I was convinced that no one would want such a book. Over lunch at the Caprice I agonised about how to tell Peter we were divorcing. It took me half an hour to come out with it. When he replied that I was still interesting with or without Bailey, and that the divorce would actually add to the book's appeal, I simply didn't believe him.

Our divorce proceedings were interminable. The law had it that before we were allowed to part without citing co-respondents or a reason, we had to spend two further years living 'separate and apart'. Crazy as it sounds, we decided to spend those two years living in the same house, just on different floors. We were still close, even though we were no longer sharing a bed, and it felt natural to carry on living together and working together. It was a strange arrangement, a sort of limbo, but it worked for us.

The news that Bailey and I were divorcing had filtered out into the newspapers, but the fact that we still went home together sent the press into flurries of confusion. We were on? Were we off? Were we doing it all for attention? 'Days after they told us they were parting Bailey and Helvin swapped sweet nothings at a ninetieth birthday celebration for Jacques Lartigue ... Later the confusing twosome could be spotted together over chicken and mash at Langan's Brasserie. Now, is this any way to split up?' asked William Hickey in the *Daily Express*. In the *Daily Mail* the same outing garnered a full page of coverage under the headline 'Divorce 1984-style'.

Baffling as it seemed to everyone, we remained truly amicable. Letters from our separate lawyers came to the same address, but we never mentioned what they said to one another. We only lost our tempers with each other once, when his lawyers had been wrangling over the terms of the settlement for so long that I lost it with him. Bailey always insisted quarrels should stay to the point – 'Don't fight mean, don't get personal' – but I am ashamed to say I broke these rules. I called him a fat pig, something I really regret. He was up all night, upset – and I was too. In the morning I went to him and said sorry.

'Let's cut short these lawyers – they're only going to make money for themselves,' I said. 'Let's have a powwow, you and me.'

'OK,' he said, 'you're right. Let's not have any lawyers at all.'

Sirens in my head went off warning me that the plan wouldn't work in my favour ... And so the wrangling resumed.

But it wasn't all gloom. The house was full of love again. Bailey was with his new girlfriend, now his wife Catherine. And as for me, a dozen white roses were arriving at Primrose Hill for me every Monday, for by now I had a new man in my life.

NINE

WHAT THE
GARDENER SAW

‏

'However many times you fall, stand up.
However many times you come close to despair, go on trusting.
However many times your heart wants to close, keep it open.'
THUKSEY RINPOCHE, Tibetan Buddhist teacher

I walked into the bedroom and slung down my holdall, gazing about me. It had evidently been a girl's room, full of pretty lacy childish things, discarded riding hats and rosettes. It was in fact the childhood bedroom of Camilla Parker Bowles, née Shand. I was staying as a guest of the Shands at their family home in Sussex, and the guest room I had been given was Camilla's room, painted Smythson blue. Decorum didn't allow for me to share the bedroom of my new boyfriend Mark, the son of the family. But decorum didn't notice when late at night he gently turned the handle to my door and came tiptoeing towards my bed.

Mark Shand was blond and handsome and kind. To me, he was heaven. He had been born into the English public-school system but it hadn't particularly suited him; instead of going to university he had run off to Australia to become a jackaroo. He'd had adventures. He'd sailed off in a boat alone, nearly drowned, washed up on the shore of Fiji and been welcomed into the arms of a half-Chinese, half-Fijian princess – it sounded like a Robert Louis Stevenson story but it was all true. Soon he went off on another trip, to Irian Jaya, which he wrote up in his first travel book, a boy's own adventure, written with Harry Fane and Don McCullin, called *Skulduggery*.

He loved travel, especially around Asia and India, which was why he had taken an interest in the article about my trip to Indonesia. It had prompted him to ask a mutual friend, Sarah Giles, to set us up. Despite a faltering start when I took umbrage one night when he didn't offer to drive me home, I soon fell for him.

Mark was tall and tanned and addicted to sport and weightlifting (he would take his sports equipment everywhere); he was really involved in his body. He had been something of a playboy, dating Caroline Kennedy and Bianca Jagger; in fact, I was sitting in the row behind him and Bianca a year or two earlier at the premiere of *The Postman Always Rings Twice*. Mark was a real action man, a sportsman and explorer whom Nigel Dempster dubbed 'He-man Shand'. He dived; he sailed; he had done the Cresta run countless times. Unlike Bailey, he loved Hawaii where he went night-diving and played tennis with my mom and all her friends – a big point in his favour.

In London, Mark borrowed his friend Bruce Chatwin's pied-à-terre in Belgravia so we would have somewhere for our trysts, a tiny, elegant place where we conducted the first blissful months of our affair. I was totally in lust with this man who had the most beautiful body I'd ever seen, and we'd spend the whole weekend in bed together. He would always buy me champagne and we'd hole up in the Belgravia flat with videos and pasta.

When he wasn't exploring he worked selling antique Cartier jewellery and objets d'art with Harry Fane (the Earl of Westmorland's son): a desk job would never have held him. He was impulsive and open-hearted, emotional where Bailey had been intellectual – and he was exactly the right man for me, especially at that time in my life of impending divorce and self-doubt.

We travelled together to the home he shared with his friends Harry and Tessa Fane in Bali, a gorgeous place at Bhatu Bling, designed by Linda Garland with traditional gardens created by Made Wijaya. In the Balinese jungle, Mark was in his element, always

This image was the basis of the cover story that relaunched me as a model when I turned 50.

I had never worked with Tim Bret Day before. I thought the photographs were just fabulous. I managed to squeeze myself into this gorgeous Versace mini-dress which later became immortalised when Beyoncé wore it to steamy effect in the 'Bootilicious' video.

With Bailey, his wife Catherine and their daughter Paloma. It gives me great pleasure to be able to share a warm friendship with Bailey and his family today.

met Lily Cole on this shoot for *Vogue*'s 90th December 2006 issue. Beautiful and bright, she is my avourite among the new faces.

opposite page When I originally retired from modelling in my forties, I spent a great deal of time exploring the world, sometimes first class, sometimes with a knapsack, this time by elephant in Jaipur, India.

Sabrina Guinness gave a lunch for Angelica Huston last year. Bianca Jagger was also there. I was proud to realise that I have known this trio of women for over thirty years.

Back home in Hawaii, riding at Kualoa Ranch in Kaawa, where they filmed *Jurassic Park*.

Beautiful Lanikai beach in Kailua on
Honolulu. The setting for the TV series
'Lost'. It used to be my favourite secret place.

I have always felt a great affinity and deep empathy with Tibetan Buddhism. Its precepts seem to sit very comfortably on my shoulders. I was privileged to meet and learn from Lama Yeshe Losal on Holy Island.

My first shoot with Nick Knight was as part of a supermodels line-up in the Millennium Issue of *Vogue*. This was my second shoot with Nick and brought me in a great deal of modelling work. I was upset that I had to wear the eye patch (I was hit by a baseball bat) but the pictures are glorious and he was fascinating to work with. They were for *W* magazine in the US.

sweet-smelling in a freshly laundered shirt, always intrepid. To approach his villa there was a long road beset by so many potholes that when our Jeep rattled over them Tessa and I used to hold our breasts, which made the men laugh. Here we had many happy times. Here, also, I thought about Suzon a great deal, and Mark could help me with this, because, in another of the strange coincidences that embroider my life, Mark had known many of Suzon's friends on Bali. I showed him a group photograph and he could place everyone in it, apart from Su.

Mark was very easy-going, tolerant of my foibles and no doubt spoiled supermodel ways. When we flew together to Bali, I booked myself into business, while he travelled in economy. Occasionally during the flight he would walk into my cabin and give me a kiss or something. He was far too self-assured to care about that kind of thing.

Once, we arrived together for Bruce Oldfield's charity fashion show, a function in aid of Barnardo's attended by Charles and Diana. As we stepped on to the red carpet, Mark tripped and fell over flat, in front of all the paparazzi. I didn't even stop to pick him up, didn't give him a backwards glance. Hey, you can't have it all, you either have a man who trips up or an unhappy marriage. Again, Mark was too magnanimous, too relaxed to mind.

At home with the Shands, I knew I had made a good impression with his mama and papa when I recognised the paintings in their dining room as Oswald Birleys. They did their best to disguise their surprise, and I was happy to confound their expectations of what a model should be like. My breakthrough with Major Shand came when I was seated at his left at the dinner table and we discovered we shared an appreciation of Rupert Brooke. I think he was pleased when I started reciting his poetry off by heart: 'Love is a flame; – we have beaconed the world's night./A city: – and we have built it, these and I ...' Major Shand was a war veteran, so of course he loved Rupert Brooke; I was also pleased to tell him about how Brooke had visited Polynesia and written poems about Tahiti and, even closer to home, Waikiki.

When Christmas came around I was invited over by the Shands for a traditional upper-class country Christmas. I had won acceptance in the Shands' eyes: this time, I was allowed to share Mark's bedroom rather than staying in Camilla's.

The festive season here couldn't have been more of a contrast to Christmas with Bailey's mum Glad; it was like going from the Royle family to the royal family.

Instead of watching *Morecambe and Wise* on telly, we played Trivial Pursuit in the drawing room. With Glad we were given Marks & Spencer jumpers; here there were expensive presents under a vast tree. At the Shands the Queen's speech was the highlight of the day, and we all had to be sitting ready and attentive when it came on. Instead of the plate piled high and topped with piccalilli there were about five courses served by staff. And there was a new discovery for me: 'bread sauce'. What was this revolting lumpy white stuff?

I was used to English upper-class formality from staying with the Lichfields at Shugborough. But breakfast there was always served in bed. So on Christmas morning I took my time getting ready, as I wanted to make a good impression. Well, I certainly made an impression.

Tara Palmer-Tomkinson recently reminded me of the entrance I made to the Shands' breakfast (how did she know? Her mother Patti is a great friend of Camilla's; evidently the story got passed around). I was the last to arrive for breakfast and the family and guests (including the two little boys, Ben Elliot and Tom Parker Bowles, and a young Laura Parker Bowles) had finished and were standing in the hall when I appeared at the top of the stairs wearing full make-up and a white satin Dior negligee and matching white satin peignoir (I had bought it especially for the stay, not realising that the correct English breakfast apparel was your husband's old pyjamas and a Barbour). As I saw them all there staring up at me aghast I wondered what I had done wrong . . . I assumed it was my socks. I had forgotten to bring slippers and had on an incongruous pair of Mark's moth-eaten ancient cricketing socks. Now I realise that, in that negligee, no one was looking at my feet.

But I soon got over it. All the Shands were really warm to me, and never tried to make me go out hunting with them, even though Mark's father the Major was Master of Hounds. (I think they could probably tell that as a keen supporter of the animal rights movement, it wasn't for me.) Mark's mother Rosalind and I would sing Fred Astaire songs in the kitchen, and I grew friendly with his sisters Camilla and Annabel, and their husbands Andrew and Simon. I even got to know Nellie, the family cook. She used to say, 'Can I come and be your cook when you and Mark are married?'

Staying at the Shands' I wrote a lot of my photographic memoir *Catwalk*. After lunch I would be closeted away in one of their grand sitting rooms, with a glass of full fat milk. I was a big milk drinker in those days, and – typical model – I had it instead of dessert.

A close friend of the Shands' was the magnificent Angela Fox, the mother of all those talented Fox men. When we discovered we were both writing our memoirs, we laughingly compared where our books were going to be serialised. Hers was published in the *Sunday Times*; mine was less exalted: extracts over three weeks in the *News of the World*.

One day Mark asked me out on a walk and told me his mother was upset. 'You see, the thing is, Marie, the gardener told the house-keeper who told Nellie who told Mama that . . . well, that there were naked pictures of you in the papers.'

I gasped into the wind. To me, there was a world of difference between doing nudes for *Vogue* and doing nudes for a tabloid news-paper. The former was art, the latter was not: it was as simple as that. If I did fashion editorial work for *Vogue*, the images might get syndicated to a newspaper, which might result in – shock, horror – the gardener, the housekeeper, the cook seeing me topless, but that was the name of the game. I don't own my image, much to my constant bafflement. And at that time the copyright laws were going crazy and newspapers were freely reprinting *Trouble and Strife* without permission. I realised with anxiety that to someone like Mark's mother, these subtleties didn't mean very much. A nude was a nude was a nude.

Later, chez the Shands, my exploits would come into their own. But all in good time. First I had my new career to launch. The painted mannequin, hitherto silent as the Sphinx, was about to start yak, yak, yakking. I was going into TV.

*

'Marie this is going to be faaaa-bulous for you.' It was my agent Mark McCormack at IMG, saying what all agents say. Only this time he seemed genuinely excited. This was *Star Games*, a really new TV idea, he said, like nothing else before. It involved ten or so famous people ('celebrities' wasn't the buzz word yet) competing in various sporting activities.

I had every reason to trust Mark, who was legendary amongst agents at the time for representing clients like Kiri Te Kanawa and Martina Navratilova. He was also legendary for taking an astonishingly big cut: twenty-five per cent. Signing up with him – and my personal agent, James Kelley – also meant being handled by their accountants, lawyers, tax consultants and investment advisers: the whole package. Whenever I bump into Anne Robinson our conversation drifts to 'Can you believe how much we were paying Mark McCormack . . .'

Star Games was going to be lighthearted entertainment, he said, presented by Michael Aspel. Contestants included: Miss World, Miss Argentina (a bit snooty), Linda Lewis (the soul singer with top notes that could shatter a chandelier), Nigel Havers (a friend of Mark's), a woman from *The Avengers*, Simon Williams (from *Upstairs Downstairs*), George Chakiris (from *West Side Story*), Alvin Stardust (what a sweetie), the actress Liza Goddard, and Doctor Who. I'm not sure which one – I don't know if I ever knew. It was just Doctor Who. Little did I realise that by appearing in that programme, one of the fledgling reality TV shows, I was about to play my part in the beginning of the end of TV as we knew it.

Bailey had an inkling of it, though. When he dropped me off (remember, we were still living together, though apart) at the hotel at six a.m. where everyone was getting changed into their short pants, he whispered to me, 'Are you sure you want to do this?'

I went ahead and ran through those hoops, hit those golf balls and swung on those monkeybars, grinning to camera all the while. It was fun, and my enjoyment of it was never spoiled because I never had to watch it back on TV. It simply went out live; this was in the days before VHS. When I got home Bailey basically said it was the most ridiculous thing he'd ever seen in his life, but well done anyway.

I also did many pilot shows, for UK and American TV. One prototype of *Through the Keyhole*, where I visited Mickie Most in his home, which he had built as a replica of the *Gone with the Wind* house, Tara; the next episode I went to film Norman St John Stevas in his townhouse in Mayfair. I also made a pilot panel show for Granada with Miriam Stoppard, Paula Yates and Charles Spencer, the Princess of Wales's brother, who was then on CNN for London: fun, but it was never commissioned.

When I started to have a TV career, my modelling work temporarily dried up. It's as simple as that: you can't combine a voluble public persona with being a high-fashion model. When Cindy Crawford started making movies, she left the catwalk. If Kate Moss were to start presenting a chat show, you can bet she wouldn't be on the cover of *Vogue* any more. Perhaps the enigmatic element essential for fashion photographs disappears once your personality becomes known; perhaps it's best not to over-analyse these things. It's just how the industry is.

My next big job was *Frocks on the Box*, with the irrepressible Muriel Gray. I'd seen her presenting *The Tube* and wondered why she was so tough with all her interviewees. I used to think, God how could she say that to Mick? But when my agent persuaded me to go for lunch at L'Escargot with Muriel and the producer of *Frocks on the Box*, we hit it off instantly. We were chatting so much the producer, Vicki Barrass didn't get a look in.

Muriel really helped me find my feet on TV. When the autocue packed up she taught me how to memorise scripts by writing them out longhand – and she encouraged me to be confident and change the words of the script to suit my style if I wanted to. She was a true professional. I would always get the giggles just as the camera was turning over for a take, and she would laugh too, but as soon as the director said 'Action!' she would be absolutely poker-faced and ready to do her piece to camera.

The producers liked our spontaneity and our jokey double act. 'Why have you got a pair of tights wrapped round your head, Muriel?' I might ask, disingenuously, about her turban. On the show, we rummaged through the wardrobes of my friends, like Jerry Hall or Eric Idle or Imran Khan. Harry Enfield, straight from his Edinburgh festival hit, was one of our sidekicks (though he always declines to put that on his CV) and he did the funny bits while we gave our advice on dressing according to your shape. You could say we were Trinny and Susannah *avant la lettre*. In fact our producer Vicki Barrass went on to devise and produce the *What Not To Wear* franchise. She was obviously thinking ahead in terms of fashion on TV. We did two series and turned down a third, preferring to quit while we were ahead.

Reading the reviews of the TV shows was a new experience for me and I took a little while to develop the hard shell of self-protection. I can still remember some of the bitchy things certain writers said. Other things just didn't bother me at all. The critics could carp all they liked about the hint of a lisp in my speech. I'd been teased for that since I was a child mumbling 'pusghetti' instead of 'spaghetti'. I was used to it. Some were nice, though – Paul Morley called me and Muriel the 'Morecambe and Wise of fashion TV'.

As I did more TV work I watched the conventions of reality TV emerging. On *Star Games* there was no mention of 'the journey', for example – which would later be the catchphrase that TV producers used incessantly. With every reality TV show I did from *Masterchef* to *Britain's Next Top Model*, the producer would insist that whatever we did, be it cooking a meal or telling some poor kid she was too short to be a fashion model, we had to take the audience with us on our 'journey' from inexperience to wisdom. In my case, on *Masterchef*, the only thing I learned was that one judge didn't like my idea of putting goat's cheese with mashed potato. But for the cameras I had to act up my hope, fear, tension, excitement . . . The whole thing

WHAT THE GARDENER SAW

is pure showbiz, as dramatically engineered as any staged play.

Judging *Britain's Next Top Model* made me, at times, really uncomfortable. I wasn't going to deal out acid put-downs to these young hopefuls just for the sake of a TV show. Giving the producers a 'journey' was one thing; giving them pure spite was another. However, for all its showbiz it does spread some vital information about the industry. I really wanted to nurture the young girls on it. They were often girls for whom high-fashion modelling was never going to be an option but they had self-belief beyond comprehension. And that is just what they need. I admired them for that. A model needs a figure like a goddess, a face like an angel and a hide like a rhinoceros. If the girls on that show believed in themselves, who was I to knock their confidence? Top models get to the top because they have that determination and spirit, not necessarily because they are perfect physical specimens.

Filming those kinds of shows was often chaotic. Ultimately, though, I didn't care who won the damn competition, as long as my agent, Karen Diamond at Models One, was happy. She was the one who was going to have to represent the winner. As it turned out the winner we picked, Lucy Ratcliffe, was brilliant and I stay in touch with her still.

Years earlier when I was represented by Storm I went to a dinner where I had to judge a model competition for them, along with lots of *EastEnders* actors and pop stars. There was so much arguing about who would win that I was completely ignored, and so was Devon Aoki, the other judge. We gave up and sat there chatting between ourselves – I'm friends with her father the restaurateur Rocky Aoki of Benihana – until someone shouted, 'Ms Helvin! Who do *you* think should win?' I drew myself to my full height and said very disdainfully, 'I will acquiesce to whichever contestant you choose.'

The whole table of *EastEnders* and assorted pop stars went quiet. They looked at me, totally nonplussed, as I had hoped they would. Gradually they went back to talking amongst themselves. I rather enjoy playing the grande dame occasionally, especially in the world of TV, which, however much fun it is to dabble in, is not my world.

*

The eighties had roared into gear by the time Jerry and I were photographed by Bailey for the cover of *Tatler*, twinned sideways with our heads top-to-tail like the twins on a tarot card. It was our third cover shoot together. We wore over-the-top jewellery and evening gloves, and had bushy eyebrows (I modelled mine on Margaux Hemingway, but in fact I probably looked more like Harpo Marx's sister) and hair so big it filled the frame. Very OTT; very 1985.

That year, the first mobile phone call was made, the Sinclair C5 was invented, and Mohamed Al Fayed bought Harrods. Shoulder pads had also come in, to my chagrin. It wasn't a good look for me. Personally I preferred something a little less uptight; Bailey had always asked me if I wanted a Chanel suit, but I still preferred Anthony Price. *The Official Sloane Ranger Handbook* was a big hit, and on television, Peter York described me as 'orchidaceous'. Back then I just hoped it meant something nice; now I know it does I'm flattered.

I was invited to 10 Downing Street around this time, when Mrs Thatcher was reaching out to the fashion industry in a sort of pre-Blair Cool Britannia moment. It backfired, of course: Katherine Hamnett turned up wearing her famous '58% Don't Want Pershing' protest T-shirt. The next year, 1985, was the year I was invited, and there was no such drama, sadly. Denis Thatcher handed out the drinks – mainly spirits, which I thought peculiar. Where was the champagne? – and I was photographed standing with Mrs Thatcher. I look terrible but she sure looks worse.

It seemed as if it was customary, then, for big households to take every Sunday newspaper, from the *Telegraph* to the *Mirror*. So one morning when Mark and I were staying at Camilla and Andrew Parker Bowles's home we came through from the breakfast room to see all the papers spread out in the morning room. The same story was on practically every front page: wild speculation about Camilla Parker Bowles and Prince Charles. Oh my God, I thought to myself, and turned the page as quickly as possible. 'Papa's furious,' Mark whispered. Luckily, on a double spread on another page I was pictured at the premiere of *Ain't Misbehavin'* wearing an amazing low-cut Fabrice dress covered in beads (I had one in red and Jerry had one in blue). Breaking the awkward silence, Annabel's husband Simon remarked, 'Oh look, Marie, they call you "the Body" in this one.'

Even Mark's papa stopped fuming and started asking questions about the pictures. 'How do you manage to look so relaxed in front of all those flashbulbs, my dear?' We'd all forgotten about the front page by noon, when Mark's father followed his time-honoured habit and opened a bottle of champagne. I was always happy to keep him company. I liked that custom!

Gradually I was introduced to all Mark's family. His aunt Elspeth was married to Sir Geoffrey Howe and after we met them for dinner at a private room in Claridge's, they then invited us to Chevening, which was the Howes' official country residence, as Geoffrey was Foreign Secretary at the time. After lunch, as we set off to explore the enormous maze in the house's beautiful grounds, Geoffrey paternally whispered to me the directions out of the maze: straight, left, left, right... before adding jovially: 'But don't tell the Italian ambassador!'

Through country house parties with the Shands I met Prince Charles a few times (I always found him a little pompous) and Princess Anne (who was great). I clearly wasn't Charles's type; once when I was chatting to him after a premiere he couldn't stop looking over my shoulder at Jerry. He patronised me a little, though only lightly. When conversation turned to photography and I mentioned a retrospective of the work of Leni Riefenstahl, he expressed surprise that I should know about her. 'Well, I'm married to a photographer, you know,' I said. I don't think he did know; he wasn't in the loop with popular culture. Princess Anne was a great deal more friendly and relaxed and even seemed to know who I was, though I couldn't imagine she studied fashion magazines.

I have never succumbed to the disease I call 'royalitis'. I devour books of British history – and I love Dr David Starkey's work – but the present royal family are, to me, no more interesting than Nellie the cook. I could see, though, that these blue bloods had love affairs of Byzantine complexity. Camilla and Charles used to have something going on – that was well known. Princess Anne once had a crush on Camilla's husband, Andrew, who was considered a real catch, a very dashing colonel – I think they even dated briefly before he was married. Camilla was instrumental in Charles meeting Diana – he even proposed to Diana at Camilla's old house. Camilla told me with gales of laughter that a Japanese news crew came to film the spot where they were standing when it happened, in amongst the cabbages and cauliflowers. Camilla obviously adored Andrew, and he her, yet all was not well in the marriage. Keeping up with all their romantic intrigue was beyond me.

There was also a sense in which the royals and their set kept themselves to themselves. I remember going to a private dinner for Prince Edward where there were fashion and film crowds intermingled with the Chelsea set and overhearing one well-bred young gel remarking grandly to another, 'It's not working, is it? You should never mix people up.'

When Sarah Ferguson married Andrew, my friend the comedian-turned psychiatrist Pamela Stephenson gave a dinner for her at a Chinese restaurant in Chelsea Harbour to introduce her to her group of female friends – there must have been forty of us. 'I expect you're all going to want to ask me questions,' Fergie announced to the party. 'So let's go round the table. You first . . .'

Inwardly, I bridled. What makes you so special? I thought. By the time it came round to me I had had quite a bit of sake to drink so I said, 'Is it true that your husband His Royal Highness is unbelievable at giving back massages and that he was taught this skill by his grandmother?'

I once went to a dinner party where Andrew, utterly charming, had confided this to me, so I knew it would strike home. Fergie was thrown into confusion and spluttered with laughter. No wonder she heads in the opposite direction every time she sees me.

Diana was very different. I met her many times before we started working on the Aids Crisis Trust together, because she was a very social princess. You got the feeling they had to drag Princess Anne to events like the Baftas but whenever I saw Diana there she always seemed to be enjoying herself, embracing the arts and fashion scene. The first time I met her I was standing with Anthony Andrews at a charity event. When she came up to us Anthony said he had thought she was in Abu Dhabi – hadn't he just seen pictures of her there? She gave a conspiratorial little grin and said, 'No rest for the wicked!' before moving on across the room. She was a breath of fresh air, no question.

Mark and I continued to be really happy. He was a great support to me even as I lived through an increasingly difficult period with Bailey in Primrose Hill. On Fridays I would commandeer our bathroom, getting ready to go out, then shout, 'Bye, Bailey,' and go off to have a naughty weekend with my boyfriend. We silently agreed that Catherine could come and stay with Bailey while I was away. I didn't mind – you can become accustomed to anything when you're in love. I would spend the weekend with Mark, but then come Monday morning I'd go back to Primrose Hill. Occasionally I'd find evidence that Catherine had been in the house over the weekend: a product in the bathroom, a piece of chicken in the fridge.

I shouldn't have let these things get to me, but I did. It was the home I had lived in for ten years, and now there was a strange woman rattling around ... 'What's your problem, Marie? It's just a fucking piece of chicken!' Bailey retaliated. I conceded he was right. It was probably tricky for him too when all Mark's flowers kept arriving for me. It was a strange situation, but we just had to be adult about it.

Then something happened to break the stalemate: Catherine became pregnant. I was out of that house within days – she was a young model of twenty-three, living on her own and carrying Bailey's baby. She belonged in Primrose Hill with him. But the two-year separation period that divorce proceedings required were not quite yet at an end. What were we to do? I acquiesced. I let Bailey divorce me on grounds of my adultery, even though he had a pregnant girlfriend. The terms of the divorce were so unfavourable to me that my lawyer had a fit. He said I shouldn't accept them, but I insisted on it. I had to get out of that house at any cost, and the hundred thousand pounds Bailey gave me was just about enough to buy a small place in central London. I was desperately keen to keep things as amicable as I could with him. He was such an important part of my life, and besides, any sense I had of my role in life was so wrapped up with him that I felt if I angered him I would never work in the fashion industry again. I agreed to pretend I was the guilty party in the divorce – and just got out of there as quickly as I could.

My packing boxes arrived and were filled up with my clothes and books. I took very little else, but Bailey still found some melodrama in the situation. When I walked out of the kitchen with a frying pan he exploded, 'Aren't you going to leave me anything?' In fact I didn't even take our wedding present from Paul and Linda McCartney, stunning hand-embroidered sheets from the heavenly shop The White House on Bond Street, which I called The Shop of God. I had thought they were too beautiful to use, and they were still in their tissue paper, hidden in some safe place – too safe for me to find before I quit the house for good.

When I left, I left. A few weeks later I rang Bailey's latest secretary, Sarah, and asked if she would send me some of the clothes I had left and maybe a sandwich toaster. But the remainder of my things had disappeared, the secretary informed me in a hushed voice. 'Yes, erm, Catherine ordered a skip, you see . . .' She had obviously gone crazy and excised every last remnant of me from the house. I don't blame her, she was young; she was pregnant; and it was an awkward situation.

Mark wanted me to move in with him in Knightsbridge – in Egerton Gardens – but, craving my own space and independence, I simply wasn't ready to live with another man. So, after a short spell of trundling my boxes round friends' houses, I found a duplex flat for about £130,000 in St George's Square in Pimlico, directly across from Young England, the nursery Princess Diana taught at. 'The address will look great on your letterhead,' said Mark, trying to be encouraging. That is such an English thing to say! I thought.

I dreamt of my own place – somewhere I could close the door

and shut the world out, after the mayhem of Gloucester Avenue. I have always been a loner, and independence for me was bliss. I filled my new flat with books, books, books … and a library ladder to reach them that used to belong to an American president, or so I was told. Although I was still a domestic incompetent (I once sat in the dark for a whole evening, waiting for the electrician to turn up to change a fuse) I soon felt totally home here, revelling in my new freedom, which I was not about to give up lightly. Poor Mark got very short shrift once when he left clothes in my closet.

When my memoir *Catwalk* was about to come out, I thought it would be prudent and civilised for Mark and me and Bailey and Catherine to meet up. This raised some eyebrows in the press, but it was all very courteous. Catherine and I chattered away and got on well immediately, though Mark and Bailey were typically male and glowered at each other across the table for the whole evening. We didn't do it again.

*

'From within … a light shines through us upon things, and makes us aware that we are nothing, but the light is all.'
RALPH WALDO EMERSON, *The Over-soul*

'Marie,' said Mark softly.

We were in the dark under a bridge gliding along a canal in a gondola in Venice. We were staying at the Gritti Palace, having made our journey to Venice on the Orient Express. It was the most fabulous, romantic trip, but when Mark took my arm and said my name in that tone of voice, it made me anxious.

His parents, keen to see their only son married, had asked once or twice if they could announce our engagement in *The Times*, which I brushed off with a laugh. His mother had even confided that if we wanted to go ahead and have children without getting married, that would be fine. But I wasn't ready for any of that. I was only just beginning to live the life I had always dreamed of, taking chances, making mistakes, experiencing all the world had to offer me. I was free in every sense of that elusive word – and I wasn't about to give it up.

Also, much as I adored Mark, sometimes I wondered if he was the man for me. I was used to working, and being with someone who worked. But Mark was a true free spirit. He would go off on crazy expeditions to far-flung places, finding himself. I questioned if I didn't need to be with someone who had already found themselves. He was the most generous boyfriend I have ever had, yet at the same time he often seemed to have no income at all. I needed someone who could provide more stability and, crucially, make me feel safe. With Bailey that was a given.

Looking back on my relationship with Mark, I couldn't have wished for anyone who was kinder, or more supportive. All my girlfriends told me he was the best thing, but, you know, when everyone tells you this, it can have the opposite effect. It can put you off.

I realise now there's no such thing as perfect – and perhaps I even knew at the time that Mark was as close to perfect as I could wish for. But something held me back. Sometimes, when you're in possession of power, you use that power to hurt. Perhaps I was annoyed with him that day; perhaps I just wanted to test him.

As the gondola emerged from the bridge into the gloomy Venetian daylight, Mark proposed, and I said no.

The flight back from Venice was fine. We both acted like everything was OK. But inside I was thinking, I wonder if he'll propose to me again one day ... I said no, but what I think I meant was: maybe later. But Mark, sitting beside me, staring at the clouds out of the window, was adjusting, deep within himself, to the new-found idea that I was never going to marry him, that we were over, and that he had to move on.

Of course he was going to take it badly. He was a deeply romantic Cancerian. They give you their heart openly, but if you hurt them, they are so wounded, it's as if you've killed them.

A few weeks later I went to Hawaii for a holiday and when I saw an envelope for me with his handwriting on it I knew what the letter was going to say. I just knew. You reap what you sow. Mark split up with me in that letter. Being a Leo I retreated into my cave. I kept it secret from my parents for days, because my mother so adored Mark.

I went back to London with the vague idea I could patch things up with him. Perhaps it wouldn't be too late. I didn't want to go straight back into a marriage, and couldn't understand why no one could comprehend this. On my return from Hawaii I tried to take control of my life and I went to Alan Carr to give up smoking, because I was in my mid-thirties and it was really time to give up my pack-and-a-half-a-day habit. Once, I looked at my ash tray and saw I had three cigarettes going at once. Alan Carr was great (he told a journalist I had come to see him wearing 'a very short skirt') and after our session I threw my cigarettes and my smart lighter, not a Dupont, but not a Cricket either, on to his mounds of rejects with a glad heart. I was a non-smoker!

That night, Mark came round to my flat and we split up once and for all. And what did I do? My face streaked with tears, I went straight round the corner and bought three cartons of cigarettes. I was going to need the crutch a little while longer.

Mark went on to marry a girl from his own background called Clio Goldsmith, whom he'd had a thing with when they were younger. They had a beautiful daughter, and are still happily married, just like Bailey and Catherine. It's important to me that both these men went on to become happy family men. I picked good guys; I just didn't keep them.

TEN

INDEPENDENT WOMAN

'Now the whole dizzying and delirious range of sexual
possibilities has been boiled down to that one big boring
bulimic word: RELATIONSHIP.'

JULIE BURCHILL

I don't celebrate my birthday in a big way (name one mature woman who does) but a party I had in my late thirties sticks in my mind. Jerry and Mick threw me a birthday dinner at their rented home in Chelsea. There were caterers and cake and Mick performed a Balinese puppet shadow show as an after-dinner amusement. The evening also ended well for David Bowie, who left with one of my girlfriends.

It was a happy occasion without any hint of awkwardness between me and Bailey. For a while there had been the inevitable fallout between any newly divorced couple and their friends. Nobody wants to take sides, but eventually, everyone is forced to. It took Jerry a long time to accept Catherine and Bailey as a couple, as she was fiercely protective of me, but eventually even she would ring up wheedling, 'Marrrieeee, do you mind *awfully* if we have Bailey and Catherine over to dinner? You can come next time . . .'

Tonight, however, Bailey came without Catherine (possibly she was on a job; possibly she felt a little nervous at the prospect of going to a dinner party thrown by one Terrible Twin for another). As my birthday present Bailey gave me a blank cheque. 'For your next trip to Hawaii, sweetheart.' Thrilled, I showed it off to everyone and hugged him wildly. Then, like a fool, I let the cheque out of my sight. I popped it in Bailey's top pocket and said I would come and get it from him another day. Did I get it back off him? Just. Was it a struggle? Yes!

Meanwhile I was loving living alone in Pimlico. People were endlessly trying to set me up with 'eligible' men and I enjoyed going on a galaxy of dates. But I was also contented being self-sufficient. I occasionally like to eat lunch out in a restaurant by myself – as my mother does, too; maybe it's a Japanese thing. I have to this day a handful of restaurants where I am really happy to sit in the corner, alone, reading, just enjoying being inward. My friends think it's peculiar but I find it relaxing, essential even. The more solitude I had, the more I wanted. 'Marie,' said Mick, who notices these things, 'if you don't start living with someone soon, you're never going to ...'

I was beginning to think he was right. But just because I didn't want to live with anyone, didn't mean I was going to lead the life of a celibate nun, right?

So I began a bachelorette existence, picking and choosing and having adventures. I hadn't devoured Erica Jong's *Fear of Flying* for nothing. I have strict ground rules for myself, though. In some ways I'm quite wild but in others I'm like your mom. I'm always safe. After the advent of AIDS I never had sex without a condom again (I can barely remember what it's like without one). I'm either in love with someone or not at all, and I can never, ever play around with more than one man at the same time. Still, I had a lot of fun.

I had a delicious fling with the chef Marco Pierre White, whose restaurant Harvey's was the talk of the town. He insisted on feeding me with his fingers, even when the restaurant was packed out with the glitterati. I soon forgot them, though, because his oyster tagliatelli was so good.

Then I saw Peter Gabriel on MTV. He was my type of man. By complete chance I met one of his agents, who wanted to represent me, and invited me down to visit his studios in Bath. As soon as we met, there was that connection, that livewire charge that tells you

you're going to have dealings with one another, whether it lasts a night or a month or several years. We had a very on/off relationship over a year or so (I was more on and he more off, to be honest) but he did manage to convince me to quit my oldest vice – of which more later.

I also succumbed, finally, to the attentions of my old flirting partner Jack Nicholson. By this time Anjelica was happily married to the renowned sculptor Robert Graham, and when Jack was in London filming *Batman*, he pursued me with renewed vigour. In the course of the same day he took me to lunch at San Lorenzo and dinner at Le Caprice. Tim Rice was in the restaurant that evening and came over to our table, seeming very excited to see us together. But he was wrong if he thought we were going to become a couple.

Now that I was, finally, attainable, the element of suspense was gone and our flirtation felt flat. We went back to my flat together with a sense of heavy-heartedness. We had waited too long: now we were free to enjoy one another, the spark was gone. 'Why have you got a picture of Elizabeth Taylor in your hall?' Jack asked. It was a portrait of me by Emma Sergeant. The evening was full of misapprehensions. When he left I didn't care if I never heard from him again. It was too depressing, this feeling of 'is that it?' What's more, I am sure the sentiment was reciprocated. If one person is feeling this way, you can bet the other is too. In the morning I received a dozen red roses, and I changed my telephone number. That was how I always reacted to a difficult situation: by running away from confrontation. I dealt with things by not dealing with them: by leaving the room; leaving the party; leaving the country.

Around that same time, Eric Clapton reappeared in my life. I had first met him at Mick and Jerry's house in around 1981, at some party with Jeff Beck and Pete Townsend and his wife. I was sitting on the floor and Eric, a drinker at the time and rather the worse for wear, stumbled over. We had a long conversation, during which I said all the wrong things, making it quite clear my hero from Cream was the singer Jack Bruce, and asking Eric about him incessantly. I also felt uncomfortable because his wife Patti was sitting on the sofa with Jerry, watching us. I kept looking sideways at her, feeling so much empathy. I had been there in my own marriage.

Now, however, things were different. Eric and I were both divorced, and he had gone through AA and emerged a different man. I helped Celia Hammond with a big party she was holding at the Hard Rock Café for her cat charity, where Eric was one of the performers (alongside Uri Geller, who bent a spoon), and when the gig was over he asked me out to Tramp, where I had a drink and he sipped a water. Then Eric drove me home to Pimlico, and I waved goodnight innocently to him, making as if to unlock my front door and get a good night's sleep. But when his car had gone I actually sneaked off and got a taxi straight over to the home of an actor I was dating called Bruce Payne. At that time I was incorrigible – living life to the full, at last.

I was still really choosy, obviously. Dodi Fayed was infamous as a playboy, so when Terry O'Neill paused in the middle of a shoot and told me, 'I know someone that wants to meet you – Dodi,' I said: 'Thanks, but I know enough to know I don't want to go there.' Terry, however, was insistent. So I let him give Dodi my number, and then when he rang me I agreed to go out for dinner, as long as Terry came along too. Dodi's car came to pick me up, but when I got out at Harry's Bar, Dodi was there on his own. How cheeky! As it turned out, though, I didn't mind at all. In fact, I rather liked his nerve. I was single and I needed to be led. Dodi was just lovely; so gently spoken and cultured, with a handsome profile and very soft dark eyes. And he was interesting too: he had been educated in Switzerland and at Sandhurst, and during his career as a film producer he had won an Academy Award for Best Picture for *Chariots of Fire*.

Immediately there was a frisson between us, but I decided not to go there. Sometimes he would call me up, very late at night, saying, 'Come on, this is silly, I'll send a car over for you now.' But he was such a playboy, I knew that if I slept with him, I would become simply another conquest. And he was too much fun to lose as a friend. Being a single female means you have to make choices and decide who is your friend and who is your lover. For me, never the twain shall meet.

I adored Dodi, despite his foibles. He was always late, running on what I called Dodi-time. If he said he was going to turn up to collect you at noon, better not expect the car to arrive till four p.m. Sitting waiting for him all dressed up was not my idea of fun, even though when he arrived he might bring a really thoughtful present, such as a box of mangoes or a special American candy that I loved, like See's chocolate lollipops. The first time he sent me roses from Harrods, they were so velvety and luscious I thought they were fake. The gorgeous roses arrived once a week – for about two months. Then I guess he gave up on me.

For Christmas he gave me a little flacon of perfume with a Chopard diamond in it. Sure, he probably gave out twenty of them, but it was still gorgeous. Straight after he gave it to me I remember he flew off to be with Michelle Pfeiffer, whom he was seeing briefly. I wonder how much bigger than mine her diamond was . . .

Despite all the stories about his supposed drug habit, I never saw any trace of this. To me, his main indulgence was chauffeurs. Wherever he went, he was driven. The only time I ever saw Dodi drive himself was once outside Harrods when we got into a sports car so low-slung we were practically horizontal.

I became a confidante of Dodi, even going along on his dates as a kind of chaperone. Who knows what the poor girls thought of me playing gooseberry? Would he ask me for my feedback on them? No, because they were usually never heard of again after the first date. Dodi was a serious player. In my head I know I did the right thing in resisting him as a lover, though sometimes my heart protests that we could have had a nice time together. But perhaps it's better to regret something you didn't do, rather than something you did.

*

'Sex is one of the nine reasons for reincarnation . . . the other eight are unimportant.'

HENRY MILLER, *Big Sur and the Oranges of Hieronymus Bosch*

One day, Sarah Doukas, who was then my booker at Laraine Ashton, rang with a routine call about work. (Sarah would go on to be one of the best agents in the business, founding Storm and spotting the fourteen-year-old Kate Moss. Already she was conspicuously good at her job, judging a model not for what she was so much as what she could become.) 'So you're doing Armani in Rome, on Tuesday, right?' Finally she wound up with: 'And by the way, do you know Warren Beatty?'

Who didn't? He was a superstar. (When the film *Shampoo* came out Bailey said, 'Thank God all the assholes are going to want to be hairdressers now, not photographers.) And in fact I had met Warren once, yes, at the Summers' house in Chelsea in 1981 when he was in the UK filming *Reds*. We had chatted for a long time, and I picked up those signals women get when someone's interested in them. In fact, we talked so intently that Terry Donovan had shouted at us, 'Oi! She's married to my best mate, you know!' So here was Warren, turning up again.

'Well, he called and asked for your number. In fact he called a few times. A girl manning the phones in the office thought it was someone pulling her leg and hung up on him. But then he got put through to me. So I'll give him your number then. It's only Warren Beatty. Might as well.'

Ears

At twelve I pierced my own ears with a sterilised, boiling hot, thick embroidery needle that I stole from the Girl Scouts. Six little girlfriends and I all teamed up and took our turn to do it, as if following a traditional Hawaiian ritual, only we all screamed all the time because we neglected an important part of the tradition: to get drunk first.

I did a terrible job, and my piercings are wonky to this day. I threaded thick embroidery skein through my earlobes, and kept my ears tucked behind my hair for the next year and a half, so Mom wouldn't notice. When she finally did, she marched me off to a proper piercing shop, Security Diamond, to get them re-done. They said I was beyond help, but a least I could wear real studs instead of loops of wool through my lobes.

Later I subjected my ears to a lot of loud rock 'n' roll (remember Blue Cheer?) and countless earring changes on shoots. But now they were about to undergo a more pleasurable experience.

*

'Hey, Marie ...' Warren's first call was relaxed and friendly; soon he was calling me every night at about eight-thirty p.m. for half an hour. He would be outside in his garden in LA – 'I've just had breakfast ... Now I'm sitting in the sun' – while I would have just raced home from the set of *Frocks on the Box*, keen to catch that call. Not that the conversation would ever get frisky – it was personal, but never too personal. For example, we talked about our fathers, who were both Virginians; later, when we were both deeply shocked by the terrorist outrage in Enniskillen, that was our topic of conversation for a few nights. He confided once that he sometimes thought perhaps Diane Keaton and he should have had a baby. Other times he told me about his producing projects, how he wanted to direct and star in a film about Howard Hughes (he left that one too late). 'You know,' he added, 'I think I'm becoming slightly reclusive myself because I realise I haven't left my house for weeks.' No wonder he was an inveterate phone caller, as he was a great conversationalist. And according to Joan Collins, he favoured multi-tasking – she reputedly said he was perfectly capable of talking to a studio executive and making love at the same time.

Perhaps Warren was my ideal boyfriend: attentive but absent. My split with Mark had kicked everything out of me. Now running home every night to speak to Warren Beatty was a real booster. Muriel Grey used to tease me on the set of *Frocks on the Box.* 'What did you do last night, Marie? Chat to Warren? I bought a cut-price shrub and painted the spare bedroom . . .' She always characterised my home life as me, sitting in a silk peignoir, stroking an expensive cat, on the phone to Warren Beatty. I suppose there was an element of truth in it. Jack Nicholson's reaction was quite different. When I told him Warren was calling me every evening, he shook his head in wonder. 'That man is relentless!'

Warren's phone calls continued for about four months. I was single, and though you could never term Warren single, he had split up from Isabelle Adjani the year before. We liked and trusted each other; sometimes there was real tenderness in his voice when he said goodbye. It was beginning to feel like the longest foreplay session in history. When Dodi Fayed invited me over to LA I was excited to have an excuse to finally meet up with Warren.

Dodi's driver and security picked me up and took me to the airport; from there I got his private plane with him over to New York. As we cruised at the low altitude of a Lear jet, a beautifully dressed hostess asked me what I would like to eat – she would make anything. I turned to Dodi to ask him what he would like and found he was gone. Like a professional traveller, he had popped a sleeping pill and retired to a private bedroom. So I settled in to my very own waitress service: 'I think I'll start with the caviar . . .'

We stopped off for the night in New York in his townhouse (the only Manhattan home I've ever been to that had a ballroom) where he disappeared off again for a massage, and I didn't see him till the morning. After a final refuelling stop at Aspen, we arrived in LA.

I booked myself into a single room at the Beverly Hills Hotel, while Dodi took a huge bungalow in the grounds. I rang Warren right away from my room, and he said he'd like to take me to some hip LA restaurant across town for lunch. I lay on my hotel bed, imagining whether we would come back there afterwards, whether we would make love, how his familiar voice would sound if it were his warm throat that was close to my ear instead of the telephone ... Before I left the room, I sprayed my tea rose perfume in the air.

The danger of a long slow courtship is anticlimax. At lunch Warren was charming, but I discerned an air of presumption about the way he treated me. It was as if it was taken for granted that we'd sleep together. Then when he mentioned a girl I knew, and told me with a grin that he'd had a threesome with her, something inside me turned. I started to lose interest in a big way.

He drove me back to my hotel and parked discreetly round the back instead of using the valet service. In the lobby everyone's heads turned as he walked past. When we got to the lift, he pressed the button, obviously expecting to come up with me. But I stepped inside, looked back at him, said, 'Thanks! Goodbye!' and watched as the lift doors closed on Warren Beatty's surprised face.

There I stood in the lift, my heart beating. Had I done the right thing? Back in my hotel room there were scores of messages from Dodi and I started to feel guilty for accepting his hospitality and then neglecting him. So I went over to Dodi's bungalow, inviting Tina Chow along with me. When I was in LA I always looked her up. She was on great form, separated now from Michael but dating Richard Gere. Moreover, she was – with great flair – designing crystal jewellery, which was unique at that time and I thought Dodi might want to stock it in Harrods.

That night I went out for dinner with Dodi and two of his friends (one was the film director Stan Dragoti, who used to be married to Cheryl Tiegs); Dodi's bodyguard sat at the bar at a discreet distance. The restaurant they chose happened to be the same one I'd been to for lunch, but I didn't want to tell them the whole Warren story, so I kept stumm and hoped the maître d' wouldn't recognise me.

The next day Warren rang and asked if he could take me out again. I thought, Hey, I'm free, I'm in LA, it's Warren Beatty – and told him that I was going out to dinner with some old friends but he was welcome to join us. The old friends in question were Helmut and June Newton, Tina Chow and Jay Johnson (whom I'd met at the Factory). I had warned Tina and Jay about Warren, so when he came over to our table they played it cool. But Helmut, so European, so uninvolved in popular culture, looked at Warren blankly. 'I know your face, young man ... You're familiar to me, but ...' Helmut trailed off, because June was kicking him so hard under the table. Tina for her part couldn't stop beaming because she was so excited for me and Warren. But I couldn't summon up much enthusiasm. I felt the golden moment of opportunity had been missed; we should have done it that lunchtime or not at all. Now it was too late.

I left LA for Hawaii, having turned down the very thing I had gone there for. Human desire is so unpredictable. I guess the fantasy, in this case, was more compelling than the act itself. When I got back to Pimlico I changed my number again. If we couldn't be lovers we certainly couldn't be friends. As I've said before, it's either one or the other with me.

Years later, I saw him once more in London because for some bizarre reason the *Dick Tracy* premiere was held in Dolphin Square, the very respectable apartment block round the corner from my home in Pimlico. So I accepted the invite and strolled round there with my good friend Bruce Oldfield. 'Is that your man?' Warren whispered to me, looking over my shoulder at Bruce. Don't be silly! I thought, and smiled.

Warren was still incredibly attractive and extremely attentive – indeed, now I had him in front of me I could see he made an art form of it, being simultaneously extremely attentive to Helena Bonham Carter with his left eye, and extremely attentive to Jenny Seagrove with his right. As I watched, Barbara Windsor elbowed her way up to him and said, 'D'you remember me?'

'Of course I do, darling,' he said, so seductively that I almost believed he did.

Warren was a legendary seducer and I was well aware there were zillions of women he'd chased. Still, it was flattering to be one of the zillions: as Woody Allen once said, 'I would like to come back as his fingertips.'

*

For a period in the eighties and early nineties I was, believe it or not, a successful entrepreneur. As well as putting my name to a perfume and body cream, I started my own brand of fashion, swimwear and bodywear that was distributed internationally. OK, so my backer George Hammer handled all the finances, and owned the company, but I threw myself into the creative and business side of the venture.

A company comprising seventy staff worked on my brand. They were a great team, including Lenny, pattern cutter extraordinaire and a production assistant who used to work for John Galliano. The first concession was in Harrods. I worked hard to promote it, doing many in-store public appearances, and to my excitement the range took off and Victoria's Secret were soon putting in orders for in excess of eighty thousand pounds. Most of the clothes were made in Redruth, Cornwall (I visited the factory and was presented with a bottle of 'Newquay Steam Lager' – not my tipple, really) and shipments were sent off as far as New York and Malaysia. The key items were casual stretch bodywear, slinky dresses, swimwear and tops in every possible colour and fabric. There were items like gold Lycra leggings, then the last word in fun fashion accessories. (They looked silly for fifteen years after that, but wouldn't you know, they're now back in again. So the great fashion wheel revolves.) At first the clothes were discreetly branded but later I copied Ossie Clark and started putting a little Marie Helvin label on the outside of the garment.

I made the kind of clothes my friends wanted to wear – or even my godchildren. I gave Lizzie Jagger her first ever pair of fake leather trousers for Christmas when she was about thirteen. Mick was horrified – '*What* have you given my daughter?!' – but Jerry was pleased.

For five years, the clothes had fantastic reviews and went down well with shoppers. We were rated the best body you could buy in a British department store by the *Sunday Times*. But then everything changed, as it does in fashion, and stretch went out. Suddenly, you couldn't sell a leotard with poppers anywhere, and even Donna Karan abandoned what had once been her defining look. It was time to move on. George my backer wanted me to try to find another niche (George's wife Ruby, a talented make-up artist, kept suggesting I start a cosmetics brand – and she and George went on to create Ruby and Millie) but I knew it was best for me to call it quits.

The press can be a cruel pack and they will rip you apart if you stand still long enough to let them. I never gave them the chance. I saw one piece, in a women's magazine, in which they put a bad spin on something I'd said (it was an article about fashion mistakes, and I'd told them I didn't have many regrets because I was really careful not to buy things I didn't like – and they twisted it to make it sound like I thought I was Miss Perfect) and I immediately decided it was time to move on to a fresh venture. Women of my generation know we have to keep on our toes. If you get complacent, you fall behind.

All my career changes seem effortless, but nothing ever is. It takes hard work, attention to detail and, sometimes, great personal restraint. You have to be nice to everyone, as the fashion world is small. Give the third assistant on the shoot ten years and she may well have become the editor-in-chief. Some day, somehow, somewhere, you will meet that one person you were rude to, and she will be running the whole show.

When we wound up the clothing company we had a sample sale at our showroom in Margaret Street, which was like mayhem. Shakira Caine and Jerry and Betty Boo all came along to get their last fix of my stretchy leggings and tight velvet dresses. This was body-con time, remember. I was happy to see it all go. Still following the lesson I learned in adolescence ('eliminate the non-essential') I only kept a few items for myself.

The patterns and raw materials, however, I felt it would be worth hanging on to. You never know when you might want to make another career turnaround. So I insisted that they were returned to me, which left me with several huge boxes. 'Where shall I put them?' I happened to say to Mick and Jerry.

'I know!' Jerry said, and suggested the warehouse in Putney where the Rolling Stones keep all their memorabilia, from cars to discs to archives. It makes me laugh to think that sitting alongside the Stones' back catalogue are several brown boxes full of bodywear patterns and useless 'Marie Helvin' brass buttons! Mick, are you reading this? Will you be chucking my boxes out on the pavement any time soon?

*

'Love is the answer, but while you're waiting for the answer, sex raises some pretty good questions.'

WOODY ALLEN

'I have this really strong feeling we could be soulmates, and I always trust my instincts . . .'

I also found it hard not to feel hopeful that Eric Clapton and I might become close, as he said this is to me in the car while driving me home from one of our dates. First, after we saw each other at the Hard Rock Café, he had invited me to his concert at the Albert Hall, and then on to dinner at San Lorenzo. At the end of the evening we had a kiss, which he sweetly described as 'the stuff that rock 'n' roll dreams are made of'.

Dinner with him, though fun (once we went out with Mickey Rourke and his wife) wasn't the easiest experience. If I had a glass of wine with my starter, and then I ordered another one with my main course he would give me a look that spelled real disapproval. 'You want *another*?' he'd ask. Jeez, I thought, I can't be with this man. He had conquered his addictions bravely and round at his flat he always offered guests a glass of champagne, but there was a residual angst in him. People who have been through rehab are rarely cosy personalities, and Eric was the least cosy person I have ever met.

Another night, over at Eric's house (a tiny little front door in Chelsea that leads you by surprise into a huge, gorgeous, comfortable home designed by David Milinaric, with a square courtyard in the middle) and other guests included John McEnroe and his wife Tatum O'Neal – yes, the lovely actress who was formerly the snotty little girl I had met all those years ago. I didn't greet her with the patronising phrase 'My, how you've grown', though I certainly thought it. She was a beautiful spirit but there was a hardness to her. After dinner the four of us headed off to Ronnie Scott's in Eric's car. As we drove his car stereo was playing opera, which didn't surprise me at all, though John McEnroe seemed to find it incredible. 'What is this?' he cried. 'Eric Clapton listening to opera? You gotta be KIDDING!' Eric tensed up and I thought he was going to flip out at these Neanderthal comments, but he stayed calm. Leaving San Lorenzo we were snapped by paparazzi, and so for a few weeks the press thought we were all best friends, although we never went out as a four before or after. Inside the dark smoky atmosphere of Ronnie Scott's a Cuban band played while John and Tatum and I giggled over a shared joint. Eric looked on disapprovingly.

He and I never found a way of being comfortable with one another, nor a steady modus operandi for a relationship. Perhaps I wasn't the only one to be a little thrown by him: he told me that when someone set him up with Cher, she said barely a word throughout the whole dinner. That wasn't the same Cher I had met when she came, full of life and charisma, to Bailey's studio to be photographed.

When Eric threw a birthday party at San Lorenzo I gave him a beautiful long white silk scarf from Brown's, a real rock star's scarf. I received, a few days later, a card from his secretary saying: 'Eric has asked me to write to thank you very much ...'

Previously, he'd sent me long handwritten letters, full of innocent affection, and I found this by contrast an insultingly impersonal note. I told him in no uncertain terms that no thank you at all would have been better than grandly getting someone else to do it. He refused even to concede that I had a point. I also always knew, with Eric, that I was one of many. At this point in his life he was single, taking scores of girls out on dates. The point was proven when the *Daily Mail* ran a double page spread of about thirty pictures of him with various girls, me and Patsy Kensit included. The girl was always different, but the restaurant was always the same: San Lorenzo. He was going there for lunch and dinner every day – it was more home to him than home. Sometimes I wondered if he was lonely.

When I heard the news that Eric's baby son Conor had died in

New York, I sent a note of condolence immediately, of course. I felt powerless to support him in any other way. What could one say or do to help someone in that dreadful situation?

A few months later, we went out on another date and afterwards he ended up coming back to my flat, for the first time. We kissed a little but I didn't feel certain that I wanted this to go further. It didn't feel altogether right. I procrastinated, made some tea, and then announced I was sleepy, and had to be up in the morning, so maybe it was time to go . . . Eric flipped out. 'I haven't come here to worship at the temple of Marie Helvin!' he memorably shouted. There was desperation in that voice, bred perhaps by his NA and AA experiences and the brutal honesty those groups encourage. Perhaps he was at a stage in his life where he had to honour his angry feelings. He stormed out, leaving me tired and confused.

An hour later, my phone went. 'Marie, I'm sorry . . . I didn't mean to be angry, it's just that, you know, I have strong feelings for you.' Of course I forgave him. Against my better judgement, I said yes when he asked if he could come back round that night.

I shouldn't have let him. Our desire was clouded by so many other feelings: hostility, pity, grief, affection . . . But I wasn't going to play act to him or to anyone else that this or that fuck had changed my life when it hadn't. By this time I had embraced feminism. The male ego may be demanding but my own ego had developed too. After our encounter that night, I didn't return his calls.

Two weeks later, I was flying out to Mustique to visit Jerry and Mick when the porter at Gatwick said something that freaked me out. 'I expect you're meeting Mr Clapton then?' Er, no – or was I? When I walked into the first-class cabin, there he was. We were practically the only two people in the whole compartment. We smiled at each other, of course, through the crackle of mutual embarrassment. He came straight over to my seat and politely suggested we have lunch together. I said I was thrilled to see him, but first I just had to watch *The Silence of the Lambs*. We could chat together afterwards.

He went back to his seat and started playing with his Game Boy.

I sat there, ostensibly absorbed in the film. But really, thoughts were racing through my head. In the years since Suzon's death I had come increasingly to rely on my old belief that everything had significance; I was learning to see symbolism in random coincidences. So what did it mean that Eric and I had been thrown together like this, so soon after that disastrous night? Was it some kind of cosmic hint that I shouldn't have dismissed him from my life so readily?

We lunched together, up there in the sky, and got on just fine. He disembarked at St Lucia, where he had a home, while I carried on to Mustique. As we parted I gave him my number at Stargroves, Mick's house in Mustique, and he asked, gently, if we could start all over again?

In Mustique I had a fun few weeks with Mick and Jerry. Of course I confided to them the whole situation with Eric. Mick was so keen to see me settled with someone, he was really encouraging: 'Go for it! You're made for one another!' Jerry too said it sounded as if it was worth pursuing. At this time I was still listening to my girlfriends when they told me I shouldn't be single at my age. So I changed my route home from Mustique – flexibility being one of the advantages of flying first class – to include three days in St Lucia.

Eric and I had a quiet time in his home there, just the two of us, being peaceful and hanging out. Once Ronnie Wood and his entire extended family dropped in for lunch, the whole happy clan of them. Another day when I went over to Eric's veranda for tea I found him in a furious mood. The head of his record company had just rung him up, asking if he had any more songs about his dead son. No wonder he was enraged by this grossly insensitive commercialism. I was really shocked on his behalf too.

Was I interested in Eric? I wasn't sure. I had thirsted, ever since Suzon's death, for knowledge and insight; seeking it out had become my guiding principle in life. But something deep within me felt that being with Eric wasn't going to bring me nearer to enlightenment. That said, I did leave the door to my room unlocked, those three nights in St Lucia. Like a true gentleman, however, he never made a move. That door remained closed.

*

'What one writer can make in the solitude of one room is something no power can easily destroy.'

SALMAN RUSHDIE, *In Defence of the Novel, Yet Again*

'I inform the proud Muslim people of the world that the author of the *Satanic Verses* book, which is against Islam, the Prophet and the Koran, and all those involved in its publication who are aware of its content are sentenced to death.'

When I heard the Ayatollah's fatwa announced on the radio, I stopped in my tracks, firstly appalled that my friend should be in such danger, and secondly deeply concerned that any head of state should attempt to silence a writer. I rang Salman immediately, but the line was ominously dead.

Salman and I had been friends ever since we had met at a party at Gita and Sonny Mehta's house. (Sonny was then the head of Picador; he went on to become head of Knopf in New York.) I had just finished *Midnight's Children*, which Bailey had bought me, and was still reeling from it. Of all his books, I love it the best. But when I went over to pay homage, he totally surprised me by complimenting me on my recent contribution to the *Independent* – I had been invited to review London Fashion Week for one of the first editions of the newspaper. It was rare, in the frenetic, narcissistic world of fashion, to get any feedback on any work you'd done so I really appreciated his comments. We exchanged numbers, but soon found ourselves coincidentally thrown together again, judging (of all things) the Jazz Awards, along with Sting. I was used to presenting prizes – in those days, if they wanted a pretty face for an event it would either be Jerry or me, depending on who was around.

I have known Salman through three wives. Our friendship has always been intense yet platonic. But I find platonic friendships are often propelled by a form of attraction, a chemistry that isn't sexual but does lead to a kind of mutual fascination.

Salman and I became close and he and Marianne Wiggins, his

second wife, visited me in Pimlico several times before the fatwa was announced. But although he was forced into hiding, it didn't mean the end of our friendship.

At Annabel's one night I was chatting to the journalist Charlie Glass when I told him how worried I was about Salman. 'What can we do for him?' I asked.

'Marie,' said Glass slowly, cautiously, 'I think I could help you get in touch with him.'

I was thrilled, and didn't even consider for a moment that it might be prejudicial to my safety. That was left to Jerry to point out a year or so later when she saw something in the papers about me and Salman, and rang me up, concerned.

I took Salman's secrecy very seriously. Charlie Glass was as good as his word and a friend of his friend contacted Salman on my behalf and a rendezvous was arranged. The night I was due to meet him, I first went to a party given by my lawyer Sir Anthony Rubenstein at Lincoln's Inn Fields, where Sir Geoffrey Robinson whispered to me, 'I think we both know the most infamous man in London.'

'Do you mean Billy Keating?' I asked, disingenuously naming my great friend the mischievous art dealer.

That put Geoffrey off the scent. When he silently mouthed, 'No, Salman!' I pretended to know absolutely nothing about him, then headed outside into a taxi, off to visit that most 'infamous' man.

First I made a detour to the famous Indian sweetmeat shop on Brick Lane, where I filled a massive box with the brightly coloured confections, one of each kind. Salman, when I met him at a secret address, was understandably very depressed about his situation, but he flipped out over the simple pleasure of the sweets.

MI5 reluctantly agreed that he could come and visit me for dinner, but only after they phoned me, vetted me and carried out a full security sweep of my premises. Then, as he was due to arrive, a security guard posted in my flat would liaise on a walkie-talkie with a guard in the street, and finally, Salman would rush furtively through the hall and into my flat, his four bodyguards all piling in after him.

So we could be private at dinner, the bodyguards would sit downstairs in my bedroom, watching television. Kathy Lette, who was also close to Salman at the time, used to joke that they liked assignments round at my place best, because they got to sit on my bed. In fact over time, I became quite friendly with them and was even invited, unbeknownst to Salman, to the security men's annual Sir Robert Peel party.

Years later, one evening at Sheekey's restaurant, I saw one of their familiar faces. 'How are you doing?' I asked. 'And who are you guarding now?'

'You'll see,' he replied; a few minutes later, in walked Robert Mugabe.

I was so shocked that the friend I was dining with, Sophie de Stempel, had to tell me, 'Close your mouth, Marie.'

I put a lot of effort into making the dinner parties special for Salman, consulting him over whom he'd like to meet and what cuisine he was hungering for. He couldn't go into the world so I wanted to bring the world to him, and I spent days preparing Thai- or Japanese- or American-themed feasts. Living on my own, I was getting really into cooking for the first time. The guests included Lou Reed and Laurie Anderson, Bailey and Catherine, Brian Eno, Brian Clarke, Peter Gabriel, Alexei and Linda Sayle, Zaha Hadid, Lorna and Kazuo Ishiguro ... Everyone was sworn to secrecy, of course – and commendably, no news about our dinners for Salman ever leaked out.

Over dinner we debated everything, from Robert Lepage's hit show *The Tales of Genji* (Salman, disallowed any theatre visits, wanted to hear all about it) to whether the monarchy could be justified. Mick once turned up at the last minute, but Jerry would never come, for reasons of safety. Alan Yentob was also a regular, and once when we were arguing over a Mel Brooks film, he memorably demanded a telephone and rang Mel Brooks directly, thus settling the argument once and for all. More to the point, it made Salman smile.

*

The period between mainstream sexual awakening and the advent of AIDS was so brief and so precious. By the early 1980s the party was over. The AIDS epidemic could no longer be ignored. Moving in fashion circles meant I had become painfully aware of it much earlier. So many people I knew fell victim, including the male supermodel Joe McDonald, who was one of the first public AIDS casualties. I had known him in his gorgeous prime, but hadn't known it would be so brief.

Most heartbreakingly, I lost Tina Chow to the disease. After I saw her in LA she stopped going out with Richard Gere, although they remained good friends. She then contracted it from someone whose identity remains unknown. As she grew sick she withdrew from her friends and the world, and died in a care home at Pacific Palisades, LA, in January 1992 leaving two beautiful children, China and Maximillian.

Even before Tina's tragic death, AIDS had a profound impact on me. Of course it did: the fashion industry was decimated by it. Every other day another star died: Perry Ellis; Gia Carangi (whom Angelina Jolie immortalised in *Gia*); Halston, so many others. I became heavily involved in the Aids Crisis Trust, founded by my friend the art dealer Adrian Ward-Jackson and the redoubtable Marguerite Littman in 1986.

Here, I learned how to play the stuffy royal protocol game for fund-raising. You couldn't just approach any old HRH, there was a strict order of precedence you had to work through each time and, moreover, the rules for newspaper coverage deemed that there was a strict rota for which paper was to be given a royal exclusive. This put me in the bizarre predicament of having to give a story about a Valentino show attended by Princess Diana to no other paper but the *Sun*.

I was really impressed by the general goodwill towards the Trust, however. Seal gave us a free Valentine's concert at Hammersmith, and when I tentatively asked Elton John if he would introduce Seal, he flew over from France like a shot. After the Christies' auction of Princess Diana's clothes in New York, the Aids Crisis Trust wound down and Elton continued the good fight with his own phenomenal AIDS foundation. Marguerite and I had approached Richard Branson for backing for the trust and he was supportive too. He had us to lunch on his boat in Little Venice, where we discussed how he could help us. As we were leaving he said he'd been expecting me to tell him I was starting a modelling agency. I wasn't interested in that, I told him, but I knew a girl who was: Sarah Doukas. And *voilà* – with some of his funds and her expertise, Storm was created.)

Then Adrian Ward-Jackson also fell ill with AIDS. Visiting him was a devastating experience, and once or twice, on my way to see him, I passed Princess Diana in the hall, her head bowed with sadness, her hand covering her tear-streaked face. She was a constant visitor, his carer told me. I also sat near her at Adrian's funeral. If she was a little wary of me because I had been Camilla Parker Bowles's brother's girlfriend – and Camilla herself had been a friend of mine, attending the launch of my book *Catwalk*, for instance – she never let it show.

One of the highlights of the Aids Crisis Trust calendar, in 1989, was the Tiffany Ball at Cliveden. I had been promoted, almost by default, to the grand role of Deputy Chairman of the Trust and was made Chair of the ball. I packed the committee with my friends – Dodi, Jerry, Shakira Caine, Catherine Bailey, Leonora Lichfield, Hugo Vickers, Susannah Constantine – and made sure they all sold tickets to the ball for £250 per head, which was then considered a huge sum. *Le tout* London was there, and more, from Tony Curtis to Yasmin Le Bon. Joan Collins drew the raffle, Dame Edna Everage entertained us (and Barry Humphries attended the dinner); Mica Paris and Courtney Pine performed and after dinner there was dancing to Georgie Fame.

Diana, the guest of honour, arrived early at the committee members' champagne reception, luminous in a white appliqué gown with a chanson collar. That night she also met someone who would go on to become a close confidante, Rosa Monckton, then the managing director of Tiffany. And there was one other important introduction, too. 'Have you met Dodi Fayed?' I remember asking. The rest, as they say, is history. Sadly, I was whisked away to deal with some formality to do with the guest list, so I couldn't eavesdrop on their first conversation.

Of course, they didn't get together till many years later. In fact, he was with another of his many girlfriends that night at Cliveden. The first I knew of his relationship with Diana was when the press got hold of it, and my phone didn't stop ringing for days. Somehow, the papers had my private number (around this time there were lots of instances of phone company employees selling celebrity phone numbers). Every journalist wanted to ask me what Dodi was like (how many times can you say, 'Lovely, no further comment'?) and every news bulletin erroneously splashed pictures of me as his former girlfriend.

I phoned Dodi and said, 'The press are going nuts here!' Then I laughed and told him to take care. Days later he left me a sweet message, sounding happy and like himself. It was the last contact we ever had.

According to Muslim custom he was buried close to twenty-four hours after his death, so I rang Mr Al Fayed's secretary to find out where I could pay my respects. The place they indicated was Brookwood cemetery in Woking, about an hour and a half out of London and near the grounds of the Al Fayed estate. My friend Lin, Peter Cook's widow, kindly drove me over there and waited in the car while I was escorted by security guards to a specially built garden enclave. As I was going in, I passed Dodi's uncle, and I simply bowed my head to him. No words of condolence seemed adequate. Dodi's grave, flanked by flaming braziers, was a large plain slab, facing Mecca. An incredible three out of five British people are of the opinion that the events in Paris that night do not make sense, and I count myself among them. Perhaps one day we will know the truth.

*

'Beauty is not in the face; beauty is a light in the heart.'

KAHLIL GIBRAN

I now reached a time in my life where I felt, quite frankly, lost. I have a distinct memory of going to Sting and Trudie's house in Wiltshire and sitting next to Alan Rickman, who turned to me and asked me, 'So what do you want to do now?'

I said, 'I just want to be.'

I can't believe I said something so trite to someone I admired, but hey, that was where my head was then. Rickman gave a squint, in that very British way. But really, I had no idea where I was in life any more. It was as if I had only just realised I was a divorced single woman of a questionable age. The concept that modelling was a young person's job only came to me very late. To be fair, I had worked pretty much constantly, so why shouldn't it have?

But now I had become curious to explore myself, to look inward. The experience of Suzon's death was still unfolding within me and it made me feel the need to live a different kind of life – broader, more spiritual, more humble. Unanswered longing and betrayal leave their scars. Which was how I came to find myself living in a tent for a month on the Hawaiian island of Kauai.

I was there on a private estate owned by a Tibetan Buddhist group, although I didn't get too deeply into the religious side of it. I mainly kept myself to myself. During the day I swam, I read, I wrote, I thought. At night I lay half-in, half-out of my tent – a bit like the pup tents we had for Scouts – and looking at the sky and listening to the water lapping and watching the stars shooting. I sat there in meditation repeating the chant:

> 'There is no other than emptiness.
> Emptiness is no other than form.
> Form is no other than emptiness . . .'

I fasted for the whole three weeks, to free my mind and body of decades of accumulated debris. The only thing I consumed was lemon water, cayenne pepper and maple syrup – what is now known as 'the Beyoncé diet' but is in fact an ancient Ayurvedic cleansing regime. People imagine that when you're fasting all you think about is doughnuts, but it's not like that. This is nothing to do with losing weight, and it's wrong to imagine it could be. Instead, it's about purity. When you come to the end of your fast you don't want to gorge. You need to reintroduce solid food slowly to your body. I feel this process is a form of rebirth, a chance to start over. Some knowledge, I believe, is more readily learned through the body than the mind.

I needed to do the retreat to cleanse my body and mind and go back to zero. Sometimes, I took a week-long fast at a country retreat in England called Shrubland Hall: sleeping, being in nature, speed-walking – when no one's looking: it looks like a modern-day Ministry of Silly Walks – and consuming nothing but lemon, honey and hot water, four times a day. Ever since Suzon died I have found it necessary to do that every once in a while: to clear out and start again.

For a period I was fascinated by Eastern medicine. On Mariella Frostrup's recommendation I went to Chiva-Som in Thailand, where I had my chakra photographed. They instruct you to take off all traces of make-up and to scrape your hair back, and then the photograph is just a burst of light, like a normal one. (The process is surprisingly expensive, though – as so many New Age things often are.) The photo showed up a strong chakra round my stomach, from which bright green rays emanated. The Thai doctor didn't explain what it meant, he merely said, 'Mmmm ... very unusual.' So much so, in fact, he asked to keep a copy to display. So, bizarrely, somewhere on the wall of this faraway spa there hangs a picture of me and my 'unusual' chakra.

I've been interested in a great many esoteric things through my life, and attracted a good many strange letters, asking: Had I travelled back and forth between the Pleiades, Clarion, Orion, Sirius? Am I a member of the Federation? Can I say when the Mother Ship will arrive? Others asked if I had a celestial connection with David Bowie.

Sometimes, on a very clear night on the beach, I stretch my arms out to the stars. 'If there's anything out there that wants me, come and get me! Beam me up! Take me back to the Rainbow Family!'

Well, Pop always said I was nutty as a fruitcake, a southern one with plenty of pecans in it. Much as the retreats helped me, they probably also confused me as well.

For example, I finally quit smoking. For this I have to thank Peter Gabriel. (Bailey had never been any help to me in this department. During the end of our marriage after he'd given up smoking effortlessly he used to say to me: 'If my stupid secretary can give up smoking, why can't you?' It was infuriating. I wasn't competing with Bailey's secretary!) Peter never smoked and through going out with him I realised that kissing me must have been like kissing an old ash tray. Going on my retreats had made me clear-sighted enough to see things from a distance.

Peter helped me think about the psychology of my addiction. He was expert at providing insight into every mental process. He made an acute observation one day that stopped me in my tracks. 'Whenever we sit down to really talk, you light up,' he said. 'Whenever you start a phone call, it's the same. You use them to help you through every difficult decision too.' He made me realise what a crutch they were for me, and started the process that led to me retreating home to Hawaii at the age of thirty-nine – and returning a forty-year-old non-smoker.

In Hawaii I wrote down all my reasons for giving up, to help fix them in my mind. It was almost like my summer assignment. I stocked up on popcorn, to chew whenever I needed an oral fix (nicotine gum never worked for me: it tasted revolting and gave me heartburn). I also discovered that the best way to quit was to keep the body alkaline, so it didn't crave the acid that comes with nicotine. When the urge to smoke came upon me I would count to ten. If that didn't work I would run outside and jump into the swimming pool, anything to jolt me out of the craving. I tried to focus on what my brain really wanted instead of the cigarette, whether that was a glass of water or just to shift position in my chair. Occasionally I would try positive visualisation techniques, spurring myself on by imagining the inside of my lungs healthy, clean and pink.

It worked, perhaps because finally, for the first time in my life, I had owned my addiction. Before when I'd tried to quit I'd been to see counsellors, hypnotherapists and other assorted experts, paid my money, bought my herbs or tinctures and handed over the responsibility for my addiction to someone or something else. Now I had accepted that the buck stopped with me. I couldn't wait to tell Peter the good news.

When I got back from Hawaii he came to pick me up from the airport and we drove on, with his ex-wife and her new boyfriend in the back of the car too, to a Stones concert.

'So don't you notice anything different about me?' I said gleefully.
'Suntan?' he asked.

When I told him, he was pleased for me, but I didn't get quite the response I was hoping for. When a lifelong smoker quits they don't want a pat on the back. They want screaming and jumping. They want a brass band parade with tickertape!

But giving up was its own reward. I felt clean, clear and had a great deal more energy. My skin began to glow again, as if it had just been scrubbed. To help with the process of giving up, I avoided alcohol and restaurants for about three months. I began to like the new me that was emerging.

I started trying to find the natural solution to every lifestyle dilemma. I guess it was a stab at being eco-friendly before the movement began. (I owe the world recompense for a lifetime of carbon emissions, after all. I have serious plane guilt!) Uneasy about the long list of chemical additives in cosmetics, I turned to my kitchen for inspiration. I seized on the humble margarine tub: body butter before it was invented! I slathered it all over my skin and loved the smooth, unctuous feeling, and the vitamins it delivered. Margarine for the face, then, and neat Flora cooking oil for the body. I even poured it straight in the bath. Delicious.

A copywriter's girlfriend read about my unusual beauty fixes in a women's magazine, and the upshot was that Flora approached me with a proposal for a huge advertising campaign, which would feature one shot of me stir frying vegetables and another of me in the shower with a bottle of Flora applying the oil all over my body. It ran for two years. Not only was it financially one of the biggest modelling contracts I'd ever had, I also loved the idea. It was something I truly did, so why not? As an older model, you either go anal, preserving your so-called dignity at all costs, or you go kooky and embrace your inner health nut. I figured life would be more fun the nutty way.

At home, I was developing my own detoxing ritual, inspired by Eastern medicine I'd discovered on my retreat. On a Friday night I would take psyllium husks, a natural fibre to aid cleansing. Then over the weekend I would fast, consuming only hot water or lemon and honey. But on a fruit fast I would eat as many grapes or apples or watermelons as I liked, my only rule being to stick to one type of fruit all day and never ever citrus fruits. The first day might bring toxin headaches if you smoke or drink caffeine, but by the end of the weekend I would be free from bloating, fatigue and tension, cleansed in body and mind – reborn, in a word.

Are you thinking what my agent was thinking? There could be a book here. And so it was that *Bodypure*, my 1995 detox manual, came about. I was really proud of it, and though it was no Carol Vorderman-style runaway bestseller, perhaps in some small way it helped prepare the ground for the detox craze that swept Britain four years later.

After I published *Bodypure*, I emerged from my searching, lost phase. I put all that to bed and emerged into the limelight again. We all go through phases in life, and sometimes I'm a recluse, while other times I'm the star of the Mardi Gras.

I went to galas and launches and premieres and cocktails, cocktails, cocktails. I threw Academy Awards parties, and Thanksgiving parties, and chaired a ball for Oxfam called 'Pink is the Navy Blue of India'. And of course they served champagne at the *Bodypure* launch party at the Halcyon Hotel. In fact the party was so much fun I threw another one the next year, and gradually it became an annual fixture. Jerry, Mick, Brian Eno, Bob Geldof and Jeanne Marine all came along, and when, one year, the party clashed with a key England match in the World Cup, I fixed huge screens up so the guests wouldn't miss out (let's face it, I feared no one would turn up otherwise). The party ended up on the front page of the *Guardian*, under the question: 'Where will YOU be tonight?' The BBC came to film the party on the nine p.m. news and they panned across the room taking in Mick and Tom Stoppard and maybe Michael Winner. 'Who *isn't* here?' the interviewer asked me. Of course it was a rhetorical question that I shouldn't have answered but by that time I was several glasses of champagne in, so I happily said: 'Gary Lineker's hopefully on his way!'

Around this time I was invited by Tony Palmer to take a part in his feature film, a Timberlake Wertenbaker adaptation of the Edith Wharton novel *The Children*. It had a great cast (Kim Novak, Karen Black, Rupert Graves, Geraldine Chaplin, Donald Sinden, Robert Stephens ...) and I had to fly to Bavaria to play a few scenes with the star, Ben Kingsley.

More than a little apprehensive about starting out my acting career opposite an actor who'd just won an Oscar for *Gandhi*, I asked Salman to write a letter of introduction to Ben from me. 'Just put "be nice to my friend Marie – it's her first serious acting job" or something like that,' I said. As soon as I got off the plane in Munich I was driven to Berchtesgaden and straight to the set to see Tony Palmer. Tony took me round to Ben Kingsley's trailer, where he was sitting alone, probably ruminating, in the way that actors do. He had a very still, powerful, charismatic presence. The first thing he said to me, with great intensity, was: 'So how do you intend to play the scene?' I hadn't even had a chance to give him the special letter of introduction; shit! I fumbled for it and stood there like a child while he read it. It must have said the right thing because his demeanour changed totally and he was very warm and encouraging after that. We also bonded when we discovered we were both reading the same book: *The Road Less Travelled*, by M. Scott Peck.

Filming was still a baptism of fire, though. I love Edith Wharton – I've read *The House of Mirth* five times at least – and was quite taken with my character, Princess Buondelmonte, and the twenties jazz age she inhabited. But I had expected at least a little rehearsal on set before we started filming. Not a chance. Perhaps Academy Award winners don't need to rehearse. It was straight in without any warning. And Ben was fantastic, from the first take. We finished shooting all my scenes after two days and the entire crew gave me a round of applause. Was that because they knew I was out of my depth? I was reassured to find out, later, that all the cast members received the same treatment.

There was a cast screening at Tony Palmer's house in Notting Hill when the film was finished. It was a complex piece of work, all right. The story, which had seemed so lucid in the script, had turned into a pan-European whirl of smoke, experimental camerawork and dramatic music by Mahler. When the credits rolled we all sat there, dumbfounded.

Still, when the film was shown at the Singapore film festival I was flown there to promote it, and my mother came over from Hawaii for the ride too. *The Children* was the opening film of the whole festival, and at the premiere Mom sat next to Giles Jacob, head of the Cannes film festival, and I sat next to Ben Kingsley, in the front row of the cinema. But when it came to my scene something came over me. I saw myself fifteen feet tall on the cinema screen and I got the giggles. My shoulders were really shaking and my knees kept hitting Ben's. God knows what he thought was wrong with me. My acting career, I felt, was not destined for greatness. The press was hilarious. Baz Bambigboye, commenting on my dowdy costume, wrote breathlessly: 'This is her first film ... Everyone says she's marvellous. But look what they've done to Britain's No 1 Model.'

*

Back in London, my second butterfly years were in full swing, and I went to a host of events. I sat next to a young Kate Moss at a prizegiving lunch, just after she'd won her three-year Calvin Klein contract. Sarah told me to give her some interview tips, because she had been chatting nineteen to the dozen to journalists, practically giving away the address of her new home. She was so sweet and gawky, yakking away in pure Croydon, and there was clearly going to be no stopping that. Soon she had a blanket ban on interviews. Clearly she was something special because the Calvin Klein contract was so impressive – and yet unlike other models, she didn't look like a breed apart. She looked like the sexiest, most beautiful girl-next-door you've ever seen. 'You gotta sign her exclusively,' I told Sarah and Simon at Storm. Putting a model under contract was unheard of, because we don't normally sign contracts with agents, but Sarah and her brother Simon knew she was exceptional and she is still represented solely by Storm.

After a lecture at Tate Modern on Francis Bacon, I went out to dinner with Brian Clarke (executor of the Bacon estate); Sir Harrison Birtwistle (wearing an aloha shirt!) and his wife; the author Gordon Burns; and the art critic, David Sylvester. With him, as with Sir Paul Getty, I found a common ground discussing the movies of the thirties and forties. 'How have you seen so many?' he asked. I never regretted skipping school to watch all those afternoon movies.

One night I was asked out to San Lorenzo by Robert Fox (the theatre producer), who was holding a private dinner there for some US angels (backers). The reason I'd been invited became clear when I saw I was sitting next to Dirk Bogarde. We'd kept in touch since Grasse and I was thrilled to chat with him. He seemed a little down, however. Natasha Richardson was sitting on the other side of him, and we both tried to reassure Dirk when he told us his career woes. His new young American agent had asked to see his showreel, he lamented. 'That's ridiculous!' Natasha and I chorused.

Another night I met Johnny Depp, when he had just finished filming *Fear and Loathing in Las Vegas*. I was out to dinner at the Ivy with Salman and as we left the restaurant I stopped at the table where my friends – the film director Terry Gilliam and Ray Cooper, the percussionist – were sitting with Johnny Depp. I introduced Salman, and they asked us what we were doing later. 'Going for a drink at Brown's nightclub – come along!' I said. Later, they called us to tell us they were on their way. I told Jake the owner of Brown's to look after them – and he sure did. He escorted us all up to a private room and practically barricaded us in there – me and these four men! I was mortified because I imagined they would rather be on the dance floor than stuck in a room with just me for female company. We had a few drinks before splitting. My abiding impression was how gracious and humble Johnny Depp was. His dark good looks put me in mind of a young Bailey before I knew him. He spoke so softly I had to try and read his beautiful lips.

At the party after the premiere of *The Remains of the Day* I sat on the same table as my friend Kazuo Ishiguro. Some prat came over and started saying loudly and clearly, as if to a foreigner, 'You must have done masses and masses of research for that film . . .' Kaz and I were kicking one another under the table – he's as British as the Queen. At another party I met the publisher Kimberly Fortier. 'You should meet a friend of mine,' she said. 'He'd love your voice.' Who was this friend of hers? David Blunkett.

I went to the Garrick wearing jodhpurs which made Robin Day boom over his bow-tie, 'Riding wear? At the Garrick?' I guess he didn't know they were by Gucci. That night I spoke to Terry Donovan, who seemed down about life and work. 'You were the best thing that ever happened to Bailey,' he said sweetly. The next day I called Bailey to tell him I was worried about Terry; three weeks later, I had a terrible call from Rosie Boycott at the *Independent* at eight on a Saturday morning.

'Terry Donovan has committed suicide,' she said. My first thought was, Oh my God, how do we tell Bailey? 'I'm sorry,' she said, 'but I have to be an editor now and ask if Bailey will write something for us . . .'

I rang him to tell him the news and he was silent for so long I almost thought he had hung up, but I could faintly hear his breathing, ragged and emotional.

I went to one party wearing a very piratical eye patch. Out in Battersea Park I had been socked in the eye by a stray baseball and was rushed to Moorfields. My eye wasn't just bruised, it was grossly swollen, like a frog's, and it stayed that way for over a week. An eye patch was the only solution – though at the party, in an excruciating coincidence, I was not the only woman wearing one. The other woman was the courageous *Sunday Times* war reporter Marie Colvin, who had lost an eye covering the Sri Lankan civil war. Snappers chased us round the party trying to photograph us together.

Once, so the story goes, Marie Colvin was pursuing Mrs Thatcher's private secretary Sir Charles Powell for a quote, though, perhaps unwilling to be pinned down by a reporter, he avoided her calls for a week. Finally, she was put through and greeted by a warm 'Hello darling!' – his secretary had mistaken her name for mine. Peter Cook, delighted by this anecdote, sent me the cutting about it from the *Evening Standard*.

Thanksgiving was another excuse for a party. If I couldn't be at home with my family, I still felt the need to mark the date. So Brian Clarke and I used to jointly host a huge feast for about 120 people, including everyone from Robocop to Salman Rushdie. Who else? Ken Livingstone, Marc Quinn, Norman and Elena Foster, Simon Kelner, Danny Huston … and most of the Fiennes: Sophie and Martha and Joe and Ralph. Once Tom Stoppard brought Glenn Close. Another time I went around introducing Ken to all my lovely single girlfriends saying proudly, 'This is our mayor' till he said to me, sotto voce: 'Marie, please, just "Ken".'

Paul McCartney and Stella and Mary always came so I had to perfect my vegetarian stuffing: pine nuts, cranberries, sage, onion … The stuffing was so in demand I made enough to fill a brand-new dustbin. The year Paul McCartney brought Heather Mills along for the first time he gave an impromptu concert at the piano, which was wonderful for all of us, even if he seemed to be addressing every song specifically to her.

One of my favourite party guests was always Tom Stoppard, my new good friend. We met through Mick, with whom he was great friends, and the connection was immediate. He had then just finished the screenplay for *Shakespeare in Love*, and was working on *The Invention of Love*. We enjoyed long conversations on the terrace at Mick's chateau, in La Forchette, the Loire, overlooking a stunning formal walled garden designed by Alvide Lees-Milne. There we would talk about anything from the work of David Lean to whether women really were from Venus.

Jerry and I would often go out with him for dinner – a peculiar trio, perhaps, to outside eyes, but to us, it worked. He gave us great advice when Jerry and I were attempting to get our Henrietta Moraes project off the ground. One night we went to a huge *Vanity Fair*-sponsored Royal Court fund-raiser together. Jerry and Mick were starting to have serious problems, and she was mainly there out of duty to their public coupledom. At the end of the evening she went home early, and said no thank you when I offered to come with her. She left without even saying goodbye to Mick – and, to his chagrin, she took the car. Mick and Tom and I carried on to the Café de Paris, where girls were dancing on podiums and the music was so loud we had to shout. Seeing the great British playwright in such a setting amused me. I am positive it was the first and the last time Tom had ever been there, but he was curious and very game to come along.

Mick and Jerry splitting up made me desperately sad because they'd been in my life as a perfect pair for so long. I was determined not to take sides: I loved them both. Suffice to say, he gave her a privileged lifestyle and she gave him four beautiful children. I will not judge who was right or wrong – that is between them. So much goes on in private between couples that no matter how close you are you will always be an outsider, not privy to people's thoughts and personal pain. When Jerry and I and Bailey and Mick were no longer a foursome, we drifted. Our friendship had been perfect in and of its time.

Tom and I were invited by our mutual friends Patrick Kinmonth the respected stage designer and Robert Carsen the acclaimed director to see their production of *Semele* by Handel at English National Opera. We both took our own dates along that night but the press got the wrong idea. It was around this time that a piece appeared in the *Daily Mail* diary column hinting that we were an item. This wasn't in fact the case, but like most press reports it became immediately accepted as gospel truth. Everyone seemed to think we were going out – apart from me. I hadn't even seen the *Daily Mail* article and I was really shocked when I read in the *Telegraph* a few months later that I was supposedly moving in with Tom.

'This just came out of nowhere!' I laughed to Tom on the phone.

'Well,' he said sheepishly, 'there was a gossip item about us a few months back, but I didn't see fit to complain . . .' In fact, he made it clear he'd rather enjoyed all the rumours. Who was I to spoil the fun? We never denied that we were together, and let the press do all the frenzied speculating they liked. They even went so far as to ask Tom's son, the actor Ed, what he thought of me and his father. I enjoyed his sardonically witty reply. 'Oh yeah, my family's straight out of Walt Disney.'

By this time I had moved out of my Pimlico home. I'd been there long enough for people to become widely cognisant of my address, and I got a lot of fan mail. Most of it was unthreatening, sweet even – Milk Tray and a teddy bear, every year, from a man who's head of a refrigeration company – but one of my fans, a man from the Netherlands, started to lose control. At first he sent me pressed flowers, mementoes, little nothings. I always wrote back just to say thank you. Then he started sending tickets – plane tickets, train tickets, tickets to the ballet . . . I sent them straight back at first, but then there were so many I couldn't keep up. Next I received abusive letters, saying he'd lost money buying these tickets for me, and finally, letters containing bundles of excrement arrived. When I gave them to the police they confirmed my worst misgivings: it was human shit.

Interpol and the local police took it all really seriously, even back then in the days before Jill Dando was murdered. They taught me that the correct way to respond to fan mail is to keep correspondence brisk and impersonal. I should never have put 'love' or drawn kisses on a reply, even though to me it had just seemed an easy way of being friendly but brief. Apparently stalkers misinterpret these sign-offs, fixating on the number of kisses. The police also advised me, quite simply, to move house.

I moved from my traditional early Victorian flat in to the modern minimalism of the Richard Rogers-designed Montevetro building in Battersea. I had a panoramic view across the Thames, and plenty of room for yoga in the mornings. I also had privacy. I made sure my lawyer took my name off the council's list of public addresses. Tom lived right across the river from me, but when we did a test – 'OK, I'm waving now' – there was a huge yew tree blocking the view and we couldn't see one another at all. My morning yoga could be naked yoga, if I felt so inclined. But a small part of me was wishing I could be practising my salute to the sun on the golden beaches of home, instead of overlooking the murky Thames.

ELEVEN

HAWAII CALLING

'The life of a man is a circle from childhood to childhood,
and so it is in everything where power moves.'

BLACK ELK, *Native American Wisdom*

$\mathcal{D}$uring the Gulf war, I became addicted to CNN. I used to sit up watching it all through the night, transfixed, addicted as if to a computer game. I couldn't believe the immediacy of it all: you watched a soldier in a plane detonating a device, and then seconds later you saw the explosion flare into light. Perhaps I was particularly moved by it because it reminded me of the intensity of my feelings as I watched the Vietnam war on TV as a teenager.

The price for my addiction to CNN was a stomach ulcer. My doctor (who was quite a character, and wrote medical mysteries under the pen name Stuart Stern) specifically told me: 'You've got to turn that bloody TV off.' So I tried to shut myself off from the war. My family were surprised that I developed ulcers, because I was always the chilled-out happy one of the family. It was Pop who was volatile, prone to flying off the handle all the time, and it was he whom everyone expected to get an ulcer, but the diagnosis made sense to me. I had always kept my feelings in, bubbling down below. No wonder I paid the price for it physically. I have learned, over the years, that I don't feel my feelings: I am my feelings. My emotions present themselves in my body.

I was sick in bed with flu watching Vivien Leigh in *Lady Hamilton* when the film was interrupted by the terrifying 9/11 news bulletin.

Shortly afterwards, there was a knock at my door from one of the Montevetro porters. 'Miss Helvin, just to reassure you, we have the building surrounded by guards.' I don't know what good they thought guards round the building would do, but it was a kind gesture. Apparently they knocked on all the Americans' doors as a priority.

After 9/11 life became more serious. I felt intensely vulnerable, an American in a strange and increasingly hostile world. My father told me to try and get hold of a fake Canadian passport or ID if I could. I knew a passenger on one of the planes: Marisa Berenson's sister Berry, the photographer. She was an acquaintance, but just to have an acquaintance on one of those planes changes you for ever. I was prescribed Prozac, the first and only anti-depressant I ever took in my life. I didn't feel comfortable on it and weaned myself off after six months. The tragedy of 9/11 made me reassess life. What was I going to do? Sit here in this beautiful Richard Rogers-designed building with my arms behind my head?

I felt the need to get out there and be industrious again. Work was also a necessity, as in the economic crash that followed 9/11, I lost a lot of money in stocks and shares. The investments I was living off simply disappeared. I had to move out of my home and for about two years before I settled in Chelsea again, I lived in borrowed homes of friends, or as their guest: Brian Clarke, Norma Heyman, Christopher Heath and Salman Rushdie (I devoured his library when I was house-sitting for him). They were all so generous to me. You always hope you can depend on your friends and then, when you need them, there they are, right beside you.

And so I relaunched my modelling career at the age of fifty. Wow, that was unexpected. I was surprised by it, so was my agent and so were my clients. According to the *Daily Mail*, my success was 'startling'.

But in a sense I had never really been away, often taking plum jobs when I fancied them. The Thierry Mugler twentieth anniversary show in 1995, for example, had been great fun. Billed by the news-papers as 'the apogee of success', the show took place in the Cirque d'Hiver in Paris, featured an all-star modelling cast including Claudia Schiffer, Amber Valetta, Linda Evangelista, Elle Macpherson, and even legends like Tippi Hedren (so tiny) and Patti Hearst (somewhat grand; when Jerry forgot her blusher, delaying our car, she sighed exaggeratedly). In one final *coup de théâtre*, James Brown appeared as the closing surprise act. It was magnificent, but even here I was thinking of home. In the wings, waiting to go on, I was chatting to Julie Newmar, who had played Catwoman to Adam West's Batman. 'I was your biggest fan as a child!' I said. 'And I knew Batman too. He was a great friend of my pop's.' She told me he always spoke of his pre-Batman life in Hawaii so fondly – and as I stepped out on to the vast cantilevered stage in the Cirque D'Hiver I felt a small pang of homesickness.

One-off jobs were fun, but to relaunch myself as a full-time model was something quite different. The newspapers made it sound so effortless, but nothing in life is ever effortless. It took a while for the ball to start rolling and for work to come in. We older models are a small band: me, Twiggy, Jerry ... Is there anyone else out there? Why not? Women my age are beautiful, not 'still' beautiful. It's like Bette Davis said: 'If you want a job well done, get a couple of old broads to do it.'

Despite the hype, employment for a model in her fifties is hard to come by. Those twenty- and thirty-somethings who work in advertising have a very old-fashioned idea of fifty. Marks & Spencer and L'Oréal have helped change the market by employing older models but more companies should do the same. All I can say is: I am what a woman in her fifties looks like today!

I've been lucky in that my genes and my lifelong moisturising routine have helped keep me looking good for my age. But my mom has always told me that Japanese women look great, great, great – until they wake up one morning and suddenly they look a thousand years old. I haven't had that morning yet, thank God, and neither has Mom.

The press coverage was great, however. 'Fabulous at Fifty' proclaimed the *Mail*. 'Do You Think I'm Sexy?' ran the *Sunday Times* headline, over a picture of me posing in a neon disco setting. 'She's got it: She's Fast, She's Filthy, She's Fifty,' continued the article inside. So what if it was a little over the top to characterise the fact that I wasn't wearing any knickers as 'a scene from *Basic Instinct*' – the article was still a great way to celebrate my second coming. It was racy enough that when my goddaughter Delilah Khomo asked to see it, her mother Ninivah censoriously cut some bits out before sending it to her at Benenden School. The Fantasy Older Woman tag was working well for me. I've found that younger men are more confident about asking me out than men my age, but unfortunately, contrary to what people imagine, I've never been interested in much younger men. Perhaps it's to do with having a kid brother.

People ask if I went back to modelling at fifty in order to prove a point about the emancipation of the older female? Not really. Life is never quite like that, is it? Things happen for more practical reasons. Part of the reason I got back into modelling was due to a few successful shoots with the great photographer Nick Knight.

One was *Vogue's* 'supermodel' line-up for their special millennium issue. About forty models struck a pose, from Carmen Dell'Orifice to Alek Wek. I was standing on the white podium for the shoot, working it, feeling the music, the wind in my hair, my eyes totally blinded by the arc lights – I was completely lost in the job. So much so that when my left breast escaped the flimsy dress I was wearing, I barely noticed: I was working. When the lights went down I heard the sound of applause and realised with a shock that there were by now quite a lot of people in the studio, and they'd all been watching. Even Kate Moss was sitting there, clapping away. It was a surprise to me. No one clapped in my day. When the pictures came out in *Vogue*, yes, you guessed it, they chose the one with my breast showing. I liked it. And so did Jerry. She rang me up afterwards: 'You look better than everyone!' she said. 'Did you screw Nick Knight or something?'

My second shoot with him was for *W* magazine. This nearly didn't happen at all. It coincided with the week my eye was hit by that baseball in Battersea Park, so my then agent Sarah Doukas reluctantly rang him up to cancel. 'She's wearing an eye patch, you see . . .'

'Great!' replied Nick. 'I want to work with that.'

I flipped out – 'This is Nick Knight! I have a black eye!' – but I got myself together, the shoot went ahead, and the results were fantastic: erotic and somehow secret, with a stolen quality. That time round, I hadn't had to work my enigmatic look: the eye patch did it all for me. Nick Knight even removed my beauty spot. I guess you can hide behind a black spot or a patch but not both.

Then Jerry and I shot the international Burberry campaign in which we're fighting over a handbag, which appeared on billboards all over the world, including Honolulu. The photographer was Mario Testino, and this time there were scores of people on set, from the art director Fabien Baron to Rosemary Bravo the head of Burberry: a crew of seventy for just one picture. It seemed as if there was a person whose designated job was to carry my bag, another who was employed to get my lunch and still another whose only role was to rub moisturiser in my legs. Val Garland was the chief make-up artist, but every way you turned there was a new face. Applause, manicurists, hair and make-up assistants: this was a whole new world for me.

When Alex Shulman had the brilliant idea of theming an issue of *Vogue* around 'ageless style', I was thrilled when she invited me to be on the cover, representing women in their fifties. The photographer was the renowned Patrick Demarchelier, and the shoot itself was funny. When I came in, Lizzie Jagger called out, 'Godmummy!' making me feel about a hundred years old. Jacquetta Wheeler was there, as delicate and beautiful as a young faun, and Yasmin Le Bon, now in her forties and the mother of three teenage girls, arrived looking as gorgeous as ever. Erin O'Connor looked amazing with bright cerise-mahogany-tortoiseshell hair and perfectly matched eyebrows. She made it clear she'd done it all herself. When I asked, 'How did you get those eyebrows?' she replied, 'It took weeks!' Cecilia Chancellor arrived, so serene and elegant.

Patrick had worked with most of us before, but could he remember any of our names? No. Well, I guess in my case it was forgivable – our last job together was thirty years ago, after all. He stood in front of the assembled seven of us, and when he wanted someone to adjust their pose he'd just shout, 'To the left a bit! You!'

'Me?' said Erin O'Connor.

'No, you!' shouted Patrick.

'Me?' said Lily Cole.

'No, you!'

'Me?' said Lizzie Jagger.

'No, YOU!'

'Me?' said Cecilia Chancellor.

'NO, YOU!!!'

'Me?' said Jacquetta Wheeler ... And so it went on. OK, so he couldn't remember our names, never mind, but you'd think it would be more efficient just to shout 'Oi, Skinny!' or 'Oi, Redhead!' or in my case maybe 'Oi, Fish face!' – that's certainly what Bailey would have done.

On hand to prepare us for the shoot was Marian Newman, the top manicurist, supported by six assistants. I'd done my own nails in preparation the night before, but the assistant took off my clear varnish and buffed up my nails instead. That's how it's done today: everyone has to be uniform.

Working with Bailey on a shoot for *Vogue*'s ninetieth anniversary issue was a real pleasure. He still, thankfully, restricts the visitors to his set to an absolute minimum. When Lily Cole and I did a double for him, there was just a handful of people in the room – the art director, make-up and hair, his son Fenton and one or two others. The camera was large format with a hood. Bailey doesn't burrow underneath it any more – his assistant does that, checking the focus – but he stands next to the camera and looks you right in the eye as he presses the shutter. Then Lily and I remained absolutely motionless, counting one-two-three-four in our heads, as the shutter of the plate camera is interminably slow.

When we did the shoot, Lily Cole was at the epicentre of the size zero hullabaloo, which was a storm in a teacup, if you ask me. Anorexia is a devastating illness and it's important that we have a debate about exactly how much fashion images exacerbate it. But governments and the media and newspaper editors go blundering in, knowing so little about the business, yet presuming to dictate to it – even trying to legislate, saying models should carry a certificate of health, should conform to a fixed body mass index figure. I find it ridiculous that a government should interfere on this issue. We are living today in a perfection-driven society, and we're bombarded by images – and that's not the fault of the fashion industry per se. Besides, Lily Cole has breasts, a bum – a perfect figure, to my mind. You couldn't dream up her look. She's a superstar. 'Magic!' Bailey said, as we looked into the lens. 'C'mon! Give me *magic!*'

I love doing this work. It's what I know, and it's what I do best.

*

'Yesterday is but today's memory, and tomorrow is today's dream.'

KAHLIL GIBRAN, *The Prophet*

'A thing is complete when you can let it be.'

GITA BELEIN

Fame: you dream about it. You visualise it, taste it, strive for it, work for it. You achieve it, embrace it – and then you find yourself doing everything in your power to distance yourself from it. Suddenly you don't want the constant invasive scrutiny it entails any more – or if you do want that, you're mad. Being famous is inevitably a twenty-four-hour thing, and it invades your entire being. Who really wants that? Surely it's not humanly possible to want that.

Joe Fiennes the actor once asked me, 'How do you deal with fame?' which I thought was a very incongruous question, this superstar actor who stunned the world in *Shakespeare in Love*, asking *me* how to cope with success – but he meant it in a genuine way.

I told him I'd realised soon after Bailey and I divorced that to become famous was to sign a Faustian pact. I wanted to publicise the good things I was doing, like charities and my memoir *Catwalk*, and I let the press into my flat, my mind, even my frickin' fridge. So much of my life became public that I wondered what was left for me. Once my mom rang me with a strange story about a friend of hers who had been to London. She had been chatting to her taxi driver about Hawaii when my name came up, and the taxi driver said, 'Do you want to see where she lives?' He had driven them right past my home in Pimlico. He even described the interior of my flat, which he'd seen in a magazine.

This kind of story freaks me out slightly – though I know it's my fault for doing those 'me and my home' interviews in the first place. I brought this on myself. Now it's my responsibility to take myself away from it.

One of the quirks of fame is that stars act as if they're all acquainted. Famous people walk into a room and assume that, as well as everyone knowing them, they know everyone. This first struck me one night at Tramp in the eighties when Liza Minnelli said to me, 'So how long have you known Tom Selleck?' Had a mutual friend, Marisa Berenson perhaps, told her about me, I wondered? Then I realised not. She was just acting on the presumption that our mutual fame was equivalent to an introduction.

Once at Tom Stoppard's summer party I met Simon Russell Beale. I'd just seen him playing Shakespeare at the National and I was really excited to meet him. But before I could tell him how much I admired his performance, he said, 'At last! I saw you in Peter Jones one day. I was standing behind you in the queue when you were buying a Hoover.'

How strange. I dread to think how I looked that day in Peter Jones. I probably thought I was 'in disguise' with dark glasses and sloppy clothes on. But there is no privacy, no anonymity once you are famous.

This is connected with why I now yearn to be at home in Hawaii. I can be free from the press there, more or less. I want an easy life on that stretch of silver sand between the sea and the sky. I want to float on my back in the middle of the Pacific Ocean thinking naughty thoughts about Clive Owen. I need to live in a place where I can be blinded by the stars at night.

And more than anything, I want to be with my parents. To my great joy they recently remarried in their eighties, so they now have each other again and I want to be with them while I can. Eventually, do we all go back to where we came from, either in terms of place or people? Is it ironic that I now crave the Polynesian paralysis I so wanted to escape as a teen – or does it make complete sense?

Of course, I'm not going just to sit on the beach in Hawaii. There are so many things I'd like to pursue – writing, and studying mysteries that have always fascinated me, like Egyptian hieroglyphs (an incredible eighty-seven per cent of them have yet to be deciphered!). I would like to get a scuba diving licence, to conquer my fear of heights, to master one yoga discipline, and to learn to become a better horsewoman. And as I expand my mind, Hawaii itself will grow. As the volcano erupts the lava flow is building up to create a new island, which already has a name: Loihi. Will it be inhabitable? I won't be around to find out.

There are so many concepts I would like to explore. For example, the Hawaiian practice of Ho'oponopono, which is the study of balance and understanding. And when I heard about the incredible Forgiveness Project, which explores conflict reconciliation through real-life human experience, I was so full of admiration. Do I have it within me to do this? I am not sure.

Have I become enlightened? Have I learned from my mistakes? I doubt it. I have, however, made peace with my imperfections. Of course I am still full of unresolved feelings and emotions about Suzon.

At home, Mom, Naomi and I like to visit the places we used to live, the fruit trees we used to pick, the streets we used to walk down. Not Pop. He abhors dwelling on the past. He resists everything from the past. He even groaned, 'Antiques time?' when we went to the

George V in Paris. 'Can't we stay somewhere a bit modern?' Was he joking? I don't even know. I think antiques make him feel like an antique himself. I try to achieve a balance between their polar approaches.

Former lovers, I let go of. They are nothing to me. I'm not the kind of cosy person who chats for ages on the phone with them. What for? Bailey is the only ex I want to see – but our relationship is more like family; I know his and he mine. Moreover, we still have a strong working partnership. Perhaps that will continue. I won't be completely in exile in Hawaii.

I will miss my friends. When I recently went to a lunch Sabrina Guinness gave for Anjelica Huston, Bianca Jagger and Nona Summers were also there. I felt so proud to have known these amazing, accomplished women for thirty years. Thirty years! It's still a shock to me that I have even lived that long. I like to hold on to the kid inside me. I could have let go of her, but instead I choose to stay innocent, excited, mystical, open.

When the first Polynesians made the two-thousand-mile journey from Tahiti to Hawaii, the navigator's star they followed was called 'Hōkūle'a'. Now I am being drawn back to Hawaii, me and my very own star – my British Blue cat is called 'Hōkūle'a' too, you see.

While Hoku watches me from her cushion, I like to water the yard in the hour just before sunset. This is my favourite time of day and my favourite thing to do in my secret Hawaii. It's like a Zen meditation in a way, this simple, repetitive, soulful activity at dusk. I like the clearness of the air and the wet earth under my feet. I like the smell of food wafting down the valley, and the way it all mingles together into a Hawaiian stew infused with the scent of the ocean and plumeria. Insect noises seem to phase in and out, humming all around me. The sound is so comforting, so familiar to me. It's a moment of total oneness as my inner reality becomes my conscious state. I am in a place where I am truly myself, within and beyond. When I come out of my fugue-like state I realise I'm still in Chelsea, and that the noise wasn't crickets – it was one of the maintenance men down the street cutting the grass. Wow. It's time to go home.

'We love the things we love for what they are.'

ROBERT FROST, *Hyla Brook*

ACKNOWLEDGEMENTS

I owe a great debt of gratitude to the many friends who have helped and encouraged me over the years, among them: Tom Stoppard, Salman Rushdie, Norma Heyman, Brian Clarke, Vimla Lalvani, Allegra Donn, Ninivah Khomo, Helen and Colin David.

I owe a special thank you to Simon Kelner who gave me the idea to do this book.

I am also indebted to David Bailey for his unfailing loyalty and generosity.

Many thanks to my indefatigable picture editor Beverly Croucher who did a brilliant job, Ian Mills at Bailey's studio, and Mark Baxtor and Martin Smith at Loup.

I am grateful for the kindness and help of Alex Shulman, Nicolas Coleridge, Hugo Vickers, Ian Webb, Lucinda McNeile, my agent Ed Victor and my model agents Karen Diamond and Elaine Dugas and all at Models 1. For their devoted encouragement and love, I would like to say *mahalo nui loa* to my family, Hugh and Linda Lee Helvin, Steve Lee Helvin and Naomi and Gerard Coste. I would also like to thank my publisher and editor the incomparable Alan Samson for his enthusiasm and his invaluable advice. A huge thank you goes to all the photographers who gave me permission to use their images in this book. It was a privilege working with you. I also owe a debt of thanks to Joanna Lumley, the original structure of whose book *No Room for Secrets* inspired the theme of body parts throughout the book.

Finally, last but not least, I wish to thank my collaborator Hermione Eyre. Without her valuable expertise and assistance this book would not exist.

*

Hermione wishes to thank her agent Charlie Campbell, her parents Sir Reginald and Lady Eyre, Tristam Davies, her former editors at the *Independent on Sunday* Ian Irvine, Nick Coleman and Elisabeth Heathcote, and her friends Richard Mason, Hannah Mackay, Beatrice Hodgkin and William Skidelsky.

A óhe lokomaika 'ii nele i ke pāna' i